Introducing Microsoft® ASP.NET AJAX

Dino Esposito

PUBLISHED BY
Microsoft Press
A Division of Microsoft Corporation
One Microsoft Way
Redmond, Washington 98052-6399

Library of Congress Control Number: 2007924643

Printed and bound in the United States of America.

2 3 4 5 6 7 8 9 QWT 2 1 0 9 8 7

Distributed in Canada by H.B. Fenn and Company Ltd.

A CIP catalogue record for this book is available from the British Library.

Microsoft Press books are available through booksellers and distributors worldwide. For further infor-
mation about international editions, contact your local Microsoft Corporation office or contact Microsoft
Press International directly at fax (425) 936-7329. Visit our Web site at www.microsoft.com/mspress.
Send comments to mspinput@microsoft.com.

Microsoft, Microsoft Press, ActiveX, IntelliSense, Internet Explorer, MSDN, MSN, PowerPoint, SQL
Server, Visual Basic, Visual C#, Visual C++, Visual Studio, Windows, Windows Media, and Windows
Vista are either registered trademarks or trademarks of Microsoft Corporation in the United States and/or
other countries. Other product and company names mentioned herein may be the trademarks of their
respective owners.

The example companies, organizations, products, domain names, e-mail addresses, logos, people, places,
and events depicted herein are fictitious. No association with any real company, organization, product,
domain name, e-mail address, logo, person, place, or event is intended or should be inferred.

This book expresses the author's views and opinions. The information contained in this book is provided
without any express, statutory, or implied warranties. Neither the authors, Microsoft Corporation, nor its
resellers, or distributors will be held liable for any damages caused or alleged to be caused either directly
or indirectly by this book.

Acquisitions Editor: Ben Ryan
Developmental Editor: Lynn Finnel
Editorial Production: Abshier House
Copy Editor: Roger LeBlanc
Technical Reviewer: Kenn Scribner
Indexer: Sharon Hilgenberg
Body Part No. X13-68385

To Silvia and Michela

"To change and to change for the better are two different things."

–German proverb

Contents at a Glance

Table of Contents

What do you think of this book? We want to hear from you!

Microsoft is interested in hearing your feedback so we can continually improve our books and learning resources for you. To participate in a brief online survey, please visit:

www.microsoft.com/learning/booksurvey/

Acknowledgments

AJAX is the next big thing for Web developers. Some action is required, and this book is designed to offer a smooth and effective start to nearly all Web developers, whatever their background might be. An introductory book on a new technology is always a challenge to write. You struggle to learn yourself while finding out the best way to explain and teach it to others.

So I was the first person to take advantage of this book. I, myself, used it to learn about ASP.NET AJAX. And I have to say that I believe I know quite a bit about it now that I'm done. I'm not sure if this means that I'm just a quick learner, or if this really proves that the book is a good one.

Scott Guthrie deserves a huge accolade for taking the time to sit with me and explain the road ahead and what the development team learned along the way—before and after the Professional Developers Conference in 2005 when the "Atlas" platform was first unveiled. Simon Calvert offered to serve as a sort of personal guide in the platform, and Stefan Schackow provided insightful answers to not necessarily smart questions. I greedily read blogs of Bertrand LeRoy and Nikhil Kothari—oh well, and the blogs of just about all of you out there—and, guess what, found them extremely useful.

While writing the book, I also had contact with a few vendors active in the AJAX arena. I want to thank Miljan Braticevic from ComponentOne, Tony Lombardo from Infragistics, and Svetozar Georgiev from Telerik. ASP.NET AJAX is great, but these guys and their teams are doing excellent work to create components for applications that work over the Web much like desktop programs.

Christian Gross just wrote a great book to help me understand what REST is and what its role is in AJAX and ASP.NET AJAX. (You'll read it all in Chapter 8).

The book you hold in your hands has a long story and at least a couple of lives. It could be said that I traveled three continents to write this book and nine different nations: Italy, the USA, France, Spain, Austria, Australia, Germany, UK, and Malaysia. My friends Greg Linwood and Brett Clarke challenged me to complete a whole chapter in a week while training, sightseeing Melbourne, and preparing a very special Microsoft PowerPoint presentation for a very special birthday. I made it—and it was really fun.

Fritz Lechnitz challenged me to finish off a chapter while a great tennis tournament was going on in Wien and I was confused in a storm of backhand and forehand shots from top players.

Andrea Saltarello challenged me to teach an ASP.NET AJAX class just one week after the official release. And we sold it out.

Finally, people at SolidQ couldn't wait for me to finish the book to start delivering some great training, at last.

Who else? Oh sure, my beloved Lynn Finnel and the whole editorial team—for being so flexible and open as to push my deadlines forward beyond imagination. Kenn Scribner discovered ASP.NET AJAX with me and put me on the right track more than once. (Sure, sometimes I returned him the favor, but this is normal with friends…)

Ben Ryan strongly wanted this book and now the book is here. Thanks Ben!

And as always, to my wife, Silvia, and to my children, Francesco and Michela, who grow taller with every book I write.

—Dino

PS: As we're speaking of AJAX, keep stamped in your mind the following words from the person considered to be the "father" of AJAX. At the very minimum, he's the man who coined the acronym. Read the whole story at *http://www.adaptivepath.com/publications/essays/archives/ 000385.php.*

The biggest challenges in creating AJAX applications are not technical. The core Ajax technologies are mature, stable, and well understood. Instead, the challenges are for the designers of these applications: to forget what we think we know about the limitations of the Web, and begin to imagine a wider, richer range of possibilities.

—Jesse James Garrett, Adaptive Path

Introduction

AJAX stands for "Asynchronous JavaScript and XML," and it's a sort of blanket term coined in 2005 to indicate rich, highly interactive, and responsive Web applications that do a lot of work on the client and place out-of-band calls to the server. An *out-of-band* call is a server request that results in a page update rather than a page replacement. The net effect is that an AJAX Web application tends to look like a classic desktop Microsoft Windows application and has advanced features such as drag-and-drop and asynchronous tasks, a strongly responsive and nonflickering user interface, and far less user frustration.

ASP.NET AJAX Extensions is a significant extension to the ASP.NET platform that makes AJAX-style functionalities possible and effective. ASP.NET AJAX Extensions is designed to be part of ASP.NET and, therefore, seamlessly integrate with the existing platform and application model.

Architecturally speaking, the ASP.NET AJAX framework is made of two distinct elements: a client script library and a set of server extensions. The client script library is entirely written in JavaScript and, therefore, works with any modern browser. Server extensions are fully integrated with ASP.NET server-based services and controls. As a result, developers can write rich Web pages using nearly the same approach they know from developing classic ASP.NET server-based pages.

Most ASP.NET AJAX developers are former ASP.NET developers and, as such, are familiar with the server-side development model based on controls. The server-centric programming model is the next big step in the evolution of the ASP.NET programming model. ASP.NET AJAX server controls are great, especially if you don't feel confident enough to create AJAX client scripts manually.

This book provides an overview of the ASP.NET AJAX framework with numerous examples to familiarize you with a variety of techniques and tools.

AJAX is a real breakthrough for ASP.NET developers and professionals. It makes cross-browser programming a reality and enables desktop-like functionalities over the Web.

Who This Book Is For

The book is recommended for virtually any ASP.NET developer and professional. As mentioned, ASP.NET AJAX is the next big thing in the ASP.NET evolution and follows a key industry trend—the AJAX model. In addition, ASP.NET AJAX goes beyond the classic AJAX model, pushing a framework that spans the client and server to provide an end-to-end solution for Web applications. As far as the Microsoft Web platform is concerned, ASP.NET AJAX Extensions weds rich functions with wide reach—an old dream of Web professionals that comes true. At last.

If you're a Web professional developing for Microsoft-based Web technologies, AJAX is your next big opportunity to seize. This book is your starting point. And even a bit more.

How This Book Is Organized

The book is divided into three parts: an overview of the platform and its building blocks, techniques to effectively enhance existing sites, and client-centric development. In the first part, you'll learn the basics of the AJAX model and the extensions made to the JavaScript language to back it. The second part is dedicated to the elements in the framework that you use to add new capabilities to existing server controls and to transform existing classic ASP.NET pages into full-fledged AJAX pages. Finally, the third part covers tools and techniques that express the real power of AJAX applications—out-of-band calls to server code.

System Requirements

You'll need the following hardware and software to build and run the code samples for this book:

- Microsoft Windows Vista, Microsoft Windows XP with Service Pack 2, Microsoft Windows Server 2003 with Service Pack 1, or Microsoft Windows 2000 with Service Pack 4

- Microsoft Visual Studio 2005 Standard Edition or Microsoft Visual Studio 2005 Professional Edition

- Microsoft SQL Server 2005 Express (included with Visual Studio 2005) or Microsoft SQL Server 2005

- 600-MHz Pentium or compatible processor (1-GHz Pentium recommended)

- 192 MB of RAM (256 MB or more recommended)

- Video monitor (800 x 600 or higher resolution) with at least 256 colors (1024 x 768 High Color 16-bit recommended)

- Microsoft mouse or compatible pointing device

Configuring SQL Server 2005 Express Edition

Some chapters of this book require that you have access to SQL Server 2005 Express Edition (or SQL Server 2005) to create and use the Northwind Traders database. If you are using SQL Server 2005 Express Edition, follow these steps to grant access to the user account that you will be using to perform the exercises in this book:

1. Log on to Windows on your computer by using an account with administrator privileges.

2. On the Windows Start menu, click All Programs, click Accessories, and then click Command Prompt to open a command prompt window.

3. In the command prompt window, type the following case-sensitive command:

   ```
   sqlcmd -S YourServer\SQLExpress -E
   ```

   Replace *YourServer* with the name of your computer.

   You can find the name of your computer by running the *hostname* command in the command prompt window before running the *sqlcmd* command.

4. At the 1> prompt, type the following command, including the square brackets, and then press Enter:

   ```
   sp_grantlogin [YourServer\UserName]
   ```

   Replace *YourServer* with the name of your computer, and replace *UserName* with the name of the user account you will be using.

5. At the 2> prompt, type the following command and then press Enter:

   ```
   go
   ```

   If you see an error message, make sure that you have typed the **sp_grantlogin** command correctly, including the square brackets.

6. At the 1> prompt, type the following command, including the square brackets, and then press Enter:

   ```
   sp_addsrvrolemember [YourServer\UserName], dbcreator
   ```

7. At the 2> prompt, type the following command and then press Enter:

   ```
   go
   ```

   If you see an error message, make sure that you have typed the **sp_addsrvrolemember** command correctly, including the square brackets.

8. At the 1> prompt, type the following command and then press Enter:

   ```
   exit
   ```

9. Close the command prompt window.

10. Log out of the administrator account.

The Northwind Traders database no longer ships with SQL Server 2005 (either version), so you'll need to download that separately. You can download the necessary installation scripts for the Northwind database from *http://www.microsoft.com/downloads/details.aspx?FamilyId=06616212-0356-46A0-8DA2-EEBC53A68034&displaylang=en*. Installation instructions are included on the download page.

Code Samples

The downloadable code includes projects for most chapters that cover the code snippets and examples referenced in the chapter. All the code samples discussed in this book can be downloaded from the book's companion content page at the following address:

http://www.microsoft.com/mspress/companion/9780735624139

Support for This Book

Every effort has been made to ensure the accuracy of this book and the companion content. As corrections or changes are collected, they will be added to a Microsoft Knowledge Base article.

Microsoft Press provides support for books and companion content at the following Web site:

http://www.microsoft.com/learning/support/books/

Questions and Comments

If you have comments, questions, or ideas regarding the book or the companion content, or questions that are not answered by visiting the site just mentioned, please send them to Microsoft Press via e-mail to

mspinput@microsoft.com

Or via postal mail to

Microsoft Press
Attn: *Introducing Microsoft ASP.NET AJAX* Editor
One Microsoft Way
Redmond, WA 98052-6399

Please note that Microsoft software product support is not offered through the above addresses.

Part I
ASP.NET AJAX Building Blocks

Chapter 1
The AJAX Revolution

Gone are the days when a Web application could be architected and implemented as a collection of related and linked pages. The advent of the so-called *AJAX* model is radically modifying the user's perception of a Web application, and it is subsequently forcing developers to apply newer and richer models to the planning and implementation of modern Web applications. But what is the AJAX model, anyway?

AJAX is a relatively new acronym that stands for *Asynchronous JavaScript and XML*. It is a sort of blanket term used to describe highly interactive and responsive Web applications. What's the point here? Weren't Web applications created about a decade ago specifically to be "interactive," "responsive," and deployed over a unique tool called the browser? So what's new today?

The incredible success of the Internet has whetted people's appetite for Web-related technology beyond imagination. Over the years, the users' demand for ever more powerful and Web-exposed applications and services led architects and developers to incorporate more and more features into the server platform and client browser. As a result, the traditional pattern of Web applications is becoming less adequate every day. A radical change in the design and programming model cannot be further delayed.

At the current state of the art, the industry needs more than just an improved and more powerful platform devised along the traditional guidelines and principles of Web applications—a true paradigm shift is required. AJAX is the incarnation of a new paradigm for the next generation of Web applications that is probably destined to last for at least the next decade.

From a more developer-oriented perspective, *AJAX* collectively refers to a set of development components, tools, and techniques for creating highly interactive Web applications that give users a better experience. According to the AJAX paradigm, Web applications work by exchanging data rather than pages with the Web server. From a user perspective, this means that faster roundtrips occur and, more importantly, page loading and refresh is significantly reduced. As a result, a Web application tends to look like a classic desktop Microsoft Windows application and has advanced features such as drag-and-drop and asynchronous tasks, a strongly responsive and nonflickering user interface, and other such features that minimize user frustration, provide timely feedback about what's going on, and deliver great mashed-up content. (Hold on! This doesn't mean AJAX Web applications *are the same as* desktop applications; they simply allow for a few more desktop-like features.)

AJAX is the philosophy that has inspired a new generation of components and frameworks, each designed to target a particular platform, provide a given set of capabilities, and possibly integrate seamlessly with existing frameworks. Microsoft ASP.NET AJAX Extensions is the AJAX addition to the ASP.NET 2.0 platform. In the next major release of the .NET Framework platform ASP.NET AJAX Extensions will officially fuse to ASP.NET and the rest of the Microsoft Web platform and application model. The next release of Microsoft Visual Studio (code-named "Orcas") will also integrate ad hoc design-time support for AJAX-specific features.

In this chapter, I'll dig deeper into the motivation for and driving force behind AJAX and then review the basic system requirements common to all AJAX frameworks.

The Paradigm Shift

We are all witnessing and contributing to an interesting and unique phenomenon—the Web is undergoing an epochal change right before our eyes as a result of our actions. As drastic as it might sound, the Web revolutionized the concept of an application. Only eight years ago, the majority of developers considered an application far too serious a thing to reduce it to an unordered mix of script and markup code. In the late 1990s, the cost of an application was sweat, blood, tears, and endless debugging sessions. According to the common and semi-serious perception there was neither honor nor fame for the "real" programmer in writing Web applications.

> **Note**   In the late 1990s, though, a number of Web sites were designed and built. Some of them grew incredibly in the following years to become pillars of today's world economy and even changed the way we do ordinary things. Want some examples? Google, Amazon, eBay. Nonetheless, a decade ago the guys building these and other applications were sort of avant-garde developers, perhaps even just smart and game amateurs.

Since then, the Web has evolved significantly. And although 10 years of Web evolution has resulted in the building of a thick layer of abstraction on the server side, it hasn't changed the basic infrastructure—HTTP protocol and pages.

The original infrastructure—one that was simple, ubiquitous, and effective—was the chief factor for the rapid success of the Web model of applications. The next generation of Web applications will still be based on the HTTP protocol and pages. However, the contents of pages and the capabilities of the server-side machinery will change to provide a significantly richer user experience—as rich as that of classic desktop Windows applications.

> **Note**   As we'll see in greater detail in Chapter 8, "Building AJAX Applications with ASP.NET," AJAX applications have a number of plusses but also a few drawbacks. Overall, choosing an AJAX application rather than a classic Web application is simply a matter of weighing the trade-offs. An AJAX application certainly gives users continuous feedback and never appears held up by some remote operation. On the other hand, AJAX applications are not entirely like desktop applications, and their capabilities in terms of graphics, multimedia, and hardware control are not as powerful as in a regular (smart) client. In the end, AJAX applications are just one very special breed of a Web application; as such, they might require some code refactoring to deliver the expected performance and results.

Classic Web Applications

Today Web applications work by submitting user-filled forms to the Web server and displaying the markup returned by the Web server. The browser-to-server communication employs the classic HTTP protocol. As is widely known, the HTTP protocol is stateless, which means that each request is not related to the next and no state is automatically maintained. (The state objects we all know and use in, say, ASP.NET are nothing more than an abstraction provided by the server programming environment.)

Communication between the browser and the Web server occurs through "forms." From a user's perspective, the transition occurs through "pages." Each user action that originates a new request for the server results in a brand new page (or a revamped version of the current page) being downloaded and displayed.

Let's briefly explore this model a bit further to pinpoint its drawbacks and bring to the surface the reasons why a new model is needed.

Send Input via Forms

Based on the URL typed in the address bar, the browser displays a page to the user. The page is ultimately made of HTML markup and contains one or more HTML forms. The user enters some data, and then instructs the browser to submit the form to an action URL.

Using the local Domain Name System (DNS) resolver in the operating system, the browser resolves the specified URL to an IP address and opens a socket. An HTTP packet travels over the wire to the given destination. The packet includes the form and all its fields. The request is captured by the Web server and typically forwarded to an internal module for further processing. At the end of the process, an HTTP response packet is prepared and the return value for the browser is inserted in the body.

Get Output through Pages

When a request is made for, say, an *.aspx* resource, the Web server passes it on to ASP.NET for processing and receives the resulting HTML markup in return. The generated markup comprises all the tags of a classic HTML page, including *<html>*, *<body>*, and *<form>*. The page source is embedded in the HTTP response and tagged with a Multipurpose Internet Mail Extensions (MIME) type to instruct the browser how to handle it. The browser looks at the MIME type and decides what to do.

If the response contains an HTML page, the browser replaces the current contents entirely with the new chunk of markup. While the request is being processed on the server, the "old" page is frozen but still displayed to the client user. As soon as the "new" page is downloaded, the browser clears the display and renders the page.

Capabilities and Drawbacks

This model was just fine in the beginning of the Web age when pages contained little more than formatted text, hyperlinks, and some images. The success of the Web has prompted users to ask for increasingly more powerful features, and it has led developers and designers to create more sophisticated services and graphics. As an example, consider advertising. Today, most pages—and often even very simple pages, such as blog pages—include ad rotators that download quite a bit of stuff on the client.

As a result, pages are heavy and cumbersome—even though we still insist on calling them "rich" pages. Regardless of whether they're rich or just cumbersome, these are the Web pages of today's applications. Nobody really believes that we're going to return to the scanty and spartan HTML pages of a decade ago.

Given the current architecture of Web applications, each user action requires a complete redraw of the page. Subsequently, richer and heavier pages render slowly and as a result produce a good deal of flickering. Projected to the whole set of pages in a large, portal-like application, this mechanism is just perfect for unleashing the frustrations of the poor end user.

Although a developer can build a page on the server using one of many flexible architectures (ASP.NET being one such example), from the client-side perspective Web pages were originally designed to be mostly static and unmodifiable. In the late 1990s, the introduction of Dynamic HTML first, and the advent of a World Wide Web Consortium (W3C) standard for the page document object model later, changed this basic fact. Today, the browser exposes the whole content of a displayed page through a read/write object model. In this way, the page can be modified to incorporate changes made entirely on the client-side to react to user inputs. (As we'll see, this is a key factor for AJAX and ASP.NET AJAX solutions.)

Dynamic HTML is a quantum leap, but alone it is not enough to further the evolution of the Web.

AJAX-Based Web Applications

To minimize the impact of page redraws, primitive forms of scripted remote procedure calls (RPC) appeared around 1997. Microsoft, in particular, pioneered this field with a technology called Remote Scripting (RS).

RS employed a Java applet to pull in data from a remote Active Server Pages (ASP)-based URL. The URL exposed a contracted programming interface through a target ASP page and serialized data back and forth through plain strings. On the client, a little JavaScript framework received data and invoked a user-defined callback to update the user interface via Dynamic HTML or similar techniques. RS worked on both Internet Explorer 4.0 and Netscape Navigator 4.0 and older versions.

Later on, Microsoft replaced the Java applet with a Component Object Model (COM) object named *XMLHttpRequest* and released most of the constraints on the programming interface exposed by the remote URL—for example, no more fixed ASP pages. At the same time, community efforts produced a range of similar frameworks aimed at taking RS to the next level and building a broader reach for solutions. The Java applet disappeared and was replaced by the *XMLHttpRequest* object.

What Is AJAX, Anyway?

The term *AJAX* was coined in 2005. It originated in the Java community and was used in reference to a range of related technologies for implementing forms of remote scripting. Today, any form of remote scripting is generally tagged with the AJAX prefix. Modern AJAX-based solutions for the Windows platform are based on the *XMLHttpRequest* object. Google Maps and Gmail are the two most popular Web applications designed according to AJAX patterns and techniques. For AJAX, these were certainly the *killer applications* that established its usefulness and showed its potential.

Two combined elements make an AJAX application live and thrive. On one hand, you need to serve users fresh data retrieved on the server. On the other hand, you need to integrate new data in the existing page without a full page refresh.

Browsers generally place a new request when an HTML form is submitted either via client-side script or through a user action such as a button click. When the response is ready, the browser replaces the old page with the new one. Figure 1-1 illustrates graphically this traditional approach.

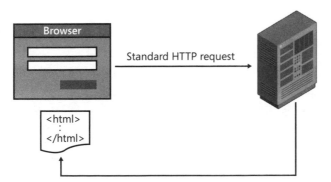

Figure 1-1   Browsers submit an HTML form and receive a new page to display.

The chief factor that enables remote scripting is the ability to issue out-of-band HTTP requests. In this context, an out-of-band call indicates an HTTP request placed using a component that is different from the browser's built-in module that handles the HTML form submission (that is, outside the traditional mechanism you see in Figure 1-1). The out-of-band call is triggered via script by an HTML page event and is served by a proxy component. In the most recent AJAX solutions, the proxy component is based on the *XMLHttpRequest* object; the proxy component was a Java applet in the very first implementation of RS.

Update Pages via Script

The proxy component (for example, the *XMLHttpRequest* object) sends a regular HTTP request and waits, either synchronously or asynchronously, for it to be fully served. When the response data is ready, the proxy invokes a user-defined JavaScript callback to refresh any portion of the page that needs updating. Figure 1-2 provides a graphical overview of the model.

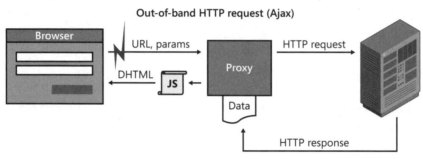

Figure 1-2   Out-of-band calls are sent through a proxy component, and a JavaScript callback is used to update any portion of the page affected by returned data.

All browsers know how to replace an old page with a new page; until a few years ago, though, not all of them provided an object model to represent the current contents of the page. (Today, I can hardly mention a single modern, commercially available browser that doesn't expose a read/write page DOM.) For browsers that supply an updatable object model for HTML pages, the JavaScript callback function can refresh specific portions of the old page, thus making them look updated, without a full reload.

The Document Object Model

The page Document Object Model (DOM) is the specification that defines a platform- and language-neutral interface for accessing and updating the contents, structure, and style of HTML and XML documents. A recognized standard ratified by the W3C committee, the DOM is now supported by virtually all browsers. The DOM provides a standard set of objects for representing the constituent elements of HTML and XML documents. All together, these objects form a standard interface for accessing and manipulating child elements of HTML pages and, more in general, XML documents.

Note that although the first working frameworks for remote scripting date back to a decade ago, the limited support browsers have had for dynamic changes in displayed documents slowed down the adoption of such technologies in the industry. Until now.

The Role of Rich Browsers

As shown in Figure 1-2, the AJAX model has two key requirements as far as browsers are concerned: a proxy component and an updatable page DOM. For quite a long time, only high-end browsers (also known as rich, up-level browsers) provided support for both features. In the past few years, only companies that could exercise strict control over the capabilities of the client browsers were able to choose the AJAX model for their sites. For too long, a *rich* browser also has meant a browser with too limited *reach*. For too long, using such a browser was definitely a bad choice for most businesses because the limited reach excluded significant portions of the customer base.

Rich vs. Reach

Perhaps due to a rare and likely unrepeatable astral conjunction, today more than 90 percent of browsers available on the market happen to have built-in support for the advanced capabilities that the AJAX model requires. Internet Explorer since version 5.0, Firefox, Netscape from version 6 and onward, Safari 1.2, Opera starting with version 8.0, and a variety of mobile devices are all browsers that fully support the AJAX programming model.

For the very first time, a *rich browser* is not synonymous with a *limited reach browser*. Finally, you don't have to choose a particular browser to enjoy advanced, programming-rich features. Designing highly interactive Web applications that implement remote scripting techniques is no longer an impossible dream to chase but a concrete opportunity to seize—whatever browsers you and your clients use.

Each platform and each vendor might have a particular framework and tool set to offer, but this doesn't change the basic fact that living the AJAX lifestyle is now possible with 90 percent of the browsers available today. It's a real breakthrough, and it is now possible to build and distribute applications that were not possible before.

Required Capabilities

Exactly what are the capabilities required of a browser to run AJAX functionalities? As mentioned, a browser needs to provide two key capabilities: a proxy mechanism to make client code able to place out-of-band HTTP calls, and an updatable DOM.

There's a W3C ratified standard for the updatable DOM. A W3C standard for the proxy component is currently being developed. It takes the form of the *XMLHttpRequest* object and is devised as an interface exposed by the browser to allow script code to perform HTTP client functionality, such as submitting form data or loading data from a remote Web site. The latest working draft is available at *http://www.w3.org/TR/XMLHttpRequest*.

In addition, browsers must support JavaScript and preferably cascading style sheets (CSS).

In the end, the AJAX lifestyle is possible and affordable for virtually every developer and nearly 90 percent of the Web audience, regardless of the platform. The tools required to make AJAX work are becoming as ubiquitous as HTML/XML parsers, HTTP listeners, and JavaScript processors. To paraphrase the catch phrase of a popular advertising campaign, I'd say that "AJAX is now." And as far as the Windows and ASP.NET platforms are concerned, AJAX takes the form of Microsoft ASP.NET AJAX Extensions.

The AJAX Core Engine

AJAX is not a particular technology or product. It refers to a number of client features, and related development techniques, that make Web applications look like desktop applications. AJAX doesn't require any plug-in modules either and is not browser specific. Virtually any browser released in the past five years can serve as a great host for AJAX-based applications. AJAX development techniques revolve around one common software element—the *XMLHttpRequest* object. The availability of this object in the object model of most browsers is the key to the current ubiquity and success of AJAX applications. In addition to *XMLHttpRequest*, a second factor contributes to the wide success of AJAX—the availability of a rich document object model in virtually any browser.

Originally introduced with Internet Explorer 5.0, the *XMLHttpRequest* object is an internal object that the browser publishes to its scripting engine. In this way, the script code found in any client page—typically, JavaScript code—can invoke the object and take advantage of its functionality.

The *XMLHttpRequest* object allows script code to send HTTP requests and handle their response. Functionally speaking, and despite the XML in the name, the *XMLHttpRequest* object is nothing more than a tiny object designed to place HTTP calls via script in a non-browser-led way. When users click the submit button of a form, or perform any action that ends up invoking the *submit* method on the DOM's *form* object, the browser kicks in and takes full control of the subsequent HTTP request. From the user's perspective, the request is a black box whose only visible outcome is the new page being displayed. The client script code has no control over the placement and outcome of the request.

The *XMLHttpRequest* Object

Created by Microsoft and adopted soon thereafter by Mozilla, the *XMLHttpRequest* object is today fully supported by the majority of Web browsers. As you'll see in a moment, the implementation can significantly differ from one browser to the next, even though the top-level interface is nearly identical. For this reason, a W3C committee is at work with the goal of precisely documenting a minimum set of interoperable features based on existing implementations.

Note   The *XMLHttpRequest* object originally shipped as a separate component with Internet Explorer 5.0 back in the spring of 1999. It is a native component of all Microsoft operating systems that have shipped since. In particular, you'll certainly find it installed on all machines that run Windows 2000, Windows XP, and newer operating systems.

The Internet Explorer Object

When the *XMLHttpRequest* object was first released, the Component Object Model (COM) was ruling the world at Microsoft. The extensibility model of products and applications was based on COM and implemented through COM components. In the late 1990s, the right and natural choice was to implement this new component as a reusable automation COM object, named *Microsoft.XmlHttp*.

Various versions of the same component (even with slightly different names) were released over the years, but all of them preserved the original component model—COM. Internet Explorer 6.0, for example, ships the *XMLHttpRequest* object in the form of a COM object. Where's the problem?

COM objects are external components that require explicit permission to run inside of a Web browser. In particular, to run the *XMLHttpRequest* object and subsequently enable any AJAX functionality built on top of it, at a minimum a client machine needs to accept ActiveX components marked safe for scripting. (See Figure 1-3.)

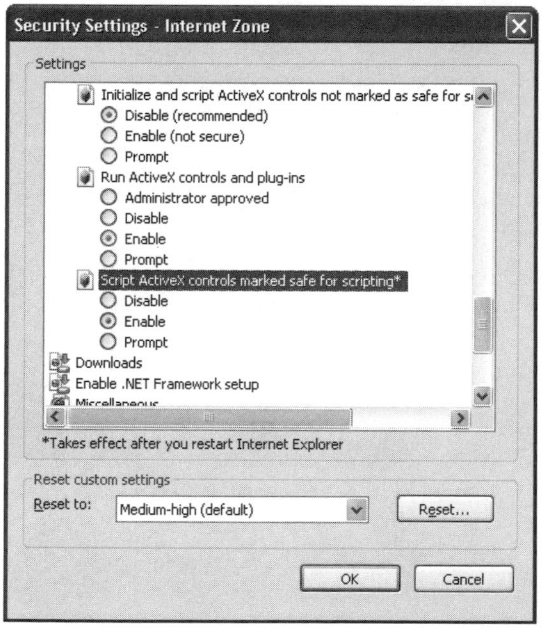

Figure 1-3   The property window used to change the security settings in Internet Explorer

The *XMLHttpRequest* object is certainly a safe component, but to enable it users need to lessen their security settings and accept any other component "declared" safe for scripting that is around the Web sites they visit.

> **Important** The internal implementation of *XMLHttpRequest* is disjointed from the implementation of any AJAX-like frameworks, such as Microsoft ASP.NET AJAX. Under the hood, any framework ends up calling the object as exposed by, or available in, the browser.

The Mozilla Counterpart

Mozilla adopted *XMLHttpRequest* immediately after its first release with Internet Explorer 5.0. However, in Mozilla-equipped browsers the *XMLHttpRequest* object is part of the browser's object model and doesn't rely on external components. Put another way, a Mozilla browser such as Firefox publishes its own *XMLHttpRequest* object into the scripting engine and never uses the COM component, even when the COM component is installed on the client machine and is part of the operating system. Figure 1-4 shows the different models in Internet Explorer (up to version 6.0) and Mozilla browsers.

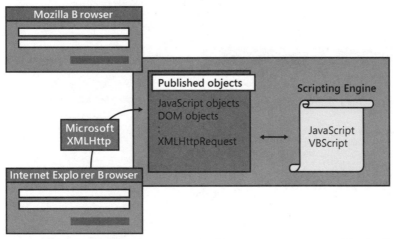

Figure 1-4 *XMLHttpRequest* is a scriptable component exposed by the browser in Mozilla and an external COM component in Internet Explorer (up to version 6.0)

As a result, in Mozilla browsers *XMLHttpRequest* looks like a native JavaScript object and can be instantiated through the classic *new* operator:

```
// The object name requires XML in capital letters
var proxy = new XMLHttpRequest();
```

When the browser is Internet Explorer, the *XMLHttpRequest* object is instantiated using the *ActiveXObject* wrapper, as shown here:

```
var proxy = new ActiveXObject("Microsoft.XmlHttp");
```

Generally, AJAX-style frameworks check the current browser and then decide about the route to take.

Needless to say, as implemented in Mozilla browsers the *XMLHttpRequest* functionality is somewhat safer, at least in the sense it doesn't require users to change their security settings for the browser.

XMLHttpRequest in Internet Explorer 7

Implemented as a COM component for historical reasons on Internet Explorer browsers, the *XMLHttpRequest* object has finally become a browser object with Internet Explorer 7.0. All potential security concerns are removed at the root, and AJAX frameworks can be updated to use the same syntax for creating the *XMLHttpRequest* object regardless of the browser:

```
var proxy = new XMLHttpRequest();
```

In addition, this change in Internet Explorer 7.0 completely decouples AJAX-like functionality in ASP.NET from an ActiveX-enabled environment.

An HTTP Object Model

I spent quite a few words on the *XMLHttpRequest* object and its expected behavior, but I still owe you a practical demonstration of the object's capabilities. In this section, I'll cover the members of the component, the actions it can perform, and details of the syntax.

As mentioned, the *XML* in the name of the component means little and in no way limits the capabilities of the component. In spite of the XML prefix, you can use the object as a true automation engine for executing and controlling HTTP requests, from client code generated by ASP.NET pages or the Windows shell, or Visual Basic 6.0 or C++ unmanaged applications. Using the *XMLHttpRequest* COM object from within .NET applications is nonsensical, as you can find similar functionality in the folds of the *System.Net* namespace in the .NET Framework.

 Important   If you're going to use Microsoft ASP.NET AJAX Extensions or any other AJAX-like framework for building your applications, you'll hardly hear about the *XMLHttpRequest* object, much less use it directly in your own code. ASP.NET AJAX Extensions completely encapsulates this object and shields page authors and application designers from it. You don't need to know about *XMLHttpRequest* to write great AJAX applications, no matter how complex and sophisticated they are. However, knowing the fundamentals of *XMLHttpRequest* can lead you to a better and more thorough understanding of the platform and to more effective diagnoses of problems.

Behavior and Capabilities

The *XMLHttpRequest* object is designed to perform one key operation: sending an HTTP request. The request can be sent either synchronously or asynchronously. The following listing shows the programming interface of the object as it results from the W3C working draft at the time of this writing:

```
interface XMLHttpRequest {
  function onreadystatechange;
  readonly unsigned short readyState;
  void open(string method, string url);
  void open(string method, string url, bool async);
  void open(string method, string url, bool async, string user);
  void open(string method, string url, bool async,
            string user, string pswd);
  void setRequestHeader(string header, string value);
  void send(string data);
  void send(Document data);
  void abort();
  string getAllResponseHeaders();
  string getResponseHeader(string header);
  string responseText;
  Document responseXML;
  unsigned short status;
  string statusText;
};
```

Using the component is a two-step operation. First, you open a channel to the URL and specify the method (GET, POST, or other) to use and whether you want the request to execute asynchronously. Next, you set any required header and send the request. If the request is a POST, you pass to the *send* method the body of the request.

The *send* method returns immediately in the case of an asynchronous operation. You write an *onreadystatechange* function to check the status of the current operation and, using that function, figure out when it is done.

Sending a Request

Most AJAX frameworks obtain an instance of the *XMLHttpRequest* object for the current browser using code that looks like the following:

```
var xmlRequest, e;
try {
  xmlRequest = new XMLHttpRequest();
}
catch(e) {
    try {
      xmlRequest = new ActiveXObject("Microsoft.XMLHTTP");
    }
    catch(e) {
    }
}
```

The code first tries to instantiate the internal *XMLHttpRequest* object and opts for the ActiveX object in the case of failure. As you can see, the creation of the object requires an exception to be caught when the browser is Internet Explorer 6.0 or any older versions. Such a code will work unchanged (and won't require any exception) in Internet Explorer 7.0.

> **Note** Checking the browser's user agent and foregoing the exception is fine as well.
> However, ASP.NET AJAX Extensions uses the preceding code because it makes the overall
> library independent from details of user agent strings and browser details. In this way, you do
> "object detection" instead of "browser detection." The final result, though, is the same. The
> exception is fired only if the browser is Internet Explorer older than version 7.0 or any other
> browser that doesn't support AJAX functionalities. If you're building your own AJAX frame-
> work, you need to check the user agent only against Internet Explorer.

The *open* method prepares the channel for the request; no physical socket is created yet,
though. To execute a POST statement, you need to add the proper content-type header. The
Boolean argument indicates whether the operation is asynchronous:

```
xmlRequest.open("POST", url, false);
xmlRequest.setRequestHeader("Content-Type",
                            "application/x-www-form-urlencoded");
xmlRequest.send(postData);
```

The *send* method opens the socket and sends the packet. In the preceding code snippet, the
method returns only when the response has been fully received.

An asynchronous request requires slightly different code:

```
xmlRequest.open("POST", url, true);
xmlRequest.onreadystatechange = CallbackComplete;
xmlRequest.setRequestHeader("Content-Type",
                            "application/x-www-form-urlencoded");
xmlRequest.send(postData);
```

The *CallbackComplete* element is a placeholder for a JavaScript function that retrieves and processes the response generated by the request.

Note that the function assigned to the *onreadystatechange* member will be invoked whenever
readyState changes value. Possible values for the state are the integers ranging from 0 through
4, which mean "Uninitialized," "Open method called successfully," "Send method called successfully," "Receiving data," and "Response received," respectively. The *CallbackComplete*
framework-specific function will generally check that state and proceed.

Receiving a Response

The response of the request is available in two formats: as raw text and as an XML document.
The *responseText* property is empty if the state is 0 through 2—that is, no data has been
received yet. When the state transitions to 3 (receiving data), the property contains the data
received so far, interpreted using the character encoding specified in the response. If no character encoding was specified, it employs UTF-8.

The *responseXml* property is not available until the full response has been downloaded and
successfully parsed to an XML document. If the body of the response is not XML or if the

parsing fails for any reason, the property returns null. It is important to note that the construction of the XML document takes place on the client once the raw HTTP response has been fully received.

Roll Your Own (Little) AJAX Framework

As mentioned, you don't need to use the straight *XMLHttpRequest* object in your AJAX-based application, regardless of the framework (for example, ASP.NET AJAX) you end up using. For completeness, though, let's briefly review the steps required to use the object in a sample ASP.NET 2.0 page. The same code can be used with ASP.NET 1.x as well. The following code represents the minimal engine you need for building homemade AJAX solutions.

> **Note**   Although a homemade AJAX framework might not be recommended, it's not impossible to write. The fact that more than 100 AJAX frameworks have been counted just demonstrates that writing AJAX homemade solutions is not a mission-impossible task. Personally, I would consider it only as a way to enrich existing applications with quick and dirty AJAX functionality limited to placing remote, non-browser-led calls.

Executing an Out-of-Band Call from an ASP.NET Page

Web pages that shoot out-of-band calls need to have one or more trigger events that, when properly handled with a piece of JavaScript code, place the request via the *XMLHttpRequest* object. Trigger events can only be HTML events captured by the browser's DOM implementation.

The JavaScript code should initiate and control the remote URL invocation, as shown in the following code:

```
<script type="text/JavaScript">
function SendRequest(url, params)
{
    // Add some parameters to the query string
    var pageUrl = url + "?outofband=true&param=" + params;

    // Initialize the XmlHttpRequest object
    var xmlRequest, e;
    try {
        xmlRequest = new XMLHttpRequest();
    }
    catch(e) {
      try {
          xmlRequest = new ActiveXObject("Microsoft.XMLHTTP");
      }
      catch(e) { }
    }

    // Prepare for a POST synchronous request
    xmlRequest.open("POST", pageUrl, false);
    xmlRequest.setRequestHeader("Content-Type",
```

```
                                      "application/x-www-form-urlencoded");
        xmlRequest.send(null);
        return xmlRequest;
}
</script>
```

The sample function accepts two strings: the URL to call and the parameter list. Note that the format of the query string is totally arbitrary and can be adapted at will in custom implementations. The URL specified by the programmer is extended to include a couple of parameters. The first parameter—named *outofband* in the example—is a Boolean value and indicates whether or not the request is going to be a custom callback request. By knowing this, the target page can process the request appropriately. The second parameter—named *param* in the example—contains the input parameters for the server-side code.

The host ASP.NET page looks like the following code snippet:

```
<html xmlns="http://www.w3.org/1999/xhtml" >
<head runat="server">
    <title>Testing Out-of-band</title>
</head>
  <body>
    <form id="Form1" runat="server">
      <h1>Demonstrate Out-of-band Calls</h1>
      <h2><%=Request.Url%></h2>
      <hr />

      <asp:DropDownList runat="server" ID="EmployeeList" />
      <input id="Button1" type="button" value="Go Get Data"
             onclick="MoreInfo()" />
      <hr />
      <span id="Msg" />
    </form>
  </body>
</html>
```

The code-behind class is shown in the following listing:

```
public partial class _Default : System.Web.UI.Page
{
    protected void Page_Load(object sender, EventArgs e)
    {
        if (IsOutOfBand())
            return;
        if (!IsPostBack)
            PopulateList();
    }

    private bool IsOutOfBand()
    {
        bool isCallback = false;
        isCallback = String.Equals(Page.Request.QueryString["callback"],
                                   "true",
                                   StringComparison.OrdinalIgnoreCase);
```

```
        if (isCallback)
        {
            string param = Request.QueryString["param"].ToString();
            Response.Write(ExecutePageMethod(param));
            Response.Flush();
            Response.End();
            return true;
        }
        return false;
    }

    private void PopulateList()
    {
        SqlDataAdapter adapter = new SqlDataAdapter(
            "SELECT employeeid, lastname FROM employees",
            "SERVER=(local);DATABASE=northwind;UID=...;");
        DataTable table = new DataTable();
        adapter.Fill(table);

        EmployeeList.DataTextField = "lastname";
        EmployeeList.DataValueField = "employeeid";
        EmployeeList.DataSource = table;
        EmployeeList.DataBind();
    }

    string ExecutePageMethod(string eventArgument)
    {
        return "You clicked: " + eventArgument;
    }
}
```

A couple of issues deserve more attention and explanation. The first one is the need to find out whether the request is an out-of-band call or a regular postback. Next, we need to look at the generation of the response. The *IsOutOfBand* method checks the *outofband* field in the posted form. If the *outofband* field is found, the request is served and terminated without going through the final part of the classic ASP.NET request life cycle—events for changed values, postback, pre-rendering, view-state serialization, rendering, and so forth. An out-of-band request is therefore short-circuited to return more quickly, carrying the least data possible.

What does the page do when an out-of-band call is placed? How does it determine the response? Most of the actual AJAX-based frameworks vary on this point, so let's say it is arbitrary. In general, you need to define a public programming interface that is invoked when an out-of-band call is made. In the sample code, I have a method with a contracted name and signature—*ExecutePageMethod*—whose output becomes the plain response for the request. In the sample code, the method returns and accepts a string, meaning that any input and output parameters must be serializable to a string.

```
string param = Request.QueryString["param"].ToString();
Response.Write(ExecutePageMethod(param));
Response.Flush();
Response.End();
```

As in the code snippet, the response for the out-of-band request is the output of the method. No other data is ever returned; and no other data except for the parameters is ever sent. In this particular implementation, there will be no view state sent and returned.

> **Important**   Although you'll probably never get to write any such code, be aware that thus far I've just provided a minimal but effective description of the underlying mechanism common to most frameworks that supply AJAX-like functionality. Each framework encapsulates a good number of details and adds new services and capabilities. At its core, though, this is how AJAX libraries work.

Displaying Results

One more step is missing—what happens on the client once the response for the out-of-band call is received? The following snippet shows a piece of client code that, when attached to a button, fires the out-of-band call and refreshes the user interface:

```
function MoreInfo()
{
   var empID = document.getElementById("EmployeeList").value;
   var xml = SendRequest("default.aspx", empID);

   // Update the UI
   var label = document.getElementById("Msg");
   label.innerHTML = xml.responseText;
}
```

According to the code, whenever the user clicks the button a request is sent at the following URL. Note that *1* in the sample URL indicates the ID of the requested employee. (See Figure 1-5.)

```
default.aspx?outofband=true&param=1
```

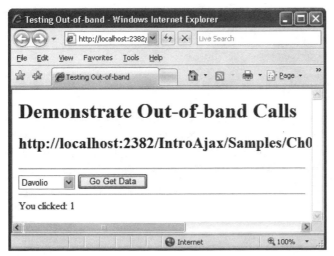

Figure 1-5   A manually coded out-of-band request in ASP.NET 1.x and ASP.NET 2.0

Displaying results correctly on most browsers can be tricky. Internet Explorer, in fact, supports a number of nonstandard shortcuts in the DOM that just don't work with other browsers. The most common snag is retrieving references to HTML elements using the *document.getElement-ById* method instead of the direct name of the element. For example, the following code works on Internet Explorer but not on Firefox and other Mozilla-equipped browsers:

```
// Msg is the ID of a <span> tag.
// This code works only with Internet Explorer
Msg.innerHTML = xml.requestText;
```

In summary, cross-browser JavaScript code is required to update the currently displayed page on the client. At the same time, a number of assumptions must be made on the server to come up with a working and effective environment. For this reason, frameworks are the only reasonable way of implementing AJAX functionalities. Different frameworks, though, might provide a different programming interface on top of an engine that uses the same common set of parts.

The Switch to the Document Object Model

Microsoft has pioneered updatable Web pages since the late 1990s. With Internet Explorer 4.0 (released back in 1997), Microsoft introduced Dynamic HTML (DHTML), which is a powerful combination of HTML, style sheets, and scripts that allows programmatic changes to any displayed page. Several companies since then have worked out their own DHTML object model—often referred to as the Browser Object Model (BOM). The W3C committee worked hard to bring vendors to agree on an interoperable and language-neutral solution for exposing Web pages through an updatable programming interface. The result is the Document Object Model (DOM), as opposed to a browser-specific BOM.

The DOM is a platform-independent and language-neutral representation of the contents of a Web page that scripts can access and use to modify the content, structure, and style of the document.

For AJAX, it's all about exchanging data with a remote server. But once the data is downloaded out-of-band on the client, what can you do with that? The DOM provides an outlet for the data to flow into the current page structure and update it.

Representation of a Document

The DOM is a standard API exposed by the browser in which a displayed page has a tree-based structure. Each node in the logical tree corresponds to an object. On the other hand, the name "Document Object Model" hints at an object model in the common interpretation of the object-oriented design terminology. A Web page—the document—is modeled through objects. The model includes the structure and behavior of a document. Each node in the logical tree is not static data; rather, it is a live object with a known behavior and its own identity.

DOM Implementation

The W3C DOM consists of three levels that indicate, for the browser, three different levels of adherence to the standard. For more information, take a look at *http://www.w3.org/DOM*.

The DOM is made of nodes, and each node is an object. For a Web page, each node maps to an object that represents an HTML tag. The object, therefore, has properties and methods that can be applied to an HTML tag. There are three fundamental operations you can accomplish on a node: find the node (including related nodes such as children, parent, or sibling nodes), create a node, and manipulate a node.

Identifying a particular node is easy as long as the page author knows the ID of the corresponding element. In this case, you use the following standard piece of code:

```
var node = document.getElementById(id);
```

In particular, if there are multiple elements sharing the same ID value, the method returns the first object in the collection. This method is supported in the DOM Level 1 and upper levels. Another interesting method to find elements is the following:

```
var coll = document.getElementsByTagName(tagname);
```

The method retrieves a collection of all objects based on the same HTML tag. For example, the method retrieves a collection of all *<div>* or all *<input>* tags in the page.

Related DOM objects are grouped in node lists. Each node has a name, type, parent, and collection of children. A node also holds a reference to its siblings and attributes. The following code snippet shows how to retrieve the parent of a node and its previous sibling:

```
var oParent = oNode.parentNode
var oPrevious = oNode.previousSibling
```

How can you modify the contents of a node? The easiest and most common approach entails that you use the *innerHTML* property:

```
var node = document.getElementById("button1");
node.innerHTML = "Hey click me";
```

The *innerHTML* property is supported by virtually all browsers, and it sets or retrieves the HTML between the start and end tags of the given object. Some browsers such as Internet Explorer also support the *innerText* property. This property is designed to set or retrieve the text inside of a given DOM object. Unfortunately, this property is not supported by all browsers. It exists in Internet Explorer and Safari but, for example, it is not supported by Firefox. Firefox, on the other hand, supports a property with a similar behavior but a different name— *textContent*.

Note   The advent of the Microsoft AJAX Client Library (discussed in Chapter 2, "The Microsoft Client Library for AJAX") shields developers from having to know much about the little differences between the DOM implementation of the various browsers. For example, you should know about *innerText* and *textContent* if you're embedding your own JavaScript in the page; however, you don't have to if you rely on the AJAX Client Library to refresh portions of the displayed page.

Note   Finally, note that you should not check the user agent string to figure out whether the current browser supports a given feature. You should check the desired object instead. For example, to know whether the browser supports *innerText*, you're better off running the following code:

```
var supportsInnerText = false;
var supportsInnerText = false;
if (temp != undefined)
supportsInnerText = true;
...
```

In this way, you directly check the availability of the property without having to maintain a list of browsers.

Nodes are created using the *createElement* method exposed only to the document object. Alternatively, you can add new elements to the document hierarchy by modifying the *innerHTML* property value, or by using methods explicit to particular elements, such as the *insertRow* and *insertCell* methods for the *table* element. Here's an example:

```
// Create an <IMG> element
var oImg = document.createElement("<img>");
...
// Create a new option for the SELECT element
var oOption = new Option(text, id);
control.options.add(oOption);
```

With this information, I have only scratched the surface of the DOM implementation in the various browsers. Nonetheless, the DOM is a key part of the AJAX jigsaw puzzle and deserves a lot of attention and skilled use. For a primer, you can take a look at *http:// msdn.microsoft.com/workshop/author/dom/domoverview.asp*.

Be Pragmatic: DHTML vs. DOM

In the beginning, only the browser's support for the DHTML object model provided JavaScript developers with the ability to update the page contents dynamically. The success of DHTML led to the definition of a standard document object model—the W3C's DOM. Quite obviously, the DOM evolved from DHTML and became much more generalized than DHTML. As mentioned, the DOM provides a tree-based model for the whole document, not just for an individual HTML tag.

Most browsers, though, support a mix of DOM and DHTML. Which one should you use? In particular, to update some contents, should you obtain a reference to the textual child node of the node that matches the intended HTML tag (the DOM way) or just grab a reference to a node and use *innerHTML* (the DHTML way)? Likewise, to add a new element, should you create a new element or just stuff in a chunk of updated HTML via *innerHTML*? Admittedly, one of the most interesting debates in the community is whether to use DHTML to manipulate pages or opt for the cleaner approach propounded by the DOM application programming interface (API).

The key fact is that the DOM API is significantly slower than using *innerHTML*. If you go through the DOM to generate some user interface dynamically, you have to create every element, append each into the proper container, and then set properties. The alternative only entails that you define the HTML you want and render it into the page using *innerHTML*. The browser, then, does the rest by rendering your markup into direct graphics.

Overall, DHTML and DOM manipulation are both useful depending on the context. There are many Web sites that discuss performance tests and DHTML is always the winner. Anyway, DOM is still perfectly fast as long as you use it the right way—that is, create HTML fragments and append them to the proper container only as the final step.

Be Pragmatic: Use Events

Let's make it clear: without events, there would be no point in adding JavaScript to Web pages. To be effective, therefore, scripts have to react to some user action as well as to actions generated by the browser, such as when loading the page. Events and event handlers are old companions to Web pages, as they appeared the first time with Netscape 2.

For quite some time, largely incompatible event models lived and thrived in different browsers—mainly in Internet Explorer and Netscape. A few years ago, the W3C standardized the event model with a paper that you can read at *http://www.w3.org/TR/2000/ REC-DOM-Level-2-Events-20001113/events.html*.

With Internet Explorer and Netscape having their own original event model, and making themselves compatible to the W3C standard, you understand that writing model-agnostic event handlers is going to be a hard task. There are a lot of events, but not all of them are supported by all browsers. The following categories of events can be considered standard: user interface events (blur, focus, scroll), device events (click, keydown), and form events (submit, select). The second big point concerns how you set event handlers. The most reliable way is still the following:

```
<a href="page.aspx" onclick="doClick()" />
```

An excellent paper that discusses the theme of events in JavaScript can be found here: *http:// www.quirksmode.org/js/introevents.html*.

> **Tip**   If you're looking for a great Web site to learn about the various aspects of JavaScript, DHTML, DOM, CSS and client-side programming in general, the right place to go is *http://www.quirksmode.org*.

Existing AJAX Frameworks for ASP.NET

Today, quite a few APIs exist to implement AJAX functionality in ASP.NET, and one of these APIs is already integrated into ASP.NET 2.0. Other APIs come from third-party vendors or take form from open-source projects. I'll briefly look at some of these APIs. Note, though, that as long as ASP.NET is your development environment, the most reasonable choice you can make is Microsoft ASP.NET AJAX Extensions. However, ASP.NET AJAX Extensions can coexist pretty well with a large number of the existing alternative AJAX frameworks. ASP.NET AJAX is not a mutually exclusive choice.

Since early 2005, some aggressive independent software vendors (for example, Telerik, Infragistics, and ComponentArt) have integrated AJAX functionality into their existing suite of controls for rapid and rich Web development. In the beginning, each vendor developed its own internal and proprietary AJAX engine and integrated it with the product. The advent of ASP.NET AJAX Extensions will likely prompt vendors to offer native ASP.NET AJAX controls or, at a minimum, provide controls that work seamlessly with ASP.NET AJAX.

Let's review some of the options you have today for developing AJAX-enabled ASP.NET Web applications. As you can see, the list is not exhaustive and features libraries from both independent software vendor (ISV) companies and open-source projects started by outstanding members of the ASP.NET community.

ASP.NET Script Callbacks

ASP.NET 2.0 contains a native API, named ASP.NET Script Callback, to implement out-of-band calls to the same URL of the current page. This API makes the out-of-band request look like a special-case page request. It transmits the view state along with original input fields. A few additional input fields are inserted in the body of the request to carry extra information. Once on the server, the request passes through the regular pipeline of HTTP modules and raises the expected sequence of server-side events up to the pre-rendering stage.

Just before the pre-rendering stage, the page method is executed, the return value is serialized to a string, and then the string is returned to the client. No rendering phase ever occurs, and the view state is not updated and serialized back.

ASP.NET Script Callback provides its own JavaScript API to wrap any needed calls to *XMLHttpRequest*. As a developer, you are not required to know about this API in detail. As a developer, you should instead focus on the programming interface of the *GetCallbackEvent-Reference* method of the *Page.ClientScript* object. This method simply returns the JavaScript code to attach to a client-side event handler to place an out-of-band call. The JavaScript code also references another piece of JavaScript used to update the page with the results generated on the server. But what happens on the server when the secondary request is made? Which page method is executed?

ASP.NET Script Callback defines an interface—the *ICallbackEventHandler* interface—that any server object that is the target of an out-of-band call can implement. The target of the out-of-band call can be either the page or any of its child controls. The execution of an out-of-band call is divided into two steps: preparation and results generation. The *RaiseCallbackEvent* method of the *ICallbackEventHandler* interface is invoked first to prepare the remote code execution. The *GetCallbackResult* method is invoked later in the request life cycle when it is time for the ASP.NET runtime to generate the response for the browser.

All in all, the programming interface of ASP.NET Script Callback is a bit clumsy. Although the programming interface shields developers from a lot of internal details, it still requires the programmer to have good JavaScript skills and is articulated in a bunch of boilerplate server code. You need server code to bind HTML elements to client-side event handlers, and you need ad hoc server code to publish a programming interface that is callable from the client. Each request carries with it a copy of the original view state and rebuilds the last known good state on the server. In other words, the original value of all input fields in the currently displayed page (regardless of any changes entered before the out-of-band call is made) are sent to the server along with any parameters for the server method. Any out-of-band calls are processed as a regular postback request up to the pre-rendering stage, meaning that all standard server events are fired: *Init*, *Load*, *LoadComplete*, and so on. Before the pre-rendering stage, the callback is prepared and executed shortly after. The requests ends immediately after the server method executes. The view state is not updated to reflect the state of the page after the out-of-band call and subsequently, it is not sent back to the client.

The advantage of using ASP.NET Script Callback is that it is a native part of ASP.NET and can be easily encapsulated in server controls. For example, the *TreeView* control in ASP.NET 2.0 uses script callbacks to expand its nodes.

ASP.NET Script Callback is not free of significant issues, however. In particular, the server method is constrained to a fixed signature and can only take and return a string. Sure, you can place any contents in the string, but the serialization and deserialization of custom objects to the string is something you must take care of entirely on your own. In addition, a page based on ASP.NET Script Callback can have only one endpoint for remote calls. This means that if a client page needs to place two distinct calls to the same remote page, you have to implement a switch in the implementation of the *ICallbackEventHandler* interface to interpret which method was intended to be executed.

The AJAX.NET Professional Library

To effectively implement out-of-band calls in application-wide scenarios, a kind of framework is required that hides all the nitty-gritty details of HTTP communication and exposes additional and higher-level controls and services.

AJAX.NET Professional (AjaxPro) is a pretty popular open-source library that adds a good layer of abstraction over the *XMLHttpRequest* machinery. Written by Michael Schwarz, the library creates proxy classes that are used by client-side JavaScript to invoke methods on the server page. The AjaxPro framework provides full data type support and works on all common Web browsers, including mobile devices. Nicely enough, the library can be used with both ASP.NET 1.1 and ASP.NET 2.0.

The key tool behind the AjaxPro library is an HTTP handler that hooks up any HTTP requests generated by the client-side part of the library:

```
<httpHandlers>
    <add verb="POST,GET" path="ajaxpro/*.ashx"
         type="AjaxPro.AjaxHandlerFactory, AjaxPro.2" />
</httpHandlers>
```

Once the *web.config* file has been correctly set up, you write JavaScript functions to trigger and control the out-of-band call. Each call targets a JavaScript object that represents the publicly callable method on the server ASP.NET page. A client-callable method is just a public method decorated with a specific attribute, as shown here:

```
[AjaxPro.AjaxMethod]
public DateTime GetCurrentTimeOnServer()
{
    return DateTime.Now;
}
```

The class with public methods, as well as any custom types used for I/O, has to be registered with the framework to have the corresponding JavaScript proxy created:

```
protected void Page_Load(object sender, EventArgs e)
{
    AjaxPro.Utility.RegisterTypeForAjax(typeof(YourAjaxClass));
}
```

If you do this, the handler guarantees that any managed .NET object that is returned by a server method will be serialized to a dynamically created JavaScript object to be seamlessly used on the client. You can return any managed type, your own classes, or enum types as you would do in plain .NET code. No view state is available during the AJAX request, meaning that you can't do much with page controls. In light of this, it is recommended that you create callable methods as static methods preferably, though not necessarily, on a separate class.

AjaxPro has some key advantages over the ASP.NET Script Callback API. It uses an attribute to mark server methods that can be called from the client. This means that you have the greatest flexibility when it comes to defining the server public interface callable from the client. In particular, you don't have to change the flow of the code or add new ad hoc methods just to comply with the requested programming interface.

In addition, you can register server types for use on the client, which provides for a strong-typed data transfer. The AjaxPro infrastructure serializes .NET types to JavaScript objects and vice versa. The AJAX.NET hooks up and replaces the standard request processing mechanism of ASP.NET—the page handler. As a result, you won't receive classic ASP.NET server events such as *Init*, *Load*, and postback. At the same time, you won't have the view state automatically transmitted with each out-of-band request. An AjaxPro request, though, is still processed by the ASP.NET HTTP runtime, meaning that the request is still subject to the modules registered with the HTTP pipeline, including session state management, roles, and authentication.

For more information about the AjaxPro library, you can take a look at *http://www.ajaxpro.info*. There you will also find a link to the CodePlex Web site to get the source code of the library.

The Anthem.NET Framework

Anthem.NET is a free, cross-browser AJAX toolkit for both ASP.NET 1.1 and 2.0, written by Jason Diamond. The library is made of a number of server controls that use *XMLHttpRequest* to post back. It sets itself apart from AjaxPro because it fully integrates with the classic life cycle of each ASP.NET request. The view state is sent across the wire, and server-side page and control events such as *Init*, *Load*, and *PreRender* are regularly fired. As a result, you write a page using the same programming model of ASP.NET, you are not required to write any JavaScript yourself, and you still leverage the beauty of the AJAX model. The only difference with a traditional ASP.NET application is that you use a different set of server controls, most of which are just subclassed versions of the original ASP.NET controls.

Extremely lean and easy to use, Anthem.NET implements AJAX functionalities through the "partial rendering" model applied at the control level. The partial rendering model is the same model that ASP.NET AJAX pushes hard. (See Chapter 4, "Partial Page Rendering.") For more information, check out *http://www.anthemdotnet.com*.

The ComfortASP.NET Framework

Conceptually similar to Anthem.NET, but significantly different in its implementation, is Daniel Zeiss' ComfortASP.NET framework. ComfortASP.NET uses a manager server control to inject script code in the client page. Invisible to the page author, the script code hooks up client postbacks and replaces them with calls to *XMLHttpRequest*.

Once back on the server, the manager component takes control of the operations and determines the delta between the current page and the page resulting from the processing of the current request. The markup that describes the changes in the displayed page is sent back and used to dynamically modify the page contents on the client via the previously emitted script. The server life cycle of the page is executed as usual, and events such as *Init* and *Load* are fired when expected.

The ComfortASP.NET framework refers to this technique as "selective update;" but in the end it is just another term to indicate what ASP.NET AJAX calls "partial rendering." (We'll cover partial rendering in Chapter 4.)

Using ComfortASP.NET couldn't be easier and faster. It only requires you to tweak the *web.config* file to add an HTTP handler for ASP.NET requests and add a manager control to each page you intend to expand with AJAX capabilities. The manager control features a few interesting properties such as compression, automatic form disabling during postback, and request timeout handling.

Taken alone, the manager control works on the page as a whole. The framework also includes a *PanelUpdater* control for you to selectively update specific portions (panels) of the page. You can learn more about the ComfortASP.NET Framework at *http://www.comfortasp.de/*.

The Telerik r.a.d.controls for ASP.NET Framework

Telerik r.a.d.controls for ASP.NET is a suite of versatile user-interface (UI) components, which offer complete interoperability with Microsoft ASP.NET AJAX Extensions. The product allows developers to build a sophisticated and largely customizable user interface based on ASP.NET AJAX. This means that r.a.d.controls are safe for use inside of any ASP.NET AJAX page and interact smoothly with any built-in ASP.NET AJAX controls.

Telerik is currently working on a special update of the r.a.d.controls suite, which will leverage the complete capabilities of the ASP.NET AJAX Framework. The new version of the product should be available by the time you read this book. Among the novelties, you can certainly expect a client-side object model that is consistent with the Microsoft AJAX Client Library conventions and controls that fully participate in the client life cycle of the request. (See Chapter 2.) In addition, the r.a.d.controls suite has rich type information similar to the .NET type descriptors, easy component discoverability and enumeration, and optimized resource management and disposal on partial page updates.

Apart from that, Telerik offers its own AJAX framework, called r.a.d.ajax. The purpose of the product is to eliminate the complexities of building JavaScript-intensive AJAX applications so that developers can take advantage of this new technology with no additional learning curve to climb. Complexities are eliminated by encapsulating the AJAX engine and all surrounding logic, including scripts, into classic ASP.NET server components, which can be configured visually with convenient builders in Visual Studio 2005. As a result, developers can simply write regular postback-based applications and turn them into AJAX-enabled ones without writing any JavaScript or server-side code.

The Telerik engine completely preserves the life cycle of the ASP.NET page, which is imperative for the proper operation of your application. The view state, event validation, and client-side scripts are also preserved as if a normal postback takes place. All form values are automatically sent to the server for processing. Telerik's framework is based on a patent-pending technology that manages AJAX postbacks internally.

For more information, visit *http://www.telerik.com.*

The ComponentArt Web.UI Framework

ComponentArt features Web.UI for ASP.NET AJAX—the first suite of controls designed specifically for ASP.NET AJAX. The library has a variety of advanced user interface controls for use in sophisticated Web applications—for example, grids, splitters, tree views, and drop-down lists. The *Callback* control, on the other hand, provides base AJAX capabilities.

The Web.UI library goes beyond mere compatibility or basic interoperability with ASP.NET AJAX. Rather, it offers deep integration into the new Microsoft AJAX framework. You find a bunch of server controls enriched with a client-side object model that fully leverages the Microsoft AJAX Client Library type system. (We'll cover the Microsoft AJAX Client Library in Chapter 2.) In particular, all controls inherit from the *Sys.UI.Control* client-side base class and expose extensive client-side methods and attributes to be invoked and set via script. Controls participate in the client-side life cycle, notify events, and communicate with native DOM elements.

All Web.UI controls have the ability to command AJAX postbacks on their own or through the ASP.NET AJAX's *UpdatePanel* control. (See Chapter 4.) For example, the *TreeView* and *Grid* controls implement their own built-in lightweight callback mechanisms for things such as load on demand or paging.

Similar to the ASP.NET AJAX *UpdatePanel*, the *CallBack* component can optionally wrap controls to update, and it can either bypass the standard page life cycle and execute server-side logic more quickly or maintain the latest state of all ASP.NET controls contained in the page through the view state. The client-side model of the *CallBack* component can be used from the client to execute server-side code. The *CallBack* control, though, is not used by any other Web.UI control internally.

For more information, visit *http://www.componentart.com.*

Infragistics's NetAdvantage for ASP.NET AJAX

NetAdvantage for ASP.NET—the Infragistics's flagship product for ASP.NET development—offers a full range of components ranging from a tree and menu, to a hierarchical grid, and even a charting engine. Infragistics employs a technique known as "Embedded AJAX" to build the AJAX functionality directly into their controls. By embedding the AJAX into the control itself, performance levels are achieved that would not otherwise be possible (when utilizing a separate AJAX engine or wrapper). In addition to the built-in AJAX features, Infragistics also supplies the "WARP Panel," which can be used to give any control(s) AJAX capabilities, much in the same manner as Microsoft's UpdatePanel.

Because the AJAX capabilities are built into Infragistics' WebControls, a developer need only know how to set a property to start using AJAX. Infragistics refers to this concept as

"No-Touch AJAX." Should you want to get your hands dirty, Infragistics provides a full client-side object model with API's and even an event model that can be programmed entirely through JavaScript. NetAdvantage for ASP.NET offers interoperability with Microsoft's ASP.NET AJAX Extensions—enabling you to use these two powerful toolsets side-by-side. Though the current level of integration with ASP.NET AJAX is not as deep as we've seen with ComponentArt's Web.UI, Infragistics manages to provide much of the same functionality through their own framework.

For more information, visit *http://www.infragistics.com/ajax*.

Categorizing AJAX Frameworks

As you can witness yourself, each AJAX-oriented framework falls into one of the following three main categories:

- RPC-style frameworks
- A suite of rich controls
- AJAX frameworks

RPC-style frameworks are ASP.NET libraries that simply provide the capability of calling back server code from the client via JavaScript. ASP.NET Script Callbacks and AjaxPro certainly have this capability.

Commercial products from popular vendors such as Telerik, ComponentArt, and Infragistics offer a suite of controls with AJAX capabilities. Currently, they don't provide the same level of integration with the ASP.NET AJAX platform; however, in the short term they will be aligned at the same level and differentiate their product offerings by extending differing levels of features and capabilities, some solidly Microsoft ASP.NET AJAX compliant (Component Art) and others to a lesser degree.

Finally, there will be pure AJAX frameworks—that is, a code library that enables pages and applications to do AJAX. Of course, ASP.NET AJAX Extensions is the most rich and powerful option, and it's certainly the standard to follow for the largest share of developers. However, a number of good frameworks (often, open-source frameworks) exist—such as Anthem.NET and ComfortASP.NET—that simply help you build AJAX pages quickly and effectively. They have anticipated most of the features you find today in ASP.NET AJAX Extensions.

ASP.NET AJAX in Person

Architecturally speaking, the ASP.NET AJAX framework is made of two distinct elements: a client script library and a set of server controls that add AJAX capabilities to ASP.NET 2.0. The client script library is written entirely in JavaScript and therefore works with any modern browser. ASP.NET AJAX offers an end-to-end programming model that spans the client and server environment. It's also seamless to use for most developers because it simply extends the popular and known application model of classic ASP.NET.

Setting Up ASP.NET AJAX Extensions

Before we delve into the ASP.NET AJAX architecture, let's briefly review some common issues related to installing, configuring, and running ASP.NET AJAX applications.

Installing ASP.NET AJAX Extensions

The setup phase of ASP.NET AJAX Extensions installs debug and release copies of the AJAX Script Library and any needed binaries. If you have any version of Visual Studio 2005 installed, the package also configures the Integrated Development Environment (IDE) to show a ready-made AJAX project template. (See Figure 1-6.)

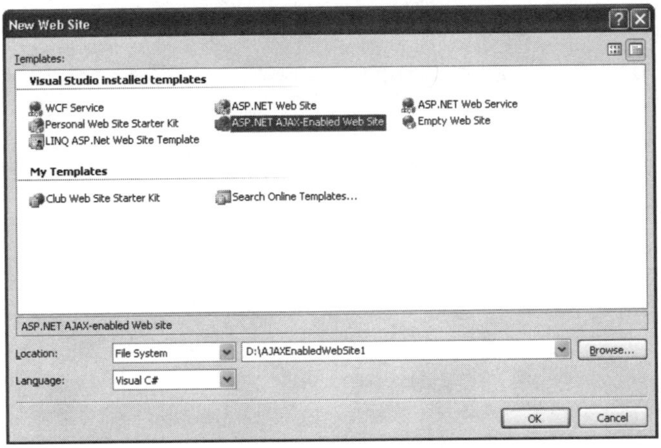

Figure 1-6   The new AJAX project template that shows up when you create a new Web site.

The ASP.NET AJAX Extensions Microsoft Windows Installer (MSI) package installs a handful of files on your computer under the following folder:

```
%DRIVE%:\Program Files\Microsoft ASP.NET\ASP.NET 2.0 AJAX Extensions\v1.0.61025
```

In addition, it places an assembly named *System.Web.Extensions.dll* in the global assembly cache (GAC). The ASP.NET AJAX assembly incorporates a bunch of JavaScript files (*.js* files) that form the client script library.

> **Note**   The official installer of ASP.NET AJAX copies the binaries in the GAC. This is still the recommended way to go. However, simply copying the *System.Web.Extensions* assembly in the Bin folder does suffice to deploy an ASP.NET AJAX Web site.

Deploying ASP.NET AJAX Applications

The simplest way to create an ASP.NET AJAX application is by choosing the Visual Studio 2005 project template. (See Figure 1-6.) Visual Studio adds to the project a *web.config* file that contains all settings required to run an ASP.NET AJAX application. In particular, the configuration file links the ASP.NET AJAX assembly to the project.

If your ASP.NET AJAX application consumes Web services, you should ensure that these Web services—local to the application—have correctly installed and can find all of their required resources.

> **Important**   Not all configuration entries created in the default *web.config* file are required in all cases. You might want to remove those that you don't need. In particular, you might want to remove HTTP handlers and HTTP modules that serve calls to Web services and page methods, respectively, if your application doesn't place remote out-of-band calls directly from JavaScript. However, when you edit the web.config file pay a lot of attention and limit yourself to commenting out parts rather than deleting them. You might inadvertently remove an important setting that breaks the whole application.

Core Components

The ASP.NET AJAX framework is made of a client and a server part. Applications use a client-side JavaScript library mostly to manage the page user interface, to call server-based components, and order partial page refreshes. Server components generate the response for the client and emit predefined client script that integrates and sometimes extends the client library. The server-side part of ASP.NET AJAX includes Web services, ad hoc controls, and the JavaScript Object Notation (JSON) infrastructure. (I discuss the JSON data interchange technology a bit later in this chapter.)

The Microsoft Client Library for AJAX

The AJAX client library is made of a set of JavaScript (*.js*) files that are linked from client pages in case of need. These *.js* files are downloaded on each client that consumes ASP.NET AJAX pages. These files are transparent to ASP.NET developers, as they are embedded in the ASP.NET AJAX assembly.

The client library provides object-oriented and cross-browser extensions to the JavaScript language such as classes, namespaces, inheritance, and data types. In addition, it defines a largely shrink-wrapped version of the .NET base class library that includes string builders, regular expressions, timers, and tracing. The key part of the ASP.NET AJAX client library is the networking layer that manages the complexity of making asynchronous calls over *XMLHttpRequest*. This layer allows the client page to communicate with Web services and Web pages through out-of-band calls.

Server-Based Components

ASP.NET AJAX is an extension to ASP.NET, and ASP.NET is a server-side development platform. Hence, ASP.NET AJAX sports a number of server-based components, including Web services and controls, that offer a double benefit. On one end, you can program these components from the client and update the current page without a full refresh; on the other hand, though, the programming model remains unaltered for the most part. In this way, at least limited to core functionalities, the ASP.NET AJAX learning curve might be pleasantly short.

Built-in Web services expose a handful of ASP.NET features to client pages, including user profiles, membership, and roles. Server controls look like classic ASP.NET server controls, except that they emit additional script code. The script code enriches the user's experience with the control by optionally taking advantage of the facilities provided by the AJAX client library. Some key AJAX server controls you will work with are *UpdatePanel*, *UpdateProgress*, and *Timer*. I'll cover them in Chapter 4.

The JSON Infrastructure

The growing use of out-of-band calls in Web applications poses a new issue—moving more and more complex data around. It's not a mere serialization issue for which the .NET Framework and other platform-specific frameworks have a ready-made solution. The serialization involved with out-of-band calls is not just cross-platform; it also involves distinct tiers and radically different tools and languages. With out-of-band calls, you move data from a client to a server and back. But the client is a browser (if not a mobile device), and JavaScript is the native format of data. The server is a Web server hosted on a variety of hardware/software platforms and running a specific Web application framework.

JSON is the emerging technology for passing structured data across the Web. It is a data interchange format and is fully described at *http://www.json.org*. Relatively easy to read for humans and to parse and generate for machines, JSON describes data using two universal data structures—collections and array—that are supported in one way or another by most modern programming languages and class libraries.

JSON is a text format that is completely language independent, although it relies heavily on a number of conventions inherited from the C family of languages.

The JSON client infrastructure can serialize a JavaScript object to an interchange format and send it over the wire to a server-side receiver. The platform-specific receiver will parse the data stream to build a platform-specific object. Likewise, the JSON server infrastructure can take any platform-specific object and serialize to an interchange format. Back on the client, the data stream is promptly transformed in a JavaScript object. As far as the .NET Framework and ASP.NET are concerned, a bit of reflection is used to examine the internal structure of classes and create proper JavaScript wrappers.

Virtually all AJAX-based frameworks implement a JSON infrastructure. ASP.NET AJAX is no exception.

> **Note**   For a while, XML has been touted as the lingua franca of the Web because it is ideal and made-to-measure for developers and architects to package and exchange data in a totally cross-platform way. Today, you find out that JSON (a non-XML technology) is sold for the same task. Is there any difference? Both JSON and XML do the same work. XML is more complex, quirky in some respects, and general-purpose, and it is preferable to describe data to be styled using an XSLT style sheet for UI purposes. For raw data, JSON is a more lightweight format that is easier to read and parse for both humans and computers.

Conclusion

Most attentive developers have been developing around interactive Web technologies since the late 1990s. Various technologies (for example, Microsoft Remote Scripting and open-source and commercial variations) have been developed without forming a critical mass of acceptance and use. Or perhaps the mass was big enough, but everyone was waiting for the spark of a killer application. Another factor that slowed down the adoption of more advanced client techniques was the lack of cross-browser support for them.

Today, the situation is radically different from what it was only three or four years ago. Now about 90 percent of the available browsers support all the minimal requirements for implementing interactive Web applications, known as AJAX applications. In addition, the W3C is standardizing the *XMLHttpRequest* object, which is the necessary communication workhorse behind all existing platforms for AJAX. The next generation of Web applications will be based on a different mechanism: it is no longer, or not just, forms posted in a change of pages, but individual requests for data and dynamic updates to displayed pages.

As a server technology aimed at the creation of Web pages, ASP.NET takes advantage of the opportunity for providing this much desired functionality. Script callbacks were the first Microsoft attempt to offer an API for building AJAX-style pages. Modeled after the classic postback event, callbacks are sometimes unnecessarily heavy and inflexible.

An add-on to ASP.NET 2.0, Microsoft ASP.NET AJAX Extensions, shows the way ahead for AJAX applications as far as the ASP.NET platform is concerned. It integrates the AJAX lifestyle into the existing application model of ASP.NET, resulting in a familiar programming model with greatly improved and richer functionality.

The Microsoft Client Library for AJAX

Most of the power of AJAX resides on the client and is strictly related to the browser's and platform's client-side functionality. Even though a large share of AJAX pages are built using a slightly different set of server controls, they couldn't work without a powerful environment available on the client and written in JavaScript. Such a script code governs the execution of out-of-band calls and often kicks in and replaces regular postbacks with AJAX postbacks. No AJAX functionality would ever be possible without JavaScript and a standard (and rich) Document Object Model (DOM). The DOM, though, is not enough.

The DOM represents the programming gateway to the page constituent elements, but it is not designed to provide programming facilities such as those you can find in a general-purpose library. Normally, the script tools you can leverage to consume objects and contents from the DOM are those provided by the JavaScript language. Not exactly a powerful toolkit. Enter the Microsoft AJAX Library.

The Microsoft AJAX library is written in JavaScript, although with a strong sense of object-orientation. The JavaScript language does support objects and allow the creation of custom objects. It does not, however, support full object-orientedness since it has no native concept of true object inheritance. Nonetheless, even excluding true object-orientation, JavaScript is still a modern and suitable language that can be used to build a class framework a la the .NET Framework. ASP.NET AJAX takes the JavaScript language to the next level by adding some type-system extensions and the notions of namespace and inheritance. In addition, the ASP.NET AJAX JavaScript supports interfaces and enumerations, and has a number of helper functions to manipulate strings and arrays.

These extensions are coded using the base set of instructions that characterize the core JavaScript language, and they're persisted to the *.js* files that form the Microsoft AJAX client runtime environment.

In this chapter, you'll first learn how to use extensions to JavaScript—such as namespaces, interfaces, and inheritance—and then take the plunge into the namespaces and classes that form the client-side AJAX framework.

JavaScript Language Extensions

Writing a rich and complex framework such as ASP.NET AJAX using only plain old JavaScript is probably beyond human capabilities. On the other hand, using another language would pose serious browser-compatibility issues and eliminate the main reason behind the today's success of the AJAX paradigm—its broad reach.

Infrastructure for Extensions

The Microsoft AJAX library adds a strong focus on typing to the JavaScript language. Top-level types such as array, Boolean, string, and number are encapsulated in classes and forced into a hierarchical structure that mirrors—to the extent that it is possible—the true .NET Framework. The Microsoft AJAX library exposes a class-oriented type system to the outside world that supports namespaces, inheritance, interfaces, enumerations, reflection, and a good deal of helper methods for strings, arrays, and other base types.

All together, these extensions enable you to code ASP.NET AJAX client functionalities in a more structured way and thereby improve maintenance, extensibility, and ease of development.

The Microsoft AJAX Library Engine

The library is made of a few *.js* files downloaded to the client browser on demand. At a minimum, the core runtime script file is downloaded. All script files are incorporated as resources in the ASP.NET AJAX assembly—the *System.Web.Extensions.dll* file—and are extracted and injected in the client page as required by the page itself.

Adding the Microsoft AJAX library to a Web application makes JavaScript programming easier, and it automatically endows the client environment with a set of new and richer objects and object-oriented capabilities.

Note   Although the Microsoft AJAX library ships as part of ASP.NET AJAX Extensions, nothing prevents you from using those *.js* files in non–ASP.NET 2.0 applications. In particular, you are encouraged to download the JavaScript files from the ASP.NET AJAX Web site and link them from, say, a PHP or ASP.NET 1.1 application, obtaining the same pleasant effect— object-oriented features from a script language. You get the files under the Microsoft permissive license agreement and are allowed to use and modify these scripts in your own applications. Find them at http://ajax.asp.net/downloads/default.aspx.

The Root Object of the Microsoft AJAX Library

Overall, JavaScript is an object-based language. (It's not truly object-oriented because it doesn't implement some of the required object-oriented concepts, such as true object inheritance.) The language features a set of built-in objects, including *Function*, *Object*, *Boolean*, *Array*, *Number*, and *String*. All intrinsic objects have a read-only property named *prototype*. You use the *prototype* property to provide a base set of functionality shared by any new instance of an object of that class. New functionality can be added to the class prototype inside of an application to extend and improve the capabilities of a given class. This is exactly what the Microsoft AJAX library does.

In the library (precisely, in the *MicrosoftAjax.js* file), all built-in JavaScript objects feature a richer prototype and incorporate new capabilities. For example, the library extends the JavaScript *Function* object with a set of methods to provide for delegates and callbacks. Here's a brief snippet from (the debug version of) *MicrosoftAjax.js* that illustrates the point:

```
// Set the type name
Function.__typeName = 'Function';

// Define a callback
Function.createCallback = function Function$createCallback(method, context)
{
    var e = Function._validateParams(...);
    if (e) throw e;

    return function() {
        var l = arguments.length;
        if (l > 0) {
            var args = [];
            for (var i = 0; i < l; i++) {
                args[i] = arguments[i];
            }
            args[l] = context;
            return method.apply(this, args);
        }
        return method.call(this, context);
    }
}

// Define a delegate (function pointer)
Function.createDelegate = function Function$createDelegate(
    instance, method)
{
    var e = Function._validateParams(...);
    if (e) throw e;

    return function() {
        return method.apply(instance, arguments);
    }
}
```

The *Function* type is then associated with the *Type* property on the *window* object in the browser DOM:

```
window.Type = Function;
```

The *window* object is the top-level object in the JavaScript hierarchy and represents a browser window. The browser creates one *window* object when it opens an HTML page and additional *window* objects for each frame it encounters. You can access all *window* members by using the member name directly—that is, without prefixing it with a name that evaluates to the current *window* object. The *window* object features a number of predefined members, including the popular *alert* method and *event* object; in addition, new dynamic members can be defined on the fly.

The native *Function* object, referred through the nickname of *Type*, is extended with a number of object-oriented methods. This is accomplished by extending the *prototype* property that characterizes any JavaScript object. The following code shows how to add the *getName* method to all Microsoft AJAX library objects:

```
Type.prototype.getName = function Type$getName()
{
    if (arguments.length !== 0)
        throw Error.parameterCount();
    return (typeof(this.__typeName) === "undefined")
            ? "" : this.__typeName;
}
```

In this way, you can ask each JavaScript object to qualify itself in a reliable and precise way. In *MicrosoftAjax.js*, the *Function* object works in a way that resembles the following pseudo-class:

```
public class Function
{
    public static Object createCallback(Object method, Object context);
    public static Object createDelegate(Object instance, Object method);
     public static Object emptyFunction();
    public static Object emptyMethod();
    public static Object getRootNamespaces();
    public static Object isClass(Object type);
    public static Object isEnum(Object type);
    public static Object isFlags(Object type);
    public static Object isInterface(Object type);
    public static Object isNamespace(Object object);
    public static Object parse(Object typeName, Object ns);
    public static Object registerNamespace(Object namespacePath);

    public Object callBaseMethod(Object instance, Object name, Object args);
    public Object getBaseMethod(Object instance, Object name);
    public Object getBaseType();
    public Object getInterfaces();
    public Object getName();
    public Object implementsInterface(Object interfaceType);
    public Object inheritsFrom(Object parentType);
```

```
    public Object initializeBase(Object instance, Object baseArguments);
    public Object isImplementedBy(Object instance);
    public Object isInstanceOfType(Object instance);
    public Object registerClass(Object type, Object base, Object interface);
    public Object registerEnum(Object name, Object flags);
    public Object registerInterface(Object typeName);
    public Object resolveInheritance();
}
```

All methods added to the prototype will be "inherited" by any other function defined in the context of any library-powered application.

Other Top-Level Types

The Microsoft AJAX library contains code that defines new objects and extends existing Java-Script objects with additional functionality. Table 2-1 lists the main global objects defined in the library.

Table 2-1   Top-Level Objects in the AJAX Library

Type	Description
Array	Extends the native *Array* object. This object groups static methods to add, insert, remove, and clear elements of an array. It also includes static methods to enumerate elements and check whether a given element is contained in the array.
Boolean	Extends the native *Boolean* object. This object defines a static *parse* method to infer a Boolean value from a string or any expression that evaluates to a Boolean value.
Date	Extends the native *Date* object with a couple of instance methods: *localeFormat* and *format*. These methods format the date using the locale or invariant culture information.
Error	Defines a static *create* method to wrap the JavaScript *Error* object and add a richer constructor to it. This object incorporates a couple of properties—*message* and *name*—to provide a description of the error that occurred and identify the error by name. A number of built-in error objects are used to simulate exceptions. In this case, the *name* property indicates the name of the exception caught.
Function	Extends the native *Function* object. This object groups methods to define classes, namespaces, delegates, and a bunch of other object-oriented facilities.
Number	Extends the native *Number* object. This object defines a static *parse* method to infer a numeric value from a string or any expression that evaluates to a numeric value. In addition, it supports a pair of static formatting methods: *localeFormat* and *format*.
Object	Extends the native *Object* object. This object groups methods to read type information such as the type of the object being used.
RegExp	Wraps the native *RegExp* object.
String	Extends the native *String* object. This object groups string manipulation methods such as trim methods and *endsWith* and *startsWith* methods. In addition, it defines static *localeFormat* and *format* methods that are close relatives of the *String.Format* method of the managed *String* type.

By simply adding a *ScriptManager* server control to an ASP.NET page, you gain the right to use any additional methods on native objects that are defined in the Microsoft AJAX library. For example, the following code will work just fine if you add such a control:

```
var s = "Dino";
alert(s.startsWith('D'));
```

The native JavaScript *String* object doesn't feature either a *startsWith* or an *endsWith* method. However, the following code in Microsoft Client library does the trick:

```
String.prototype.endsWith = function String$endsWith(suffix)
{
    var e = Function._validateParams(...);
    if (e) throw e;

    return (this.substr(this.length - suffix.length) === suffix);
}
String.prototype.startsWith = function String$startsWith(prefix)
{
    var e = Function._validateParams(...);
    if (e) throw e;

    return (this.substr(0, prefix.length) === prefix);
}
```

Discovering Type Information

JavaScript objects are not truly strongly-typed objects. In particular, there's no fully reliable mechanism to know the type of the object you're working with. The *toString* method and the *typeof* operator help only partially. The former is designed to provide a string representation of the object, so it merely returns the contents of the object for strings and numbers. The latter always returns *object* regardless of the name of the custom object you're manipulating. Consider a class *IntroAjax.Person* defined as shown here:

```
Type.registerNamespace("IntroAjax");

// Constructor
IntroAjax.Person = function IntroAjax$Person(firstName, lastName)
{
    IntroAjax.Person.initializeBase(this);
    this._firstName = firstName;
    this._lastName = lastName;
}

// Add a FirstName property to the class prototype
IntroAjax.Person.prototype.get_FirstName =
    function IntroAjax$Person$get_FirstName() {
        // Raise an error if the number of arguments doesn't match
        if (arguments.length !== 0)
            throw Error.parameterCount ();
        return this._firstName;
    }
```

```
IntroAjax.Person.prototype.set_FirstName =
    function IntroAjax$Person$set_FirstName(value) {
        // Automatic arguments validation
        var e = Function._validateParams(arguments,
                    [{name: "value", type: String}]);
        if (e)
            throw e;
        this._firstName = value;
    }

// Add a LastName property to the class prototype
IntroAjax.Person.prototype.get_LastName =
    function IntroAjax$Person$get_LastName() {
        if (arguments.length !== 0)
            throw Error.parameterCount();
        return this._lastName;
    }
IntroAjax.Person.prototype.set_LastName =
    function IntroAjax$Person$set_LastName(value) {
        var e = Function._validateParams(arguments,
                    [{name: "value", type: String}]);
        if (e)
            throw e;
        this._lastName = value;
    }

IntroAjax.Person.registerClass('IntroAjax.Person');
```

Imagine that you now create an instance of this class and then need to know about its exact type. A new method added to the *Object* object provides for exact type recognition. The method to use is *Object.getTypeName*:

```
var p = new Person("Dino", "Esposito");
alert(Object.getTypeName(p));
```

The message box now shows *IntroAjax.Person* instead of a more generic "object" string. It's interesting to take a look at the source code of the *getTypeName* method:

```
Object.getTypeName = function Object$getTypeName(instance)
{
    var e = Function._validateParams( ... );
    if (e) throw e;

    return Object.getType(instance).getName();
}
Object.getType = function Object$getType(instance)
{
    var e = Function._validateParams( ... );
    if (e) throw e;

    var ctor = instance.constructor;
    if (!ctor || (typeof(ctor) !== "function") ||
        !ctor.__typeName || (ctor.__typeName === 'Object'))
```

```
    {
        return Object;
    }
    return ctor;
}
```

In the end, the *getName* method on the root *Type* object is used to resolve the type name. (As mentioned earlier, *Type* is a global *window* object that evaluates to the JavaScript *Function* object.)

```
Type.prototype.getName = function Type$getName()
{
    if (arguments.length !== 0)
        throw Error.parameterCount();
    return (typeof(this.__typeName) === "undefined")
            ? "" : this.__typeName;
}
```

As you can see, the *getName* method simply returns the value of an internal variable. It turns out that each new object sets the *_typeName* variable to the string that represents the class name. For example, in the Microsoft AJAX library the type name of the *Object* class is explicitly set to the string "Object":

```
Object._typeName = 'Object';
```

All built-in JavaScript objects are modified in the Microsoft AJAX library to feature an additional type name property.

Note JavaScript clearly has a number of useful similarities with C-like languages such as C# and Java. Yet it is a script language with a number of shortcuts and special extensions. One is the === (triple =) operator; another is its opposite, the !== operator. The === operator is a variation of the classic == (is-equal-to) operator and checks for both value and type, whereas the classic equality operator is limited to checking values. As an example, consider the following code snippet:

```
var x = 1;
var y = "1";
```

If you compare *x == y*, you get *true*—the same value. If you compare *x === y*, you get *false*—the same value, but not the same type.

The bottom line is that the Microsoft AJAX library builds a thick abstraction layer on top of the core JavaScript native objects that transforms a script language in a sort of object-oriented script framework. If you forget for a while about most common JavaScript concepts and syntax elements you know and think of it as a brand new language, you could easily envision the library as a shrink-wrapped version of the .NET Framework and the ASP.NET AJAX JavaScript language as simplified C#.

> **Note**   You might have noticed that JavaScript functions used to implement methods on objects are named rather than being plain anonymous functions. This approach is a change in the Microsoft AJAX library that occurred with the Beta stage of ASP.NET AJAX, and it's also a technique that is not that common among JavaScript writers. In the Microsoft AJAX library, functions are pseudo-named so that you get additional information, such as obtaining context within a stack trace. This change will help Visual Studio "Orcas" to do a great job with debugging and Microsoft IntelliSense.

Reflection Capabilities

Earlier in the chapter, I showed a pseudoclass named *Function* to represent the real capabilities of the JavaScript *Function* type in the Microsoft AJAX library. Table 2-2 provides more information regarding what most of those methods really do. All methods in the table are invoked on library classes to help you discover type information and manage it dynamically. Static methods are invoked from the *Type* object directly.

Table 2-2   Methods on the *Type* Object

Name	Description
callBaseMethod	Returns the value of the base method, or null if a base method is not found.
getBaseMethod	Returns the implementation method of a method in the base class, or null if the implementation method is not defined.
getBaseType	Returns the base type of an instance.
getInterfaces	Returns the interfaces implemented by the specified instance.
getName	Returns the name of the base type of the instance.
implementsInterface	Determines whether the type implements a specified interface.
inheritsFrom	Determines whether the type inherits from the specified parent type.
initializeBase	Initializes the base type in the context of the defined instance.
isImplementedBy	Determines whether an instance implements the specified interface.
isInstanceOfType	Determines whether an object is an instance of a specified type or one of its derived types.
parse	Static method, returns an instance of the type defined by specified type name as represented as a string.
registerClass	Registers a class defined by the constructor, with an optional base type and with interfaces.
registerEnum	Creates a new enumeration type.
registerInterface	Registers an interface, represented by its constructor.
registerNamespace	Static method, registers and creates a namespace.
resolveInheritance	Static method, enables you to reflect on the inherited members of a derived type.

The methods listed in Table 2-2 help you to reflect type information programmatically and create objects in an indirect manner.

The *$get* Alias

Before we take a look at more juicy object-oriented extensions such as namespaces and inheritance, let's discuss a few shortcuts you can use in your script code to speed up development.

One of the most common mistakes that occurs when writing script code inside of Web pages is to use direct access to HTML elements instead of resorting to the *getElementById* method of the DOM. Suppose you have a text box element named *TextBox1* in your client page. The following script code won't work on all browsers:

```
alert(TextBox1.value);
```

The correct form ratified by the W3C paper for the HTML DOM standards is shown here:

```
alert(document.getElementById("TextBox1").value);
```

The correct form is clearly more verbose and bothersome to write over and over again. Microsoft Client library comes to the rescue with the *$get* global function. Simply put, the *$get* function is a shortcut for the *document.getElementById* function. In an ASP.NET AJAX page, the following expression is fully equivalent to the one just shown:

```
alert($get("TextBox1").value);
```

More precisely, the *$get* function is an alias for a piece of code defined as follows:

```
var $get = Sys.UI.DomElement.getElementById = function
        Sys$UI$DomElement$getElementById(id, element)
{
    var e = Function._validateParams( ... );
    if (e) throw e;

    if (!element)
        return document.getElementById(id);
    if (element.getElementById)
        return element.getElementById(id);

    var nodeQueue = [];
    var childNodes = element.childNodes;
    for (var i = 0; i < childNodes.length; i++)
    {
        var node = childNodes[i];
        if (node.nodeType == 1)
            nodeQueue[nodeQueue.length] = node;
    }

    while (nodeQueue.length) {
        node = nodeQueue.shift();
        if (node.id == id) {
            return node;
        }
```

```
        childNodes = node.childNodes;
        for (i = 0; i < childNodes.length; i++) {
            node = childNodes[i];
            if (node.nodeType == 1) {
                nodeQueue[nodeQueue.length] = node;
            }
        }
    }

    return null;
}
```

If you simply call *$get* passing the sole ID, the function falls back into *document.getElement-ById*. Alternatively, you can specify a root element. If this element supports the *getElementById* method, the function returns the output of *element.getElementById*; otherwise, the *$get* function uses the DOM interface to explore the contents of the subtree rooted in the element to locate the node with the given name.

> **Note**   Before the Beta stage, ASP.NET AJAX defined a global alias named *$* that mapped to the *document.getElementById* function. The *$* alias has been changed to *$get* to avoid conflicts with other AJAX frameworks developers might use along with ASP.NET AJAX.

Similar shortcuts exist also to look up components in the runtime hierarchy and to create them and add and remove event handlers. We'll return to this point later in the chapter as we make our way through the library components.

Closures vs. Prototypes

When it comes to JavaScript classes (more exactly, pseudoclasses), there are mainly two models to use when creating them. One is known as a *closure*; one is based on the *prototype*. In early builds of the Microsoft AJAX library, the ASP.NET team used the closure model. They switched to the prototype model in the Beta stage.

A closure is a general concept of programming languages. When applied to JavaScript, it can be summarized as follows: A closure is a JavaScript function that can have variables and methods defined together within the same context. In this way, the outermost (anonymous or named) function "closes" the expression. Here's an example of the closure model for a function that represents a *Person* type with two properties:

```
registerNamespace("IntroAjax");

// Closure: Constructor and members
IntroAjax.Person = function()
{
    var _firstName;
    var _lastName;
    this.get_FirstName = function() { return this._firstName; }
    this.get_LastName = function() { return this._lastName; }
}
IntroAjax.Person.registerClass('IntroAjax.Person');
```

As you can see, the closure is nothing more than the constructor of the class. Again, JavaScript classes are not classes in the sense understood in the .NET Framework, but we'll refer to them as classes for convenience.

In a closure model, the constructor contains the member declarations and members are truly encapsulated and private to the class. In addition, members are instance based, which increases the memory used by the class.

The prototype model entails that you define the "public" structure of the class through the JavaScript *prototype* object. The following code sample shows how to rewrite the preceding *Person* class to avoid a closure. The resulting code is nearly identical to the code presented earlier for the *IntroAjax.Person* class—that is, the recommended way to write classes in the Microsoft AJAX library.

```
registerNamespace("IntroAjax");

// Prototype: Constructor
IntroAjax.Person = function()
{
    // Ctor creates private fields
    this._firstName = "";
    this._lastName = "";
}

// Prototype: Members
IntroAjax.Person.prototype.get_FirstName = function() {
    return this._firstName;
}
IntroAjax.Person.prototype.get_LastName = function() {
    return this._lastName;
}

IntroAjax.Person.registerClass("IntroAjax.Person");
```

In the prototype model, the constructor and members are clearly separated and a constructor is always required. As for private members, the Microsoft AJAX library convention is to name them with a "_" prefix. In the prototype model, members are shared by all instances, which reduces the memory used by each instance and provides for faster object instantiation. Aside from syntax peculiarities, the prototype model makes defining classes much more similar to the classic object-oriented programming (OOP) model than the closure model.

Note   The goal of the ASP.NET AJAX team was deliver a model that provided the best quality and performance on the largest number of browsers. Prototypes have a good load time in all browsers; and indeed, they have excellent performance in Firefox. (In contrast, closures have a better load time than prototypes in Internet Explorer.) Prototypes provide better support for IntelliSense, and allow for tool-based statement completion when used in tools that support this feature, such as Visual Studio "Orcas". Prototypes can also help you obtain type information by simply using reflection. You won't have to create an instance of the type in order to query for type information, which is unavoidable if closures are used. Finally, prototypes allow you to easily view private class members when debugging. Debugging objects derived using the closure model requires a number of additional steps.

If you're simply going to write client script that uses built-in classes in the library, you don't need to learn about closures and prototypes. If you happen to write a custom JavaScript class to extend the Microsoft AJAX library, you should use the prototype model.

> **Note** If you want to learn more about JavaScript closures, go to the following URL: *http://www.jibbering.com/faq/faq_notes/closures.html.*

Object-Oriented Extensions

In JavaScript, the *Function* object is the main tool you use to combine code with properties and forge new components. In the Microsoft AJAX library, the *Function* object is extended to incorporate type information, as well as namespaces, inheritance, interfaces, and enumerations. Let's see how.

Adding Namespace Support

A namespace provides a way of grouping and classifying types belonging to a library. A namespace is not a type itself, but it adds more information to the definition of each type it contains to better qualify the type. Conceptually, a namespace is related to a directory in much the same way a type is related to a file. The unit of data you work with is ultimately the file, and you identify the file by name. However, files with the same name defined in different directories appear as completely distinct entities to any programming environment.

By default, all custom JavaScript functions belong to the global space of names. In the Microsoft AJAX library, you can associate a custom function with a particular namespace for purely organizational reasons. When declaring a custom type in the Microsoft AJAX library, you can do as follows:

```
Type.registerNamespace("IntroAjax");
IntroAjax.Person = function IntroAjax$Person(firstName, lastName)
{
    this._firstName = firstName;
    this._lastName = lastName;
}

// Define the body of members
function IntroAjax$Person$ToString() {
    return this._lastName + ", " + this._firstName;
}
...

// Define the prototype of the class
IntroAjax.Person.prototype = {
    ToString:       IntroAjax$Person$ToString,
    get_FirstName: IntroAjax$Person$get_FirstName,
    set_FirstName: IntroAjax$Person$set_FirstName,
    get_LastName:  IntroAjax$Person$get_LastName,
```

```
    set_LastName:  IntroAjax$Person$set_LastName
}

// Register the class
IntroAjax.Person.registerClass("IntroAjax.Person");
```

The *Type.registerNamespace* method adds the specified namespace to the runtime environment. In a way, the *registerNamespace* method is equivalent to using the *namespace {...}* construct in C# or the *Namespace .. End Namespace* construct in Microsoft Visual Basic .NET.

 Note   Because the Microsoft AJAX library expresses the capabilities of a runtime framework rather than the syntax of a programming language, the correspondence between *Type.registerNamespace* and a C# or Visual Basic .NET language construct is purely logical. Internally, *Type.registerNamespace* is limited to adding information to the current DOM to track the current namespace.

The *IntroAjax.Person* function defined following the namespace declaration describes a type *Person* in the *IntroAjax* namespace. Finally, the newly defined function must be registered as a class with the Microsoft AJAX library framework. You use the *registerClass* method on the current function. The *registerClass* method is defined in the prototype of the *Function* object; as such, it is inherited by all functions. Internally, the *registerClass* method sets the *_typeName* property of the function to the first parameter of the method—the actual name of the class.

The *registerClass* method takes a number of parameters. The first parameter is mandatory, and it indicates the public name that will be used to expose the JavaScript function as a class. Additional and optional parameters are the parent class if there is any and any interface implemented by the class.

As mentioned, in the definition of a new class, you can use an anonymous function or a named function. In terms of syntax, both solutions are acceptable. The convention, though, is that you opt for named functions and name each function after its fully qualified name, replacing the dot symbol (.) with a dollar symbol ($).

Adding Inheritance Support

Let's define a new class *Citizen* that extends *Person* by adding a couple of properties: address and a national identification number. Here's the skeleton of the code you need:

```
// Declare the class
IntroAjax.Citizen = function IntroAjax$Citizen(firstName, lastName, id)
{
    ...
}

// Define the prototype of the class
```

```
IntroAjax.Citizen.prototype = {
    ...
}
```

```
// Register the class
IntroAjax.Citizen.registerClass("IntroAjax.Citizen", IntroAjax.Person);
```

Note that the first argument of *registerClass* is a string, but the second one has to be an object reference. Let's flesh out this code a bit.

In the constructor, you'll set some private members and call the base constructor to initialize the members defined on the base class. The *initializeBase* method (defined on *Function*) retrieves and invokes the base constructor.

```
IntroAjax.Citizen = function IntroAjax$Citizen(firstName, lastName, id)
{
    IntroAjax.Citizen.initializeBase(this, [firstName, lastName]);
    this._id = id;
    this._address = "";
}
```

You pass *initializeBase* the reference to the current object as well as an array with any parameters that the constructor to call requires. You can use the *[...]* notation to define an array inline. If you omit the *[...]* notation, be ready to handle a parameter count exception.

Quite often, developers derive a class because they need to add new members or alter the behavior of an existing method or property. Object-oriented languages define a proper keyword to flag members as overridable. How is that possible in JavaScript? By simply adding a member to the class prototype, you mark it as overridable in derived classes. In addition, if the member already exists on the base class, it is silently overridden in the new one. Here's the prototype of the *Citizen* class:

```
IntroAjax.Citizen.prototype =
{
    ToString:    IntroAjax$Citizen$ToString,
    get_ID:      IntroAjax$Citizen$get_ID,
    get_Address: IntroAjax$Citizen$get_Address,
    set_Address: IntroAjax$Citizen$set_Address
}
```

The class has a read-only *ID* property and a read-write *Address* property. Furthermore, it overrides the *ToString* method defined in the parent class.

```
function IntroAjax$Citizen$ToString()
{
    var temp = IntroAjax.Citizen.callBaseMethod(this, 'ToString');
    temp += "  [" + this._id + "]";
    return temp;
}
```

You use *callBaseMethod* to invoke the same method on the parent class. Defined on the *Function* class, the *callBaseMethod* method takes up to three parameters: instance, name of the method, plus an optional array of arguments for the base method.

As mentioned earlier, the *ToString* method on the *Person* class returns a *LastName, FirstName* string. The *ToString* method on the *Citizen* class returns a string in the following format: *LastName, FirstName [ID]*.

> **Note**   In the prototype model, a derived class has full access to the private members of the parent class. To be precise, in JavaScript the notion of private members is not the same as in classic OOP. As mentioned earlier, in the Microsoft AJAX library private members exist by convention; they're not enforced by any syntax rules. In other words, the language allows you to access, say, the member *_firstName* of class *Person* straight from class *Citizen*. You should avoid that, though, as base class accessor implementations may provide additional logic over and above simply returning the field value.

Adding Interface Support

An interface describes a group of related behaviors that are typical of a variety of classes. In general, an interface can include methods, properties, and events; in JavaScript, it contains only methods.

Keeping in mind the constraints of the JavaScript language, to define an interface you create a regular class with a constructor and a prototype. The constructor and each prototyped method, though, will just throw a not-implemented exception. Here's the code for the sample *Sys.IDisposable* built-in interface:

```
Type.registerNamespace("Sys");

Sys.IDisposable = function Sys$IDisposable()
{
    throw Error.notImplemented();
}

function Sys$IDisposable$dispose()
{
    throw Error.notImplemented();
}

Sys.IDisposable.prototype =
{
    dispose: Sys$IDisposable$dispose
}

Sys.IDisposable.registerInterface('Sys.IDisposable');
```

The following statement registers the *Citizen* class, makes it derive from *Person*, and implements the *IDisposable* interface:

```
IntroAjax.Citizen.registerClass('IntroAjax.Citizen',
         IntroAjax.Person, Sys.IDisposable);
```

To implement a given interface, a JavaScript class simply provides all methods in the interface and lists the interface while registering the class:

```
function IntroAjax$Citizen$dispose
{
   this._id = "";
   this._address = "";
}

IntroAjax.Citizen.prototype =
{
   dispose: IntroAjax$Citizen$dispose
   ...
}
```

Note, though, that you won't receive any runtime error if the class that declares to implement a given interface doesn't really support all the methods.

> **Note**   If a class implements multiple interfaces, you simply list all required interfaces in the *registerClass* method as additional parameters. Here's an example:
>
> ```
> Sys.Component.registerClass('Sys.Component', null,
> Sys.IDisposable,
> Sys.INotifyPropertyChange,
> Sys.INotifyDisposing);
> ```
>
> As you can see, in this case you don't have to group interfaces in an array

Core Components

The AJAX client library is made up of three main logical layers: JavaScript extensions, core framework classes, and user-interface (UI) framework classes. (See Figure 2-1.)

As mentioned in the previous sections, JavaScript extensions add new methods and capabilities to native JavaScript objects and enable registration methods to simulate object-oriented constructs such as classes, namespaces, inheritance, and interfaces. The UI framework includes base components to define client behaviors, controls, DOM elements, and input devices such as keyboard and mouse buttons. The UI framework also incorporates as private elements classes that provide the client object model for a couple of ASP.NET AJAX server controls, namely *Timer* and *UpdateProgress*. We'll cover these controls in Chapter 4, "Partial Page Rendering."

The core framework classes form a sort of base library that incorporates a set of commonly used classes for event handling, string manipulation, Web services, debugging, and network operations. As you saw earlier, the Microsoft AJAX library supports namespaces, so classes in the client library belong to a particular namespace. Most classes in the base framework layer of the library belong to the *Sys* namespace.

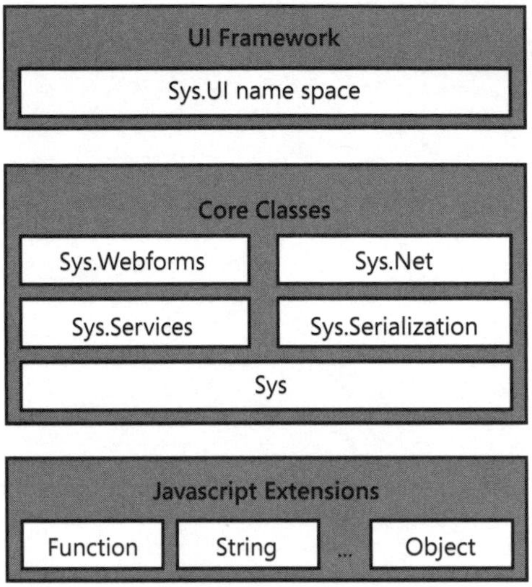

Figure 2-1   A graphical view of the AJAX client library

In the remainder of this chapter, we'll take a look at the main functionality implemented in the Microsoft AJAX library, starting with the *Application* object.

The *Sys.Application* Object

The execution of each ASP.NET AJAX page is controlled by an application object that is instantiated in the body of the library. The application object is an instance of a private class—the *Sys._Application* class. As mentioned, JavaScript has no notion of private members; therefore, private members are conventionally indicated by the underscore symbol (_) in their names.

Whenever an ASP.NET AJAX page is loaded in the browser, an instance of the *Sys._Application* class is promptly created and assigned to the *Sys.Application* object:

```
Sys.Application = new Sys._Application();
```

In addition, each ASP.NET AJAX page is injected with the following script code:

```
<script type="text/javascript">
<!--
Sys.Application.initialize();
// -->
</script>
```

This code is placed immediately after the closing tag of the page's form, and it commands the loading of any script files registered for loading with the page's script manager. More details on script loading are unveiled in Chapter 3, "The Pulsing Heart of ASP.NET AJAX." As a result, the *Sys.Application* object is the nerve center of the ASP.NET AJAX page.

Generalities of the *Sys._Application* Class

The *Sys._Application* class derives from *Component* and is the entry point in the page hierarchy to locate client-side components either bound to server controls or programmatically added to the application. Table 2-3 lists some of the methods available on the *Sys._Application* class.

Table 2-3   Members on the *Sys._Application* Class

Member	Description
addComponent	Adds the specified Microsoft AJAX library component to the page hierarchy
beginCreateComponents	Starts adding new Microsoft AJAX library components to the page
endCreateComponents	Ends adding new Microsoft AJAX library components to the page
findComponent	Looks up the specified Microsoft AJAX library component in the page
getComponents	Gets the list of Microsoft AJAX library components found in the page
initialize	Ensures that all referenced script files are loaded
notifyScriptLoaded	Called by script files to notify the application object that the script has been successfully loaded
queueScriptReference	Queues a new script reference for loading
removeComponent	Removes the specified component from the page hierarchy

The application object serves two main purposes: providing access to page components, and loading external script files registered with the page script manager. Note that each external script file registered with the script manager needs to place a *notifyScriptLoaded* call at the bottom of its source to notify the application of success.

Looking Up Components

The *findComponent* method scrolls the runtime hierarchy of components for the current page until it finds a component with a matching ID. The method has two possible prototypes:

```
Sys._Application.findComponent(id);
Sys._Application.findComponent(id, parent);
```

The former overload takes the ID of the component and uses it to look up and navigate the hierarchy all the way down from the root. When a non-null *parent* argument is specified, the search is restricted to the subtree rooted in the context object. The *id* parameter must be a string; the *context* parameter must be an Microsoft Client library object. The method returns the object that matches the ID, or it returns null if no such a object is found.

Microsoft Client library also supports a shortcut for retrieving runtime components—the *$find* method. The *$find* method is an alias for *findComponent*.

```
var $find = Sys.Application.findComponent;
```

You can use this method to locate all components created by server controls and extenders, as well as by your own JavaScript code and, if supported, by XML-Script declarations.

Events in the Page Lifetime

Table 2-4 lists the events fired by the *Sys._Application* class. Listeners for these events can be added via script code.

Table 2-4   Client Events on the *Sys._Application* Class

Event	Description
Init	Occurs when the page is first initialized
Load	Occurs when the page is loaded
loadTimedOut	Occurs when the loading step takes too much time to complete
scriptLoadFailed	Occurs when one script fails to load for whatever reason
Unload	Occurs when the page is unloaded

When an ASP.NET AJAX page first loads up, the *load* event is fired for the client code to perform any required initialization. Note that the event refers to the page lifetime, not the application lifetime. So whenever a classic postback occurs, you receive a new *load* event. You don't receive events for any AJAX-style postback. Likewise, the *unload* event is fired when the page is unloaded.

The *load* event occurs after an ASP.NET AJAX page has been loaded and initialized completely. For such a page, the *load* event is preferable to the browser's *onload* for initialization purposes. Only when you get the Microsoft AJAX library *load* event, therefore, can you be sure that the page is ready for user interaction.

The *unload* event occurs just before the Microsoft AJAX library runtime releases the page and all of its resources. For the sake of the application's stability, you should use this event instead of the browser's *onunload* event for clean-up tasks.

The following code shows how to add handlers to the *load* and *unload* events via script:

```
Sys.Application.add_load(_pageLoadHandler);
Sys.Application.add_unload(_pageUnloadHandler);
```

You add this code to a *<script>* tag you import in the page. Note that this *<script>* tag must be placed past the definition of the script manager control, as shown here:

```
<form id="Main" runat="server">
   <asp:ScriptManager runat="server" ID="scriptManager" />
   <script type="text/JavaScript" language="JavaScript">
      Sys.Application.add_load(_pageLoadHandler);
      Sys.Application.add_unload(_pageUnloadHandler);
   </script>
   ...
</form>
```

An even easier way to define *load* and *unload* handlers is by means of predefined function names: *pageLoad* and *pageUnload*. These functions need to be global and parameterless.

```
<script type="text/JavaScript" language="JavaScript">
    function pageLoad()
    {
        alert("Being loaded");
    }
    function pageUnload()
    {
        alert("Being unloaded");
    }
</script>
```

Because this piece doesn't directly call into any of the Microsoft AJAX library objects—including *Sys.Application*—you can safely place it everywhere, even at the top of the ASP.NET AJAX page.

The *Sys.Component* Object

Generally, the term *component* denotes an object that is reusable and can interact with other objects in the context of a framework. The term *control*, on the other hand, denotes an object that is sort of a specialized component. The main trait that differentiates components and controls is the user interface. Components are non-UI objects; controls are primarily UI-based objects.

In the Microsoft AJAX library, the root component class is *Sys.Component*. The root class for controls is named *Control* and, guess what, lives in the *Sys.UI* namespace. In the Microsoft AJAX library, *Sys.UI.Control* derives from *Sys.Component*. Let's learn more about the common properties of components; we'll work with controls later in the chapter.

The *Sys.Component* Class

Derived from the JavaScript native type *Object*, the *Sys.Component* class defines a number of properties and events shared by all components. Table 2-5 lists the properties of the *Sys.Component* class.

Table 2-5   Properties of the *Sys.Component* Class

Property	Description
events	Lists all events fired by the class
id	Gets and sets the ID used to identify the component
isInitialized	Indicates whether the component has been initialized
isUpdating	Indicates whether the component is in the middle of a batch update operation

The *Sys.Component* class features an *initialize* method that is used to start up the component. The base implementation of the method simply sets an internal flag to denote that the component has been initialized. Derived classes can further specialize the method to accomplish additional tasks. Table 2-6 lists the methods of the *Sys.Component* class.

Table 2-6   Methods of the *Sys.Component* Class

Method	Description
beginUpdate	Starts a batch operation aimed at updating the state of the component
dispose	Disposes of all resources associated with the class
endUpdate	Signals that an update operation has terminated
initialize	Performs any task required to initialize the component
raisePropertyChanged	Raises the *propertyChanged* event.

In addition to the members considered so far, the class fires a couple of events: *disposing* and *propertyChanged*. The former event occurs when the component is being disposed of; the latter event occurs when the state of the component is updated. The *propertyChanged* event is part of the *INotifyPropertyChange* interface.

Detecting Property Changes

The *Sys.Component* class features a built-in mechanism to detect ongoing changes to the properties of a component. When this happens, the *propertyChanged* event is fired. The method *raisePropertyChanged* on the base class allows derived components to fire the *propertyChanged* event to notify callers that the value of a given property has been updated. Here's a sample implementation of a component property:

```
this.set_MyProperty = function(value) {
    _myProperty = value;
    this.raisePropertyChanged("MyProperty");
}
```

Generally, derived components place a call to *raisePropertyChanged* in the *set* method of a given property. For a derived component, using the property changes mechanism is optional and not mandatory.

Batched Updates

The *Sys.Component* class also provides facilities when too many properties are going to be updated at the same time. To minimize screen updates, you can tell the object to perform property updates in a batch. To do so, you group updates in calls to the *beginUpdate* and *endUpdate* methods. When a batch update operation is in progress, the value of the *isUpdating* property is automatically set to *true*.

Depending on the specific component, batch updates can improve performance and minimize screen updates.

The $create Alias

The *$create* alias provides a concise syntax for creating an Microsoft AJAX library component. It is mapped to the static method *create* on the *Sys.Component* class with the following prototype:

```
var $create = Sys.Component.create = function Sys$Component$create(
    type, properties, events, references, element)
{
    ...
}
```

Of all the arguments just shown, only the *type* argument is mandatory; all others are optional. For example, the following code creates an instance of *Samples.UI.Button* and assigns it a click event handler, *button1_Click*, and ties it to the DOM element control *sendDataButton*:

```
$create(Samples.UI.Button,
        {},
        {'click':'button1_Click'},
        {}
        $get('sendDataButton')
);
```

The *$create* method defines the type to create, a list of properties, event handlers, and even an optional DOM element if any exists. The *$create* alias can also handle scenarios in which components have references to other components. In addition, objects are automatically registered with *Sys.Application*, thus allowing components to be found through *$find*.

Component Disposing

The *Sys.Component* class implements two interfaces that revolve around the disposal of any component instance: the *Sys.IDisposable* and *Sys.INotifyDisposing* interfaces. The *Sys.Disposable* interface features the *dispose* method; the *Sys.INotifyDisposing* interface lists the sole *disposing* event.

Components are required to be disposable so that you can free all of their client resources when used in the context of updatable panels. In addition, you should make sure the *dispose* method handles being called more than once. Here's an example:

```
dispose: function()
{
    // Check whether childObject1 has been disposed of
    if (!_childObject1_disposed)
    {
        ...
    }
}
```

In this case, the _childObject1_disposed_ member is an internal member of the particular component that tracks whether or not the present component has gotten rid of its child objects and resources, including handlers. It is recommended that you use internal flags to check whether any child components (for example, event handlers) being manually disposed have already been disposed of when the whole component is destroyed.

The Network Stack

AJAX libraries in general, and ASP.NET AJAX Extensions in particular, owe their growing popularity to their ability to execute out-of-band Web requests from the client. In particular, ASP.NET AJAX Extensions allows you to invoke Web service methods as well as static methods defined on the server ASP.NET page class. This ability leverages the networking support built into the Microsoft AJAX library.

The *Sys.Net.WebRequest* Class

In the Microsoft AJAX library, a remote request is represented by an instance of the *Sys.Net.WebRequest* class. Table 2-7 lists the properties of the class.

Table 2-7   Properties of the *Sys.Net.WebRequest* Class

Property	Description
body	Gets and sets the body of the request
executor	Gets and sets the Microsoft Client library object that will take care of executing the request
headers	Gets the headers of the request
httpVerb	Gets and sets the HTTP verb for the request
timeout	Gets and sets the timeout, if any, for the request
url	Gets and sets the URL of the request

The *WebRequest* class defines the *url* property to get and set the target URL and the *headers* property to add header strings to the request. If the request is going to be a POST, you set the body of the request through the *body* property. A request executes through the method *invoke*. The event *completed* informs you about the completion of the request.

Each Web request is executed through an internal class—the Web request manager—that employs an "executor" to open the socket and send the packet. The default executor class is *XMLHttpExecutor*. All executors derive from a common base class—the *Sys.Net. WebRequestExecutor* class.

The XML HTTP Executor

The Microsoft AJAX library defines just one HTTP executor—the *Sys.Net.XMLHttpExecutor* class. As the name suggests, this executor uses the popular *XMLHttpRequest* object to execute the HTTP request. Table 2-8 lists the properties of the class.

In addition, the XML HTTP executor features methods to start and abort the request. Table 2-9 lists the methods of the class.

Table 2-8   Properties of the *Sys.Net.XMLHttpExecutor* Class

Property	Description
responseAvailable	Boolean property, indicates whether the response is available
responseData	Gets the response of the request as raw text
started	Boolean property, indicates whether the request has started
statusCode	Indicates the status code of the HTTP response
statusText	Indicates the status text of the HTTP response
timedOut	Boolean property, indicates whether the request has timed out
xml	Gets the response of the request as an XML document object

Table 2-9   Methods of the *Sys.Net.XMLHttpExecutor* Class

Property	Description
abort	Aborts the ongoing request, if any
executeRequest	Sends the request to its target URL
getAllResponseHeaders	Gets all response headers in a single collection object
getResponseHeader	Gets the value of the specified header

Note that the *abort* method aborts the current *XMLHttpRequest* call, which simply closes the socket through which the client is expecting to receive response data, sets the *aborted* flag to true, and then fires the *completed* event. None of this affects any operation that might be executing on the server.

> **Note**   AJAX libraries are associated with the *XMLHttpRequest* browser object. So what else could an executor be other than an instance of the *XMLHttpRequest* class? In general, an HTTP executor is any means you can use to carry out a Web request. An alternative executor—which was removed from the Microsoft AJAX library in the Beta stage—is based on HTTP frames. The idea is to use a dynamically created inline frame to download the response of a given request and then parse that result into usable objects.

The *Sys.WebForms.PageRequestManager* Class

The *Sys.Net.WebRequest* class and its derivatives serve the purpose of issuing client requests to a server resource. This is the engine behind client Web service calls. ASP.NET AJAX Extensions provides a large share of its functionalities through updatable panels. (See Chapter 4.) Updatable panels are portions of the page that can be refreshed independently of others and the same page as a whole. The *PageRequestManager* class is the Microsoft AJAX library class in charge of controlling the update of individual panels. Table 2-10 lists the members of the class.

For reasons that will become clear in Chapter 4, only one instance of this class is allowed per page. The class defines an event model that page authors can leverage to hook up the various stages in a panel refresh. We'll return to this point in detail in Chapter 4.

Table 2-10   Members of the *Sys.WebForms.PageRequestManager* Class

Member	Description
isInAsyncPostback	Boolean property, indicates whether the class is engaged in a panel refresh (also known as, asynchronous postback).
abortPostback	Method used to abort an ongoing panel refresh. The operation closes the underlying socket and prevents any further page updates.
getInstance	Static method used to return the singleton instance of this class available in the page space.

User-Interface Components

The Microsoft AJAX library doesn't define concrete user-interface components, such as classes that provide the client-side behavior of server controls. Instead, in the library you find only base classes to define three key categories of user interface components: behaviors, controls, and DOM elements. Web developers, as well as third-party vendors, can use these base classes to provide additional behaviors and client-side controls.

The *Sys.UI.Behavior* Class

Client behaviors are components derived from the *Sys.UI.Behavior* class and are triggered by client events, such as mouse movements, keystrokes, timer ticks, and DOM-based events. When triggered, behaviors can do virtually everything: update properties, run animations, implement drag-and-drop, and more. The goal of client behaviors is to enrich the behavior of an HTML element.

Multiple behaviors can be attached to the same HTML element; based on its functionality, the same behavior can be attached to distinct elements. The Microsoft AJAX library defines only the base class of client behaviors, but no built-in behaviors.

The constructor of the behavior class determines the binding between the behavior and a DOM element. The *Sys.UI.Behavior* class also features static methods to retrieve all behaviors attached to an element as well as look up behaviors by name and type.

The *Sys.UI.Control* Class

The *Sys.UI.Control* class derives from *Sys.Component* and wraps a DOM element—ideally, the DOM subtree of the matching server control. The binding between a *Sys.UI.Control* object and a DOM element is set in the class constructor.

```
Sys.UI.Control = function Sys$UI$Control(element)
{
   ...
}
```

The class provides methods to add, remove, and toggle the cascading style sheet (CSS) style of the control and to initialize the underlying DOM subtree. The *raiseBubbleEvent* method bubbles up any DOM event detected in the control's subtree. When this happens, the *onBubbleEvent* event is fired.

The *Sys.UI.DomElement* Class

The *Sys.UI.DomElement* class represents a native DOM element. The class inherits from Java-Script's *Object* and, as such, it's not an Microsoft AJAX library component. The class has methods to add, remove, toggle, and check CSS styles and to locate child elements by ID. In addition, you can find methods to get and set the location of the element in the host page (x,y coordinates) and to get the bounding rectangle of the element.

Handling DOM Events

DOM events are wrapped by instances of the *Sys.UI.DomEvent* class. The class lists methods to add a single handler, add multiple handlers, remove one handler, and clear all handlers. Table 2-11 details all methods.

Table 2-11   Methods of the *Sys.UI.DomEvent* Class

Method	Alias	Description
addHandler	*$addHandler*	Adds a handler for the event on the specified DOM element
addHandlers	*$addHandlers*	Adds a collection of event handlers
clearHandlers	*$clearHandlers*	Removes all handlers set on a given DOM element
preventDefault		Prevents the execution of the default task for the event
removeHandler	*$removeHandler*	Removes a given handler set on the specified DOM element
stopPropagation		Stops the propagation of the event up the DOM subtree

As you can see, the Microsoft AJAX library provides a shorthand notation to create DOM event hookups and removal. For example, you can use the *$addHandler* and *$removeHandler* aliases to add and remove a handler. Here's the syntax:

```
$addHandler(element, "eventName", handler);
$removeHandler(element, "eventName", handler);
```

Table 2-12 lists properties of the *Sys.UI.DomEvent* class.

Table 2-12   Properties of the *Sys.UI.DomEvent* Class

Property	Description
altKey, ctrlKey, shiftKey	Boolean properties denoting whether the Alt, Ctrl, and Shift keys were pressed when the event occurred.
button	Indicates the mouse button that was clicked, if any. Values are taken from the *Sys.UI.MouseButton* enumeration.
charCode	Gets the character code of the key that raised the associated event.

Table 2-12 **Properties of the *Sys.UI.DomEvent* Class (Continued)**

Property	Description
clientX, clientY	X,Y coordinates of the mouse event in the client area of the browser.
keyCode	Indicates the key that was hit, if any. Values are taken from the *Sys.UI.Key* enumeration.
offsetX, offsetY	X,Y offsets of the mouse position with respect to the clicked DOM element.
rawEvent	Gets the native event object as originated from the current browser.
screenX, screenY	X,Y coordinates of the mouse event in the screen.
target	Gets the DOM object that caused the event.
type	Indicates the type of event that occurred.

In many cases, you'll want to hook up several handlers to a DOM event for a component. Rather than manually creating all the required delegates and related handlers, you can use a condensed syntax to add and remove multiple handlers:

```
initialize: function()
{
   var elem = this.get_element();
   $addHandlers(
       elem,
       {[
           'mouseover': this._mouseHoverHandler,
           'mouseout': this._mouseOutHandler,
           'focus', this._focusHandler,
           'blur', this_blurHandler
       ]},
       this);
}
```

The *$clearHandlers* alias, conversely, removes all handlers set for a particular DOM element in a single shot.

> **Important**   If you write a component and wire up some events, it is essential that you clear all handlers when the component is unloaded, or even earlier, if you don't need the handler any longer. For example, you should do that from the component's *dispose* method to break circular references between your JavaScript objects and the DOM. Correctly applied, this trick easily prevents nasty memory leaks.

A Cross-Browser Model for Events

Building cross-browser compatibility for events is not an easy task. Internet Explorer has its own eventing model and so do Firefox and Safari. For this reason, the event model of the Microsoft AJAX library is a new abstract application programming interface (API) that joins together the standard W3C API and the Internet Explorer nonextensible model. The new API is closely modeled after the standard W3C API. In addition to using different method names (*add/removeEventListener* is for Firefox, and *attach/detachEvent* is for Internet Explorer), browsers differ in the way they pass event data to event handlers. In Internet Explorer, an event handler receives its data through the global *window.event* object; in Firefox, the event data is passed as an argument to the handler. In the Microsoft AJAX library, event handlers receive a parameter with proper event data. You use the members on the *Sys.UI.DomEvent* class to execute common event-related operations regardless of the host browser.

Another significant difference is in the way mouse and keyboard events are represented. The Microsoft AJAX library abstracts away any differences between browsers by providing ad hoc enumerated types, such as *Sys.UI.Key* and *Sys.UI.MouseButton*. Here's some sample code:

```
function button1_Click(e)
{
  if (e.button === Sys.UI.MouseButton.leftButton)
  {
    ...
  }
}
function keyboard_EnterPressed(e)
{
  if (e.keyCode === Sys.UI.Key.enter)
  {
    ...
  }
}
```

From within an event handler, the *this* pointer represents the DOM element the event was attached to. Note that the referenced DOM element isn't necessarily the element that triggered the event. For example, if the event is bubbled up you might catch an event from, say, a *<div>* that was fired by a child button. In this case, you reach the trigger element using the *target* property listed in Table 2-12. Finally, if you're registering handlers from a component and use delegates to reference event handlers, the *this* keyword refers to your component, not DOM elements.

Note   You won't receive any event data if you bind the handler via markup—for example, by setting the *onclick* attribute of an *<input>* tag. Everything said here applies only to event handlers added via methods (and aliases) of the *Sys.UI.DomEvent* class. Events bound through attributes are still processed, but you have to resort to your knowledge of the browser's event model to correctly grab associated information.

Other Components and Functionalities

The Microsoft AJAX library contains a number of other miscellaneous components to provide additional facilities to ASP.NET AJAX developers. Let's briefly focus on a few of them, starting with the script version of a popular .NET Framework managed class—the *StringBuilder* class.

String Manipulation

The *Sys.StringBuilder* class adds advanced text manipulation capabilities to ASP.NET AJAX pages. As the name suggests, the class mimics the behavior of the managed *StringBuilder* class defined in the .NET Framework.

When you create an instance of the builder object, you specify initial text. The builder caches the text in an internal array by using an element for each added text or line. Table 2-13 details the members of the class.

Table 2-13   Members of the *Sys.StringBuilder* Class

Member	Description
append	Adds the specified text to the internal array
appendLine	Calls append, and adds a new line character
clear	Clears the text stored in the builder
isEmpty	Checks whether the builder contains any text
toString	Returns the contents of the array as a plain string of text

The *StringBuilder* object doesn't accept objects other than non-null strings. The *toString* method composes the text by using the *join* method of the JavaScript *array* class.

The Microsoft AJAX library *String* class is also enriched with a *format* method that mimics the behavior of the *Format* method on the .NET Framework *String* class:

```
alert(String.format("Today is: {0}", new Date()));
```

You define placeholders in the format string using *{n}* elements. The real value for placeholders is determined by looking at the *n*.th argument in the *format* method call.

Debugging Facilities

Another class that is worth mentioning is the *Sys._Debug* class. An instance of this internal class is assigned to the *Sys.Debug* global object.:

```
Sys.Debug = new Sys._Debug();
```

In your pages, you use the *Sys.Debug* object to assert conditions, break into the debugger, or trace text. Table 2-14 details the methods available on the object.

Table 2-14   Methods of the *debug* Object

Method	Description
assert	Asserts that the specified condition parameter is true.
clearTrace	Erases the trace output.
fail	Breaks into the debugger. The method works only if the browser is Internet Explorer.
trace	Writes the text argument to the trace output.
traceDump	Displays the specified object in a readable form.

The *assert* method has the following prototype:

```
assert(condition, message, displayCaller);
```

If the condition is met, the method just exits and the execution continues with the next instruction. If the condition is *false*, the method displays a message box with the specified message. If the *displayCaller* parameter is *true*, the method also displays information about the caller.

The *clearTrace* method takes no arguments and clears the portion of the page where ASP.NET AJAX-related trace messages are displayed. More precisely, the *clearTrace* method just hides the panel component that shows all trace messages.

The *traceDump* method writes the contents of the specified object in a human-readable format in the Microsoft Client library trace area. The trace area is expected to be a *<textarea>* element with an ID of *traceConsole*. You can place this element anywhere in the page:

```
<textarea id="traceConsole" cols="40" rows="10" />
```

The *traceDump* method accepts two parameters, as shown here:

```
Sys.Debug.traceDump(object, name)
```

The *name* parameter indicates descriptive text to display as the heading of the object dump. The text can contain HTML markup. Figure 2-2 shows the results.

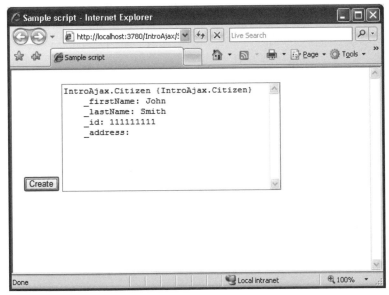

Figure 2-2   The Microsoft AJAX library debugging tracer in action

Any text output through tracing is displayed in the Visual Studio 2005 Output window.

The *trace* method writes the text argument to the trace output. It takes only one parameter—the text to render.

The *fail* method breaks into the debugger, but only if the browser is Internet Explorer. What if you're testing your ASP.NET AJAX application under another browser? You can't use the Visual Studio debugger to step through client code running in Firefox or other Mozilla-based browsers. However, a Firefox debugger implemented as a Firefox extension can be downloaded from *http://www.mozilla.org/projects/venkman*.

Conclusion

Microsoft Client library is a set of JavaScript classes that represent the client-side engine of the ASP.NET AJAX Extensions framework. In the library, you find a bunch of functionalities to support ASP.NET AJAX server controls as well as to command client Web requests. A set of helper classes complete the Microsoft AJAX library to make it easier and more comfortable for developers to create JavaScript callbacks to update a page on demand.

The key trait of the Microsoft AJAX library is the set of extensions to transform JavaScript into an object-oriented language. JavaScript is not a true OOP language even though it always has supported objects and also provides a rudimentary mechanism for prototyping classes and derived classes. The Microsoft AJAX library builds on top of this basic functionality to add namespace and interface support.

The Microsoft AJAX library defines base classes for client controls, behaviors, and components, including classes that wrap DOM elements abstracting from browser differences. No concrete UI classes are defined, but all further details are left to developers and third-party vendors. Finally, the library enriches the native top objects of JavaScript (strings, dates, regular expressions, and numbers), and it has a variety of helper classes, such as debugging facilities, string builders, and the whole network stack to place remote calls.

Part II
Adding AJAX Capabilities to a Site

Chapter 3
The Pulsing Heart of ASP.NET AJAX

Microsoft ASP.NET AJAX Extensions is a framework that brings AJAX-style functionality to the ASP.NET 2.0 platform. Unlike other similar frameworks, it is designed to be part of ASP.NET and therefore seamlessly integrate with the existing platform and application model. ASP.NET AJAX will be fully integrated with the next release of Microsoft Visual Studio (codenamed "Orcas"), and along with LINQ it will be one of the pillars of the future ASP.NET platform.

Right from the start, you should think of ASP.NET AJAX Extensions as a native part of the ASP.NET platform and not just as a bolted-on and more or less unobtrusive external library. In the context of ASP.NET, the role of the AJAX subsystem is fairly clear and defined. It is the ingredient that spices up the whole platform and makes it a high-productivity platform for a new generation of Web applications. With AJAX aboard, you can finally write Web applications that work with Internet Explorer, Firefox, Navigator, and Safari browsers with ubiquitous reach and easy deployment.

ASP.NET AJAX Extensions brings enhancements on both the server and client side of the Web platform. It comes with a rich suite of components and controls to make AJAX coding easy and, more importantly, mostly transparent to ASP.NET developers.

There are two main approaches for building ASP.NET AJAX pages—server-centric and client-centric. In the server-centric model, you incrementally add AJAX-based user interface enrichment to new and existing applications. You keep the core part of your user interface and application logic on the server mostly written with Microsoft Visual Basic .NET or C#. At the same time, your applications benefit from the browser's capabilities through JavaScript code. Your exposure to JavaScript, though, is minimal if not close to zero. Choosing a server-centric model allows ASP.NET developers to add a good deal of interactivity to Web applications with an extremely short learning curve.

The real power of AJAX, however, is harnessed when you can fully leverage JavaScript and the browser's DOM, in a client-centric model. In this way, you can provide a significantly richer, more interactive, and more immersive user experience. You can build mash-ups and make the application react to user's input in a way that closely resembles a desktop application.

In the client-centric model, you need good client-side programming skills. You keep control of everything, trigger server operations, grab results, and refresh the user interface. The bandwidth consumption is minimal, but your efforts are significant; and therefore, so is the likelihood of adding bugs and memory leaks.

In the server-centric model, everything is easier. A special component takes care of most of this burden and accomplishes tasks in a more reliable way at the cost of more bandwidth. In the server-centric model of AJAX, a component acts as the manager of the page and takes care of postbacks and page updates. You don't write code for that; you just have to add a handful of new server controls to pages and tweak the configuration file.

This is currently the most common way to approach AJAX development in the industry. Virtually any AJAX frameworks out there expose an AJAX manager component and a bunch of settings. In this chapter we'll take a look at the manager component and configuration file of ASP.NET AJAX Extensions pages.

Configuration of ASP.NET AJAX

When you create the project of an AJAX-enabled ASP.NET Web site, everything looks like a classic ASP.NET application at first glance. After a second look, though, you can see that the configuration file contains some changes in the form of new sections and new runtime components. In particular, the runtime components—made-to-measure HTTP modules and HTTP handlers—play a key role in the implementation of ASP.NET AJAX.

The *web.config* File

In ASP.NET, the *web.config* file stores application settings that apply to the folder where it is located and to child subfolders. Each application can have a variety of *web.config* files to apply different settings at different folder levels.

The *web.config* file is a text file written in accordance with a well-known XML schema. The standard schema file features a built-in number of sections and elements, but new sections can be added to configure custom services and components. As mentioned, ASP.NET AJAX Extensions 1.0 is just an extension to ASP.NET, and it can be easily seen as a new service that requires its own set of extensions to the configuration syntax.

New Configuration Sections

The ASP.NET configuration file has a root element named <*configuration*>. A particular configuration file that contains information for a custom service can optionally define new sections. All nonstandard sections used in a configuration file must be declared in the initial <*configSections*> section. The following code snippet shows the new sections defined in the root *web.config* file of an ASP.NET AJAX application:

```
configuration>
  <configSections>
    <sectionGroup name="system.web.extensions" ...>
      <sectionGroup name="scripting" ... />
        <section name="scriptResourceHandler" ... />
        <sectionGroup name="webServices" ... >
          <section name="jsonSerialization" ... />
          <section name="profileService" ... />
          <section name="authenticationService" ... />
        </sectionGroup>
      </sectionGroup>
    </sectionGroup>
  </configSections>
  ...
</configuration>
```

As you can see, everything goes under the *<scripting>* section which, in turn, is a child of
<system.web.extensions>. Under the *<scripting>* section, you find another child section named
<webServices>. Let's dig out the *<scripting>* section first.

> **Note**   Sections are a necessary syntax element in configuration files. However, you don't
> need to declare all sections in all application-specific *web.config* files. When processing
> a *web.config* file, in fact, ASP.NET builds a configuration tree starting from the root
> *machine.config* file. Because all standard sections are already declared in the *machine.config*
> that ships with the .NET Framework, your application needs to declare only custom sections
> you plan to use.
>
> Because ASP.NET AJAX Extensions 1.0 is an extension to ASP.NET, new and specific sections
> are to be declared in the *web.config* file of each AJAX-enabled application. To avoid that, you
> can define new sections in the *machine.config* file located in the *%Windows%\Microsoft.NET\
> Framework\v2.0.50727\Config* folder of the Web server machine.

The *<scripting>* Section

The *<scripting>* section might contain a child section named *<scriptResourceHandler>*. The
child section determines how ASP.NET AJAX system scripts should be served to the client and
handled. The *<scriptResourceHandler>* section features two attributes: *enableCaching* and
enableCompression. Both are Boolean values and are set to *true* by default:

```
<scripting>
  <scriptResourceHandler enableCaching="true" enableCompression="true" />
</scripting>
```

The *enableCaching* attribute indicates whether the system script files (as well as any other
linked scripts and resources) are to be cached locally or downloaded for each request. System
script files are a key element of AJAX frameworks, and ASP.NET AJAX Extensions is no exception. The more the framework is rich with features, the more the size of such script files
becomes large.

To keep the overall size of system script files below the threshold of a few KBs, compression is required. You can enable or disable compression through the *enableCompression* attribute. When the attribute is turned on, script files that are embedded as resources in an assembly and string resources are compressed.

> **Warning**   Compression and caching applies only to scripts and resources served by the ASP.NET AJAX script resource handler—*ScriptResource.axd*. To use the handler, you have to place scripts and resources in an assembly and link them to the *ScriptManager* control. Just linking a *.js* file through a *<script>* tag doesn't afford you the benefits of caching and compression. When static, file-based scripts are referenced, you will need to provide compression through IIS or through some other compression utility. (For more information, take a look at the following: http://support.microsoft.com/default.aspx/kb/322603.) Note also that the script resource handler doesn't apply compression and caching to scripts and resources for versions of Internet Explorer older than 7.0. The reason is explained in this article: http://support.microsoft.com/kb/321722.

The *<webServices>* Section

Under the *<webServices>* section, you find a number of child sections, as detailed in Table 3-1.

Table 3-1   Children of the *<webServices>* Section

Section	Description
authenticationService	Configures the ASP.NET AJAX authentication service. With this service active, you can authenticate the user credentials without being redirected to a login page. Authentication can optionally be configured to occur only on secure channels. We'll return to this topic in Chapter 6, "Built-in Application Services."
jsonSerialization	Defines the list of custom JSON serializers registered to work in the application. Serializers are grouped under the child *<converters>* section. The *maxJsonLength* attribute indicates maximum length in bytes for a JSON string. The default value is 500.
profileService	Configures the ASP.NET AJAX profile service. With this service active, you can manipulate the properties of the ASP.NET user profile from Java-Script. To allow profile properties to be retrieved and modified from within ASP.NET AJAX applications, you add each property name to the *readAccessProperties* and *writeAccessProperties* attributes of the section. We'll return to this topic in Chapter 6.

The *<webServices>* section is not necessary if you don't plan to use Web services from within ASP.NET AJAX pages.

The Runtime Engine

As an extension to ASP.NET, ASP.NET AJAX Extensions can't help but rely on the extensibility model of ASP.NET. Some of its key functionalities are implemented using additional runtime components such as HTTP modules and handlers. When these components are required, you register them in the *web.config* file, as shown in the following sections.

The *ScriptResource* HTTP Handler

ASP.NET AJAX needs to register an HTTP handler to effectively manage any system and user-defined script that is being added to each page. The ASP.NET AJAX script manager injects the Microsoft AJAX library and other scripts via a made-to-measure handler named *ScriptResource.axd*. It is defined as follows:

```
<httpHandlers>
    <add verb="GET,HEAD" path="ScriptResource.axd" validate="false"
        type="System.Web.Handlers.ScriptResourceHandler,
            System.Web.Extensions, ..." />
</httpHandlers>
```

If the *validate* attribute is *false*, ASP.NET does not attempt to load the specified handler class until an actual request comes for *ScriptResource.axd*. This behavior potentially delays any runtime errors, but it improves the startup time. Basically, the script resource handler works on JavaScript files and Web resources (images, strings) embedded into assemblies and optimizes the way in which those are injected into your client pages. The handler takes care of serving scripts efficiently for you. For example, it ensures that scripts are cached by the browser and compressed using GZip. Furthermore, it helps you with localization by reading the right version of the resource based on the current culture.

In addition, ASP.NET AJAX might require a second HTTP handler. The configuration code is shown here:

```
<httpHandlers>
    <remove verb="*" path="*.asmx" />
    <add verb="*" path="*.asmx" validate="false"
        type="System.Web.Script.Services.ScriptHandlerFactory,
            System.Web.Extensions, ..."/>
</httpHandlers>
```

As you can see, the default handler for ASP.NET Web services is removed (**.asmx* files) and replaced with an AJAX-specific handler that falls back to the standard one in some cases. In particular, the new handler for **.asmx* resources examines the ongoing HTTP request and lets it go as usual if it can't find anything in the request that qualifies it as an ASP.NET AJAX request. You don't need this handler if you're not going to use ASP.NET Web services from within ASP.NET AJAX client pages.

The *ScriptModule* HTTP Module

The HTTP module named *ScriptModule* serves the purpose of executing remote page method calls in JavaScript from within client pages:

```
<httpModules>
  <add name="ScriptModule"
       type="System.Web.Handlers.ScriptModule, System.Web.Extensions, ..." />
</httpModules>
```

Without this module, you can't invoke a properly decorated method on the ASP.NET code-behind class. (We'll return on this in Chapter 7, "Remote Method Calls with ASP.NET AJAX".) Of course, if you don't plan to do so, you don't need register the *ScriptModule* HTTP module. This speeds up request processing slightly since the request isn't routed through this module.

The Script Manager Component

Virtually any AJAX library needs a component or a tool that makes some JavaScript code available on the client. This script code represents the client infrastructure necessary for the library to work. An AJAX library, on the other hand, can't be entirely based on server-side code and does need a lot of script code. The point is, which component or tool is ultimately responsible for injecting this code?

Had AJAX come along ten years ago, the answer would have been quite obvious: the developer is in charge of linking the client page to each script resource that proves necessary. This approach requires the developer to know quite a bit about the script, including location, name, and functionality.

Today, in the age of codeless and declarative programming, AJAX libraries tend to offer a server-side, often parameterless, component that when dropped on the page automatically outputs any required scripts. This component is generally known as the *AJAX manager* or *script manager*. The script manager accomplishes a number of tasks. In addition to ensuring that the proper script is linked to the page, the script manager typically enables and supports partial page rendering, generates proxy code to call remotely into server-side methods and objects, and sets up auxiliary services.

In ASP.NET AJAX, the script manager component takes the form of the *ScriptManager* server control.

The ASP.NET *ScriptManager* Control

The main control in the server infrastructure of ASP.NET AJAX Extensions is the *ScriptManager* control and its twin *ScriptManagerProxy* control. You will find just one instance of the *ScriptManager* control in each ASP.NET AJAX page. No AJAX capabilities can be enabled in ASP.NET pages that lack a reference to one *ScriptManager* control. The *ScriptManagerProxy* control is used only in master pages scenarios.

The *ScriptManager* control manages and delivers script resources, thus enabling client scripts to make use of the JavaScript type system extensions and other JavaScript features we covered in Chapter 2, "The Microsoft Client Library for AJAX." The *ScriptManager* control also supports features such as partial page rendering and Web service calls.

```
<asp:ScriptManager runat="server" ID="ScriptManager1" />
```

The preceding code shows how to insert the script manager in an ASP.NET page. The control produces no user interface, works exclusively on the server, and doesn't add extra bytes to the page download.

Properties of the *ScriptManager* Control

The *ScriptManager* control features a number of properties for you to configure its expected behavior. Table 3-2 details the supported properties.

Table 3-2   Properties of *ScriptManager*

Property	Description
AllowCustomErrorsRedirect	Indicates whether custom error redirects will occur during an asynchronous postback. The property is set to *true* by default.
AsyncPostBackErrorMessage	Gets and sets the error message to be sent to the client when an unhandled exception occurs on the server during an asynchronous postback. If not set, the native exception's message will be used.
AsyncPostBackSourceElementID	Gets the ID of the server control that triggered the asynchronous postback. If there's no ongoing asynchronous postback, the property is set to the empty string.
AsyncPostBackTimeout	Gets and sets the timeout period in seconds for asynchronous postbacks. A value of zero indicates no timeout. The property is set to *90* by default.
AuthenticationService	Gets an object through which you can set preferences for the client-side authentication service.
EnablePageMethods	Indicates whether static page methods on an ASP.NET page can be called from client script. The property is set to *false* by default.
EnablePartialRendering	Indicates whether partial rendering is enabled for the page. The property is set to *true* by default.
EnableScriptGlobalization	Indicates whether the *ScriptManager* control renders script in the client that supports parsing and formatting of culture-specific information. The property is set to *false* by default.
EnableScriptLocalization	Indicates whether the *ScriptManager* control retrieves script files for the current culture, if they exist. The property is set to *false* by default.
IsDebuggingEnabled	Indicates whether the debug versions of client script libraries will be rendered. The *debug* attribute on the @*Page* directive doesn't affect this property.

Table 3-2 Properties of *ScriptManager* (Continued)

Property	Description
IsInAsyncPostBack	Indicates whether the current page request is due to an asynchronous postback.
LoadScriptsBeforeUI	Indicates whether scripts are loaded before or after markup for the page UI is loaded.
ProfileService	Gets an object through which you can set preferences for the client-side profile service.
ScriptMode	Gets and sets the type (debug or retail) of scripts to load when more than one type is available. Possible values come from the *ScriptMode* enumeration type: *Auto*, *Inherit*, *Debug*, or *Release*. The default value is *Auto*, meaning that the type of script is determined on the fly.
ScriptPath	Indicates that scripts should be loaded from this path instead of from assembly Web resources.
Scripts	Gets a collection of script references that the *ScriptManager* control should include in the page.
Services	Gets a collection of service references that the *ScriptManager* control should include in the page.
SupportsPartialRendering	Indicates whether a particular browser or browser version can support partial page rendering. If this property is set to *false*, regardless of the value of the *EnablePartialRendering* property, no partial rendering will be supported on the page. The property is set to *true* by default.

Some properties in the table refer to features that we'll cover in future chapters, such as partial page rendering and asynchronous postbacks (Chapter 4, "Partial Page Rendering") or client-side services (Chapter 6). Other properties, on the other hand, refer to the core functionalities of the script manager and will be further discussed in a moment.

Figure 3-1 shows the message box you receive if an asynchronous postback takes too much time to complete. (See the entry for the *AsyncPostBackTimeout* in Table 3-2.)

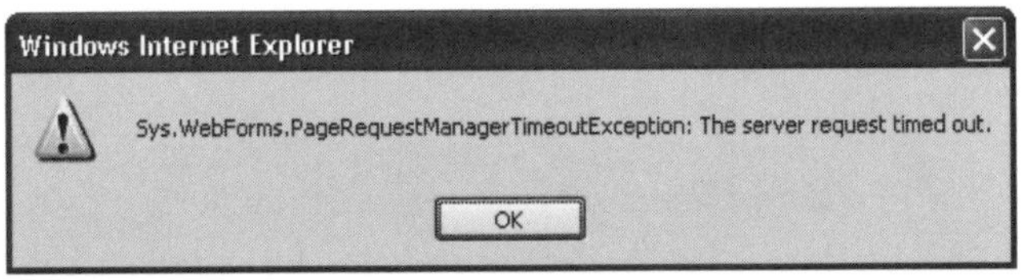

Figure 3-1 The timeout message box for asynchronous requests that time out

You get the error shown in Figure 3-1 if, for example, you set a breakpoint somewhere in the server code and then hang out for a couple of minutes before stepping out of the debugger.

Methods of the *ScriptManager* Control

Table 3-3 lists the methods defined on the *ScriptManager* control.

Table 3-3   Methods of *ScriptManager*

Method	Description
GetCurrent	Static method, returns the instance of the *ScriptManager* control active on the current page.
RegisterArrayDeclaration	Static method, ensures that an *ECMAScript* array is emitted in a partial rendering page.
RegisterAsyncPostBackControl	Takes note that the specified control can trigger an asynchronous postback event from within an updatable panel.
RegisterClientScriptBlock	Static method, ensures that the specified script is emitted in a partial rendering page.
RegisterClientScriptInclude	Static method, ensures that the markup to import an external script file through the *src* attribute of the *<script>* tag is emitted in a partial rendering page.
RegisterClientScriptResource	Static method, ensures that the markup to import an external script from the page's resources is emitted in a partial rendering page.
RegisterDataItem	Registers a string of data that will be sent to the client along with the output of a partially rendered page.
RegisterDispose	Registers controls that require a client script to run at the end of an asynchronous postback to dispose of client resources.
RegisterExpandoAttribute	Static method, ensures that the markup to import a custom, nonstandard attribute is emitted in a partial rendering page.
RegisterExtenderControl	Registers an extender control with the current ASP.NET AJAX page.
RegisterHiddenField	Static method, ensures that the specified hidden field is emitted in a partial rendering page.
RegisterOnSubmitStatement	Static method, ensures that that client-side script associated with the form's *OnSubmit* event is emitted in a partial rendering page.
RegisterPostBackControl	Takes note that the specified control can trigger a full postback event from within an updatable panel.
RegisterScriptControl	Registers a script control with the current ASP.NET AJAX page.
RegisterScriptDescriptors	Registers a script descriptor with the current ASP.NET AJAX page.
RegisterStartupScript	Static method, ensures that client-side script is emitted at the end of the *<form>* tag in a partial rendering page. In this way, the script will execute as the page refresh is completed.
SetFocus	Allows you to move the input focus to the specified client element after an asynchronous postback.

All static methods emit some form of script and markup in the client page. These static methods are the AJAX counterpart of similar methods defined on the page's *ClientScript* object that you should know from ASP.NET 2.0. The static *RegisterXXX* methods on the *ScriptManager* class ensure that the given piece of script and markup is properly emitted only once in each partial update of the ASP.NET AJAX page.

Similarly, other nonstatic *RegisterXXX* methods should be seen as tools to emit proper script code in ASP.NET AJAX pages—especially script code that is associated with custom controls. We'll return to script loading in a moment.

Events of the *ScriptManager* Control

Table 3-4 details the two events fired by the *ScriptManager* control.

Table 3-4   Events of *ScriptManager*

Event	Description
AsyncPostBackError	Occurs when an exception goes unhandled on the server during an asynchronous postback.
ResolveScriptReference	Occurs when the *ScriptManager* control is going to resolve a script reference.

Both events are much more than mere notifications of something that has happened on the server. Both give you good chances to intervene effectively in the course of the application. For example, by handling the *AsyncPostBackError* event, you can edit the error message being returned to the client. Furthermore, by handling the *ResolveScriptReference* event, you can change the location from where the script is going to be downloaded on the client.

The *ScriptManagerProxy* Control

Only one instance of the *ScriptManager* control can be added to an ASP.NET AJAX page. However, there are two ways in which you can do this. You can add it directly on the page using the *<asp:ScriptManager>* tag or indirectly by importing a component that already contains a script manager. Typically, you can accomplish the second alternative by importing a user control, creating a content page for a master page, or authoring a nested master page.

What if a content page needs to add a new script reference to the manager? In this case, you need a reference to the script manager. Although it's defined in the master page (or in a user control), the script manager might not be publicly exposed to the content page. You can use the static method *GetCurrent* on the class *ScriptManager* to get the right instance:

```
// Retrieve the instance of the ScriptManager active on the page
sm = ScriptManager.GetCurrent(this.Page);
```

The *ScriptManagerProxy* class saves you from this sort of coding. In general, in cases where you need features of the *ScriptManager* control but lack a direct reference to it, you can instead include a *ScriptManagerProxy* control in the content page.

You can't have two script managers in the context of the same page; however, you can have a script manager and a proxy to retrieve it. The *ScriptManagerProxy* control enables you to add scripts and services to nested components, and it enables partial page updates in user controls and nested master pages. When you use the proxy, the *Scripts* and *Services* collections on the *ScriptManager* and *ScriptManagerProxy* controls are merged at runtime.

> **Note**   The *ScriptManagerProxy* class is a very simple wrapper around the *GetCurrent* method of the *ScriptManager* class, and its programming interface is not an exact clone of the *Script-Manager*. From within the proxy, you have access only to a limited number of properties, including *Scripts*, *Services*, *AuthenticationService*, and *ProfileService*. If you need to modify anything else, refer to the *GetCurrent* static method of the *ScriptManager* class.

Script Loading

By extensively relying on client capabilities, ASP.NET AJAX requires a lot of script code. The framework itself links a lot of code, as do custom controls and actual user pages. It turns out that registering and loading script and resources—such as hidden fields, styles, and arrays—is a key factor. The *ScriptManager* control manages resources created to be used by all controls participating in partial page updates.

You add script files using the *Scripts* collection, either declaratively or programmatically.

Adding Script Resources

The *ScriptManager* control automatically emits in the client page any ASP.NET AJAX required script. As a page developer, you don't have to worry about the script code necessary to support JavaScript extensions, the *UpdatePanel*, or perhaps the *Timer* control. In addition, you have the *Scripts* collection available as a tool to register optional and custom scripts. The *Scripts* collection can be populated programmatically or declaratively through the *<asp:ScriptReference>* element.

The following example illustrates the script loading model you can use to load optional scripts:

```
<asp:ScriptManager runat="server" ID="ScriptManager1">
  <Scripts>
    <asp:ScriptReference
        Name="Microsoft.Web.Resources.ScriptLibrary.PreviewGlitz.js"
        Assembly="Microsoft.Web.Preview" />
    <asp:ScriptReference
        Path="~/Scripts/MyLib.js" />
  </Scripts>
</asp:ScriptManager>
```

You can reference scripts from an in-memory assembly or from a disk file. The second option is faster, as no extra effort is required to extract scripts from the assembly's resources.

Table 3-5 lists the properties of the *ScriptReference* class by means of which you can control the loading of scripts.

Table 3-5   Properties of *ScriptReference*

Property	Description
Assembly	Indicates the assembly that contains in its resources the script to download on the client.
IgnoreScriptPath	Boolean value, indicates whether the *ScriptPath* value optionally set at the top *ScriptManager* level has to be ignored. This property is set to *false* by default.
Name	Name of the script to download on the client.
NotifyScriptLoaded	Boolean value, indicates whether the script resource loader should automatically append a script loaded notification statement to let the *Sys.Application* object know when the script is loaded. This property is set to *true* by default.
Path	Indicates the server path where the script to download on the client can be found.
ResourceUICultures	A comma-delimited string of valid user-interface (UI) cultures supported by the path.
ScriptMode	Specifies the algorithm for choosing between the debug and release versions of the script file. If no debug version exists, the *ScriptReference* class automatically falls back to release code. Feasible values for the property come from the *ScriptMode* enumeration type.

Mapping Script Paths

You can reference script files, including ASP.NET AJAX system scripts, either from an assembly or from a disk file. There are a couple of benefits of using disk files. First, you gain something in performance because less work is required to download. Second, you make JavaScript debugging more pleasant, as you can easily step through the source code. Let's see what's required to have script files stored in binaries served from the file system instead. We'll see it for the principal ASP.NET AJAX script file—*MicrosoftAjax.js*—which alone contains two-thirds of the Microsoft AJAX library . The technique is also valid for any custom script file, however.

Normally, you don't take care of *MicrosoftAjax.js*—you just find it downloaded care of the script manager. If you examine the HTML source of an ASP.NET AJAX page, you can hardly find a reference to such a file. Here's what you find instead:

```
<script src="/IntroAjax/ScriptResource.axd?d=...&amp;t=..."
        type="text/javascript">
</script>
```

Script references obtained from embedded Web resources are served by the *ScriptResource.axd* HTTP handler. In ASP.NET AJAX, this handler replaces the old acquaintance *WebResource.axd* handler—a native component of ASP.NET 2.0. What's the difference? In addition to serving script references, the *ScriptResource.axd* handler also appends any localized JavaScript resource types for the file.

As a result, you have no system scripts that are an explicit part of your application. To avoid that, you create a directory structure that roots under a custom folder the following subdirectories:

```
System.Web.Extensions\1.0.61025.0
```

The first directory name must match the name of the assembly that contains the script. The name of the ASP.NET AJAX Extensions assembly is *System.Web.Extensions*. The second directory matches the version number of the assembly. You can read this version number from the *web.config* file.

Now set the *ScriptPath* property on *ScriptManager* to, say, *JS*:

```
<asp:ScriptManager ID="ScriptManager1" runat="server"
    ScriptPath="~/JS" />
```

All of a sudden, the *MicrosoftAjax.js* script file is now referenced as shown here:

```
<script
    src="~/JS/System.Web.Extensions/1.0.61025.0/MicrosoftAjax.js"
    type="text/javascript">
</script>
```

Needless to say, your pages will fail if no such script files can be found in the specified directory path.

When you install ASP.NET AJAX Extensions, it copies debug and release versions of all system scripts. You can copy these files into your application's folder from the installation path of ASP.NET AJAX. The typical path looks like the following:

```
<DRIVE>:\
```

Program Files\Microsoft ASP.NET\ASP.NET 2.0 AJAX Extensions\v1.0.61025\MicrosoftAjax-Library\System.Web.Extensions\1.0.61025.0 Release and debug files live in the same directory. Debug files have the *.debug* string in front of the *.js* extension. For example, the debug version of *MicrosoftAjax.js* is named *MicrosoftAjax.debug.js*.

> **Note**   ASP.NET AJAX uses a special naming convention to distinguish between debug and release script files. Given a release script file named *script.js,* its debug version is expected to be filed as *script.debug.js.*

Now, thanks to the effect of the *ScriptPath* property, the source files will be picked up from the disk. Finally, note that you can still define a local *Path* attribute on a script reference to override the *ScriptPath* value. It is also possible to force the use of an assembly for a given script reference by using the *IgnoreScriptPath* attribute on individual script references.

Resolving and Overriding Script Files

In summary, the *ScriptPath* property allows you to pick up scripts otherwise located in an assembly from a disk folder. The *Path* attribute, though, can override the global *ScriptPath* setting for a particular script reference. An interesting use of this feature is when you override a system script, as shown here:

```
<asp:ScriptManager runat="server" ID="ScriptManager1">
  <Scripts>
    <asp:ScriptReference Name="MicrosoftAjax.js"
        Path="~/Scripts/MicrosoftAjax2.js" />
  </Scripts>
</asp:ScriptManager>
```

In this case, instead of the original *MicrosoftAjax.js*, the client receives a customized version saved with a different name.

For each script reference, including the client framework scripts, you can also handle the *ResolveScriptReference* event and dynamically change the script location. For example, you can redirect the script from a server that is geographically nearer to the user. The following example illustrates how to handle the *ResolveScriptReference* event to redirect to a different script file:

```
<asp:ScriptManager runat="server" ID="ScriptManager1"
    OnResolveScriptReference="ResolveScript">
   ...
</asp:ScriptManager>

<script runat="server">
void ResolveScript(object sender, ScriptReferenceEventArgs e)
{
    // Changes the location of the script. Note scripts must
    // exist in this new location else load error.
    e.Script.Path = "~/MyScripts2/" + e.Script.Name;
    ...
}
</script>
```

The script manager fires the *ResolveScriptReference* event to allow modifications to script references before they are rendered.

Script Globalization

Globalization is a programming feature that refers to the code ability of supporting multiple cultures. A request processed on the server has a number of ways to get and set the current culture settings. For example, you can use the *Culture* attribute on the *@Page* directive, the

Culture property on the *Page* class, or perhaps the *<globalization>* section in the *web.config* file. How can you access the same information on the client from JavaScript?

Defined on the script manager, the Boolean *EnableScriptGlobalization* property enables the *ScriptManager* control to generate and emit the client culture information. When the *Enable-ScriptGlobalization* property is *true*, the *ScriptManager* emits proper script code that sets up a client global *Sys.CultureInfo* object that JavaScript classes can consume to display their contents in a culture-based way. The JavaScript snippet is shown next. It consists of a global variable named *__cultureInfo* that is called back by Microsoft AJAX library classes with locale-specific formatting options. The variable is given a value that corresponds to the JSON serialization of a *Sys.CultureInfo* object. Note that you won't see any of this code in your page unless you explicitly set a culture for your page. No injection will ever take place for the default, invariant culture.

```
<script type="text/javascript">
<!--
var __cultureInfo = '{"name":"it-IT", ... }';
// -->
</script>
```

The following code snippet shows how to consume culture information from the client:

```
<script type="text/javascript" language="Javascript">
function ShowDate()
{
    var d = new Date();
    var strDate = d.localeFormat("dddd, dd MMMM yyyy HH:mm:ss");
    $get('Label1').innerHTML = strDate;
}
</script>
```

The desired date format is set explicitly—weekday, day, month name, year, and time—but it contains culture-specific information, such as the name of the weekday and month. By default, on an English operating system, you get something like the following:

```
Friday, 02 February 2007 15:52:43
```

You get this result regardless of the culture settings you might have set in the ASP.NET page. This is because in the example the output is generated in JavaScript, where you have no access to the culture information. Try the following now:

```
<%@ Page Language="C#" Culture="it-IT" ... %>
...
<asp:ScriptManager ID="ScriptManager1" runat="server"
    EnableScriptGlobalization="true" />
```

When you re-run the page, with the *EnableScriptGlobalization* flag turned on, you get a different result, as shown in Figure 3-2.

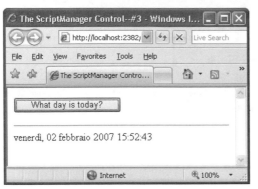

Figure 3-2   Showing culture-specific information in a globalized script

Only a few methods on a few JavaScript objects support globalization. In particular, it will work for the *localeFormat* method of *Date*, *String*, and *Number* types. Custom JavaScript types, though, can be made global by simply calling into these methods or accepting a *Sys.CultureInfo* object in their signatures.

Script Localization

Script files can have localizable elements such as text strings for messages and user-interface elements. When the *EnableScriptLocalization* property is set to *true* and a UI culture is properly set in the page, the script manager automatically retrieves script files for the current culture, if any.

Unlike globalization, localization is driven by the *UICulture* attribute in the *@Page* directive and the *UICulture* property in the *Page* class. So in an ASP.NET AJAX page that supports both script globalization and localization, you might have the following directive:

```
<%@ Page Language="C#" UICulture="it-IT" Culture="it-IT" ... %>
```

This information is not enough for the *ScriptManager* to pick up localized scripts, if any. You also need to specify which UI cultures you intend to support for each script reference. You indicate the supported cultures through the *ResourceUICultures* property on individual script references. The property is a comma-separated string of culture symbols. Here's an example:

```
<asp:ScriptManager ID="ScriptManager1" runat="server"
    EnableScriptLocalization="true">
  <Scripts>
    <asp:ScriptReference Path="Person.js" ResourceUICultures="it-IT" />
  </Scripts>
</asp:ScriptManager>
```

Note that the *ResourceUICultures* is ignored if the *Path* attribute is not specified on the script reference tag.

At this point, if the page requires a script named *Person.js* and the culture is set to *it-IT*, the *ScriptManager* object attempts to retrieve a script file named *Person.it-IT.js* from the same path.

The Script Registration Model

The *ScriptManager* control exposes a slew of registration methods you can use for managing individual script blocks, hidden fields, arrays, and expando attributes programmatically. If you're familiar with ASP.NET 2.0, you'll likely be reminded of similar registration methods defined on the *ClientScriptManager* class. What's the difference between *ClientScriptManager* and the ASP.NET AJAX *ScriptManager*?

Registration methods on *ScriptManager* serve the purpose of partial page rendering. Any array, expando attribute, or hidden field you need to carry back and forth over each partial page update must be registered in advance with the script manager. To register scripts and other resources that are not needed for partial page updates, you use methods of the *ClientScriptManager* class instead.

With explicit registration, the script manager knows what scripts are going to be present and processed during an asynchronous postback. The alternative would be quite costly and error-prone—parsing the contents of the updatable panel looking for the *<script>* tag. This technique was implemented in early builds of ASP.NET AJAX and proved to be quite poor. Along with the registration step, some dispose logic is also required so that when an updatable panel is cleared out during a postback, any scripts inside of it can tear down anything they need. The ultimate goal is having all controls working properly when hosted in updatable panels, each with its own required piece of script in place. This is an essential point to know if you plan to write custom controls based on ASP.NET AJAX.

Script Error Handling

In ASP.NET AJAX, the theme of script-related error handling is mainly two-fold. It is made of the usual techniques and issues related to generic error handling local to the code you write. This means, for instance, handling undefined references, checking error codes, types, parameter count, and return values. As we saw in Chapter 2, the Microsoft AJAX library provides some built-in tools that go beyond the basic set of capabilities offered by the original Java-Script language. In addition, an advanced feature of the *ScriptManager* control allows you to define debug and release versions of your script files and let it decide which one to load based on your input and runtime conditions (that is, are you really debugging your code?).

Next, there's a second aspect of script-related error handling that is specific to ASP.NET AJAX; in particular, it refers to partial page rendering. Let's tackle debug and release versions of script files first.

Handling Debug and Release Scripts

In general, the main difference between debug and release scripts is that the release scripts remove unnecessary blank characters, comments, trace statements, and assertions. Even though it is common today to download script files, even from popular Web sites, that are filled with comments and blank lines, in an AJAX context where script is no less than essential, every little bit you can save is welcome. So AJAX scripts might come in debug and release versions, and you should be ready to write both for your own JavaScript classes.

The question is, which version should be served to the client? And based on what considerations? The easiest approach is to leave the burden on the developer's shoulders and ask her to link different files as required by the context.

In ASP.NET AJAX Extensions, the logic to choose between debug and release versions has been entirely incorporated in the *ScriptManager* control. You tell the *ScriptManager* about the desired script mode—debug or release—and the script manager infers debug files based on a naming convention. A file named *MyScript.debug.js* is considered to be the debug version of the file *MyScript.js*. If the file is subject to localization, the corresponding localized (Italian) debug file is *MyScript.debug.it-IT.js*. This rule applies to both system and custom script files.

The *ScriptMode* property of the *ScriptManager* control determines the global algorithm to use for scripts. Each script reference, though, has its own local mode property so that you can have, say, release versions of the Microsoft Client library system files and debug versions of your custom files.

Note   The *ScriptMode* property is totally ignored both on *ScriptManager* and *ScriptReference* when the *retail* attribute of the *<deployment>* element is set to *true*. In this case, the release versions of client scripts will be used throughout the Web site. Note that the *retail* attribute is set to *false* by default in machine.config.

The *ScriptMode* property on both *ScriptManager* and *ScriptReference* accepts values from the *ScriptMode* enumeration and applies them to all referenced scripts and an individual script, respectively. Feasible values for the *ScriptMode* property are defined in the *ScriptMode* enumerated type and are listed in Table 3-6.

Table 3-6   Script Modes

Value	Description
Auto	The *ScriptManager* or the *ScriptReference* class decides which type of script to include. The algorithm produces different results based on the location of the script (static file, assembly) and class that invokes it and the runtime conditions. (I'll say more about this later.)
Debug	The *ScriptManager* loads the debug version of the script unless a made-to-measure script reference overrides the setting. The *ScriptReference* loads the debug version of the specified script.
Inherit	In a *ScriptManager* control, the setting is equivalent to *Auto*. In a *ScriptReference* control, the value from *ScriptManager* determines which version of the client script to use.
Release	The *ScriptManager* loads the release version of the script unless a made-to-measure script reference overrides the setting. The *ScriptReference* loads the release version of the specified script.

At the end of the look-up algorithm, a file name is determined. If the determined script file doesn't not exist, an error will be raised.

Let's see how the script version to load is determined in the script manager when *ScriptMode* equals *Auto* or *Inherit*. The version of client scripts is first determined by looking at value of the *debug* attribute of the *@Page* directive. If the page is running in debug mode, debuggable scripts are used. The actual setting, though, might be overridden if a matching entry exists for the script in the *<Scripts>* section that provides a different value for *ScriptMode*. In the end, the *Auto* value is equivalent to *Debug* when the *debug* attribute of the *@Page* directive is *true*. In all other cases, it is equivalent to *Release*.

When assigned to the *ScriptMode* property of a *ScriptReference* control, the value *Auto* is equivalent to *Release* for static files. It is equivalent to *Inherit* for script references defined in an assembly. For a script reference, *Inherit* means that the script mode is inherited from the script manager.

The following settings guarantee that whatever you set on script manager is replicated by child references:

```
<asp:ScriptManager ID="ScriptManager1" runat="server" ScriptMode="Auto">
    <Scripts>
        <asp:ScriptReference path="person.js" ScriptMode="Inherit" />
    </Scripts>
</asp:ScriptManager>
```

If a debug script must be loaded, the file *person.debug.js* must be available. If not, a script error occurs on the client.

> **Important**   The debug version of the Microsoft AJAX library is around 200 KB; the release version is around 70 KB. Does it mean that all this script will be downloaded (and then cached) on the client? Not exactly. In ASP.NET AJAX Extensions, both release and debug scripts may optionally go through a compression HTTP module, and the release scripts are also "crunched" to reduce size further. As a result, you should have approximately 20 KB for release scripts.

Custom Error Handling and Redirection

What if an exception is thrown during the execution of a partial page refresh? The client page receives a pop-up message that replicates the contents of the Message property of the original exception. What can you do about it?

The property *AsyncPostBackErrorMessage* on the script manager class can be used to edit or replace the default message. You can set the property either declaratively in the page markup or during the *ScriptManager*'s *AsyncPostBackError* event. If the value is empty, the exception's message will be used. Here's an example:

```
void AsyncPostBackError(object sender, AsyncPostBackErrorEventArgs e)
{
    string msg = "An error occurred and its description is: {0}";
    msg = String.Format(msg, e.Exception.Message);
    ScriptManager1.AsyncPostBackErrorMessage = msg;
}
```

When executed, the client-side error message appears as you see in Figure 3-3.

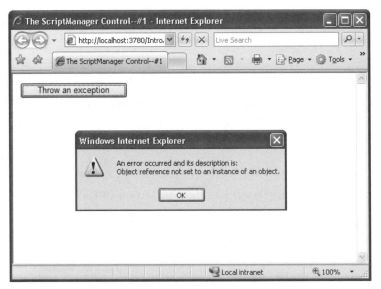

Figure 3-3   An error occurred during a partial page refresh.

What if you don't like popups and want to redirect the user to an error page instead? In this case, you configure the page to use the traditional error-handling mechanism for ASP.NET pages. You configure the *<customErrors>* section in the *web.config* file and indicate HTML error pages to reach in case of specific errors. Here's a quick example:

```
<customErrors mode="On" defaultRedirect="GenericErrorPage.htm">
    <error statusCode="404" redirect="site404.htm" />
    ...
</customErrors>
```

Alternatively, you can use the global *Error* event in *global.asax* and, for example, log the error and programmatically redirect to a custom error. This behavior is fully supported by ASP.NET AJAX and can be disabled by setting to *false* the value of the *AllowCustomErrorRedirects* property of the *ScriptManager* object. When *AllowCustomErrorRedirects* is set to *false*, the *Script-Manager* overrides custom error redirects and instead sends the error to the client, where you can display error information without redirecting the user to another page. On the client, though, you get a pop-up message. Is there a way to show a message instead? You bet.

By adding the following script to the page, you register a handler for the *endRequest* event of the *PageRequestManager* client object. (See Chapter 2, "The Microsoft Client Library for AJAX".)

```
<script type="text/JavaScript" language="JavaScript">
function pageLoad()
{
   // Register handlers for UpdatePanel client events
   var manager = Sys.WebForms.PageRequestManager.getInstance();
   manager.add_endRequest(endRequest);
}
function endRequest(sender, args)
{
   $get("ErrMessage").innerHTML = args.get_error().message;
   args.set_errorHandled(true);
}
</script>
```

The *endRequest* client event fires at the end of a partial page refresh operation. The event handler receives an *EndRequestEventArgs* class through the *args* parameter. As we'll see more clearly in Chapter 4, the *EndRequestEventArgs* class features two key properties: *error* and *errorHandled*.

The property *error* returns a JavaScript object that represents the server-side exception. From this object, you get the error message. The *errorHandled* property is a Boolean value that indicates whether the script is done with the error. By setting this property to *true*, you disable the popup and get output like that shown in Figure 3-4.

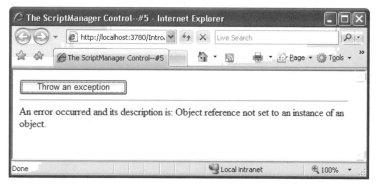

Figure 3-4   Incorporating the error message in the page

Conclusion

The *ScriptManager* control is in some sense the heart and soul behind each ASP.NET AJAX page. It orchestrates partial page refreshes, bootstraps the Microsoft AJAX library by loading scripts, generates proxies for local Web services, and coordinates the work of updatable panels. The *ScriptManager* control also provides functionality to control developers writing AJAX-enabled controls.

Understanding the behavior of this control is key to setting up effective, no-surprises ASP.NET AJAX pages that load custom script and perform the most common and popular AJAX-style operation—partial page rendering. In the next chapter, we'll take the plunge into the *UpdatePanel* control—that is, the brains behind partial page rendering.

Chapter 4
Partial Page Rendering

The key concept behind AJAX development is that much more work than usual should occur on the client. For the time being, working on the client side also means using a script language, which is not something that would make most developers jump for joy. A large share of Web developers have a love-hate relationship with JavaScript and with script languages in general. Either they love it and can achieve virtually any results by leveraging the flexibility of the syntax, or they hate it and feel ill just at the appearance of a client *<script>* tag.

By design, any AJAX-enabled page inherently requires a bit of JavaScript code to start a remote operation and refresh the portion of the page affected by the results of the operation. The richer and more sophisticated the AJAX functions, the larger the developer's exposure is to JavaScript. No AJAX framework can change this basic fact, and ASP.NET AJAX Extensions are no exception.

Given that client script can't be avoided in AJAX, many frameworks, instead of trying to avoid using it, will hide as many details as possible of the required script. They tend to shield the developer from JavaScript and present a familiar programming model—mostly a server-based programming model. According to this model, server-side components generate required script code and silently inject it into the client page. What does it mean in the context of ASP.NET?

By using a handful of new server controls, ASP.NET developers can easily experience the thrill of using AJAX in their applications and they can do so with a very short learning curve. As you'll see in this chapter, you need not learn a new programming model or significantly improve your script skills to build effective AJAX applications. At the same time, though, you must be aware that what's covered in this chapter is only a relatively small portion of the AJAX capabilities. You still need a good grasp of JavaScript and client-side technologies to take full control of the ASP.NET AJAX platform.

Defining Updatable Regions

ASP.NET AJAX Extensions comprise two distinct but not mutually exclusive APIs: client and server. You can build AJAX functionalities using direct client-side programming, traditional server-side programming, or any combination of the two. We'll focus on server-centric programming features in this chapter and leave the client-side model for Chapter 6, "Built-in Application Services" and Chapter 7, "Remote Method Calls with ASP.NET AJAX."

As mentioned, any AJAX-based page requires some client-side JavaScript code to do its job; it isn't necessary, however, to leave the writing of such a script code to the ASP.NET programmer. A framework, in fact, could generate made-to-measure script code as the output of a server-side control. The server control, though, can take a variety of forms. It can be the AJAX version of a traditional server control—for example, an AJAX-enabled drop-down list that supports client insertions and moves them back to the server without a full page postback. It can also be a generic control container that takes care of refreshing all of its children without a full page postback.

As you can see, opposing philosophies underly these two approaches. If you opt for self-enabled AJAX controls, you need a new family of server controls that have a deep impact on existing pages. If you opt for containers instead, you need to learn and use only one new server control with a subsequent limited impact on existing code and your learning curve. ASP.NET AJAX Extensions chooses this second route.

In ASP.NET AJAX, page updates can be governed by a piece of client code automatically injected by a server control—the *UpdatePanel* control. By wrapping portions of ASP.NET pages in an updatable panel, you automatically transform any postbacks originated by embedded controls in a lightweight AJAX postback. This form of indirect page updating is by far the simplest way to add AJAX capabilities to new and existing ASP.NET 2.0 pages.

Generalities of the *UpdatePanel* Control

The *UpdatePanel* control represents the nerve center of the server-centric programming model of ASP.NET AJAX. It groups collections of server controls in updatable panels and ensures that the panel is refreshed using AJAX postbacks. It lets you execute server-side code and return updated markup to the client browser.

You might wonder how this differs from classic postbacks. The difference is in how the postback is implemented—instead of using a full page refresh, the *UpdatePanel* control sends an out-of-band request for fresh markup and then updates the Document Object Model (DOM) tree when the response is ready. Let's investigate the programming interface of the control.

The *UpdatePanel* Control at a Glance

The *UpdatePanel* control is a container control that enables partial rendering in an ASP.NET page. Defined in the *System.Web.Extensions* assembly, it belongs specifically to the *System.Web.UI* namespace. The control class is declared as follows:

```
public class UpdatePanel : Control
{
    ...
}
```

Although it's logically similar to the classic ASP.NET *Panel* control, the *UpdatePanel* control differs from the classic panel control in a number of aspects. In particular, it doesn't derive from *Panel* and, subsequently, it doesn't feature the same set of capabilities as ASP.NET panels, such as scrolling, styling, wrapping, and content management.

The *UpdatePanel* control derives directly from *Control*, meaning that it acts as a mere AJAX-aware container of child controls. It provides no user interface (UI) related facilities. Any required styling and formatting should be provided through the child controls. In contrast, the control sports a number of properties to control page updates and also exposes a client-side object model.

The Programming Interface of the Control

Table 4-1 details the properties defined on the *UpdatePanel* control that constitute the aspects of the control's behavior that developers can govern.

Table 4-1   Properties of the *UpdatePanel* Control

Property	Description
ChildrenAsTriggers	Indicates whether postbacks coming from child controls will cause the *UpdatePanel* to refresh. This property is set to *true* by default. When this property is *false*, postbacks from child controls are ignored. You can't set this property to *false* when the *UpdateMode* property is set to *Always*.
ContentTemplate	A template property, defines what appears in the *UpdatePanel* when it is rendered.
ContentTemplateContainer	Gets the template container object you can use to programmatically add child controls to the *UpdatePanel*.
IsInPartialRendering	Indicates whether the panel is being updated as part of an asynchronous postback. This property is designed for control developers. (More detail is provided later in this chapter.)
RenderMode	Indicates whether the contents of the panel will be rendered as a block *<div>* tag or as an inline *<span>* tag. The feasible values for the property— *Block* and *Inline*—are defined in the *UpdatePanelRenderMode* enumeration. The default is *Block*. (More detail is provided later in this chapter.)
Triggers	Defines a collection of trigger objects, each representing an event that causes the panel to refresh automatically.
UpdateMode	Gets or sets the rendering mode of the control by determining under which conditions the panel gets updated. The feasible values— *Always* and *Conditional*—come from the *UpdatePanelUpdateMode* enumeration:. The default is *Always*. (More detail is provided later in this chapter.)

To add child controls programmatically to an updatable panel, you use the *ContentTemplate-Container* property. In ASP.NET 2.0, to add or remove a child control, you use the *Controls* property. Why should you use the *ContentTemplateContainer* property with an *UpdatePanel* control? The reason is that what you really need to do with the *UpdatePanel* control is add or remove controls to the content template, not the control directly. That's why *Controls* doesn't work and you have to opt for the actual container of the template.

For example, consider this line of code:

```
UpdatePanel1.Controls.Add(new LiteralControl("Test"));
```

If you try to add a child control programmatically to the *Controls* collection—as in the preceding code snippet—all that you get is a runtime exception.

> **Note**   As mentioned, no ASP.NET control can remove or hide the *Controls* property, but that doesn't mean you should use it in the case of the *UpdatePanel* control. The *UpdatePanel* control doesn't need it because *UpdatePanel* is a templated control. All child controls, therefore, should be added to the template container. Period.
>
> Although such an explanation might be sufficient for novice or non-curious ASP.NET developers, seasoned ASP.NET developers might wonder how it's possible that you get an exception as soon as you try to add a new element to the *Controls* collection. For this to happen—they would argue—you need a homemade type of collection. And that's exactly what happens!
>
> The real type of the object returned through the *Controls* property is not the default *ControlCollection* type; rather, it's an internal *SingleChildControlCollection* type. The *Add* method of this collection type throws the exception. In ASP.NET control development, the trick to replacing the object behind the *Controls* property in a control is overriding the *CreateControlCollection* method. This is just what *UpdateControl* does.

Programmatic Updates

In addition to the properties listed in Table 4-1, the *UpdatePanel* control also features a public method with the following signature:

```
public void Update()
```

The method doesn't take any special action itself, but is limited to requiring that the child controls defined in the content template of the *UpdatePanel* control be refreshed. By using the *Update* method, you can programmatically control when the page region is updated in response to a standard postback event or perhaps during the initialization of the page.

An invalid operation exception can be thrown from within the *Update* method in a couple of well-known situations. One is if you call the method when the *UpdateMode* property is set to *Always*. The exception is thrown in this case because a method invocation prefigures a conditional update—you do it when you need it—which is just the opposite of what the *Always* value of the *UpdateMode* property indicates. The other situation in which the exception is thrown is when the *Update* method is called during or after the page's rendering stage.

So when should you get to use the *Update* method in your pages? You resort to the method if you have some server logic to determine whether an *UpdatePanel* control should be updated. As mentioned, this requires that you set the *UpdateMode* property to *Conditional*. In addition, if you need the decision of updating the panel to be strictly determined by your server logic, set the *ChildrenAsTriggers* property to *false* and make sure no triggers are defined for the panel. We'll return to this point later in the chapter.

The Eventing Model of the Control

The *UpdatePanel* control doesn't fire custom events. The only supported events are those it inherits from the base *Control* class and that are common to all ASP.NET controls: *Init*, *Load*, *PreRender*, *DataBinding*, and *Unload*.

The control defines internal handlers for all these events except *DataBinding*. During the pre-rendering stage, the control checks for conflicts between the current values of *ChildrenAsTriggers* and *UpdateMode* and raises an exception if *UpdateMode* is *Always* and *ChildrenAsTriggers* is set to *false*.

Your handler for the *Init* event (as well as handlers for other events) will be invoked before the control does its own scheduled job for the event.

Enabling Partial Rendering

An ASP.NET AJAX page looks almost identical to a normal ASP.NET page, except that it includes a *ScriptManager* control and one or more *UpdatePanel* controls. Each copy of the *UpdatePanel* control refers to a page region that can be updated independently from other regions and the remainder of the page. *UpdatePanel* controls can also be placed inside user controls and on both master and content pages. In addition, it can be nested inside of another *UpdatePanel* control and, like any other ASP.NET server control, created and appended dynamically to the page.

Partial rendering divides the page into independent regions, each of which controls its own postbacks and refreshes without causing or requiring a full page update. This is desirable when only a portion—and perhaps only a small portion—of the page needs to change during a postback. Partial updates reduce screen flickering and allow you to create more interactive Web applications. As an AJAX programmer, in fact, you can afford more postbacks than is reasonably possible if the entire page has to be refreshed on each and every postback.

> **Important** Like any other ASP.NET AJAX feature, partial rendering requires a *ScriptManager* control in the page. It is essential, though, that the *EnablePartialRendering* property on the manager be set to *true*—which is the default case. If the property is set to *false*, *UpdatePanel* works like a regular panel.

Defining the Updatable Contents

The contents of the *UpdatePanel* control are expressed through a template property—
ContentTemplate. You typically define the template declaratively, using the *<ContentTemplate>*
element. However, the *ContentTemplate* property can be set to any object that implements the
ITemplate interface, including a Web user control, as shown here:

```
void Page_PreInit(object sender, EventArgs e)
{
    string ascx = "customerView.ascx";
    UpdatePanel1.ContentTemplate = this.LoadTemplate(ascx);
}
```

Note that the *ContentTemplate* property of an *UpdatePanel* control cannot be set after the template has been instantiated or the content template container has been created. This means
that you can safely load the content template only in the *PreInit* event. If you move the preceding code to the page's *Init* or *Load* handler, you'll get an exception.

Normally, ASP.NET controls included in a template are not visible at the page level. To get a
valid reference to any control in a template, you have to use the *FindControl* method on the
control instance that holds the template. Let's consider the following code snippet:

```
<asp:UpdatePanel id="UpdatePanel1" runat="server" …>
  <ContentTemplate>
    <asp:textbox runat="server" id="TextBox1" ... />
    <asp:button runat="server" id="Button1" onclick="Button1_Click" ... />
    ...
  </ContentTemplate>
</asp:UpdatePanel>
```

What do you think the following code will do at run time? Will the text box's value be
retrieved or will the assignment throw a null-reference exception?

```
void Button1_Click(object sender, EventArgs e)
{
    string temp = TextBox1.Text;
}
```

The *TextBox1* control is defined inside a template and, as such, it's not scoped to the page. In
ASP.NET 1.x, the preceding code will just fail; in ASP.NET 2.0, though, it might work fine if the
template property is decorated with the *TemplateInstance* attribute. As you can see in the following code snippet, this is exactly the case for the *UpdatePanel*'s *ContentTemplate* property:

```
[Browsable(false)]
[PersistenceMode(PersistenceMode.InnerProperty)]
[TemplateInstance(TemplateInstance.Single)]
public ITemplate ContentTemplate
{
    get { return _contentTemplate; }
    set { _contentTemplate = value; }
}
```

In the end, any control defined in the *ContentTemplate* property can be accessed directly from any event handler defined within the host page.

Defining Regions Programmatically

The *ContentTemplate* property lets you define the contents of the updatable region in a declarative manner. What if you need to edit the template programmatically and add or remove controls dynamically? The following template defines a button and a label:

```
<asp:UpdatePanel ID="UpdatePanel1" runat="server">
    <ContentTemplate>
        <asp:Button runat="server" ID="Button1"
            Text="What time is it?" OnClick="Button1_Click" />
        <br />
        <asp:Label ID="Label1" runat="server" Text="[time]" />
    </ContentTemplate>
</asp:UpdatePanel>
```

The button is associated with a *Click* event handler that sets the label to the current time:

```
protected void Button1_Click(object sender, EventArgs e)
{
    Label1.Text = DateTime.Now.ToShortTimeString();
}
```

As you click the button, the page posts back and updates the label. You author the page in the traditional way. When controls you drag and drop onto the designer's surface are hosted in an updatable panel, however, those controls interact with the server using AJAX postbacks instead of classic whole-page postbacks. We'll return to the mechanics of AJAX postbacks in a moment. Figure 4-1 shows the page in action. The page works as expected, except that there is no indication on the browser's status bar signals that a full page postback is taking place.

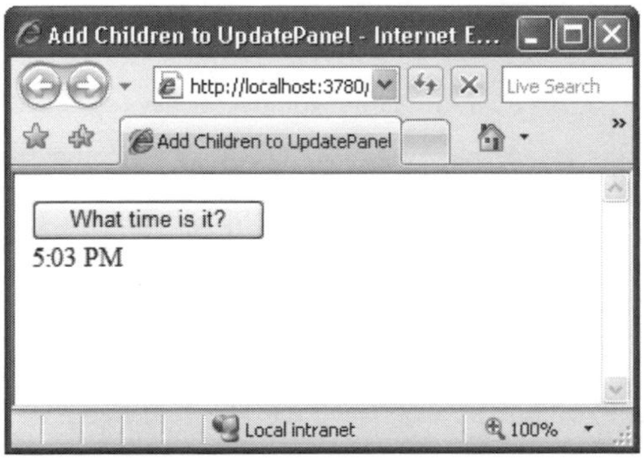

Figure 4-1   A sample ASP.NET AJAX page in action

To add controls to or remove controls from an updatable panel, you use the *ContentTemplate-Container* property. The following code shows how to build the same user interface shown in Figure 4-1, but in this case creating it programmatically. In addition to defining the template on the fly, the following code also adds the *UpdatePanel* control dynamically to the page via code:

```
public partial class Samples_Ch04_Simple_Dynamic : System.Web.UI.Page
{
    private Label Label1;

    protected void Page_Load(object sender, EventArgs e)
    {
        UpdatePanel upd = new UpdatePanel();
        upd.ID = "UpdatePanel1";

        // Define the button
        Button button1 = new Button();
        button1.ID = "Button1";
        button1.Text = "What time is it?";
        button1.Click += new EventHandler(Button1_Click);

        // Define the literals
        LiteralControl lit = new LiteralControl("<br>");

        // Define the label
        Label1 = new Label();
        Label1.ID = "Label1";
        Label1.Text = "[time]";

        // Link controls to the UpdatePanel
        upd.ContentTemplateContainer.Controls.Add(button1);
        upd.ContentTemplateContainer.Controls.Add(lit);
        upd.ContentTemplateContainer.Controls.Add(Label1);

        // Add the UpdatePanel to the list of form controls
        this.Form.Controls.Add(upd);
    }

    protected void Button1_Click(object sender, EventArgs e)
    {
        Label1.Text = DateTime.Now.ToShortTimeString();
    }
}
```

You can add an *UpdatePanel* control to the page at any time in the life cycle. Likewise, you can add controls to an existing panel at any time. However, you can't set the content template programmatically past the page's *PreInit* event.

Rendering Modes

The contents of the panel can be merged with the host page in either of two ways: as inline markup or as block-level elements. You control this setting through the *RenderMode* property. The feasible values for the property are listed in Table 4-2.

Table 4-2   The *UpdatePanelRenderMode* Enumeration

Value	Description
Block	The contents of the panel are enclosed by a *<div>* element.
Inline	The contents of the panel are enclosed by a *<span>* element.

By default, the contents of the panel form a new block and are wrapped by a *<div>* tag, as demonstrated by the following sample code:

```
<div id="UpdatePanel1">
   ...
</div>
```

If you opt for the *Inline* option, the contents flow with the page, as you can see in the following example:

```
<form id="form1" runat="server">
    <asp:ScriptManager runat="server" ID="ScriptManager1" />

    <big>This panel has been generated (inline) at:
        <asp:UpdatePanel ID="UpdatePanel1" runat="server"
            RenderMode="inline">
          <ContentTemplate>
              <b style="background-color:lime">
              <% =DateTime.Now %>
              </b>.<hr />
              <asp:Button ID="Button1" runat="server" Text="Refresh" />
          </ContentTemplate>
        </asp:UpdatePanel>
    </big>

    <br /><br /><br />

    <big>This panel has been generated (block) at:
        <asp:UpdatePanel ID="UpdatePanel2" runat="server"
            RenderMode="block">
          <ContentTemplate>
              <b style="background-color:lime">
              <% =DateTime.Now %>
              </b>.<hr />
              <asp:Button ID="Button2" runat="server" Text="Refresh" />
          </ContentTemplate>
        </asp:UpdatePanel>
    </big>
</form>
```

The preceding code produces output like that shown in Figure 4-2.

The updatable part of the page might not be a block of markup; it can also be simply an inline fragment of a paragraph.

Detecting Ongoing Updates

During a postback, the *IsInPartialRendering* read-only Boolean property indicates whether the contents of an *UpdatePanel* control are being updated. You access the property during postback code and the property returns *true* if the current request is being executed as a result of an AJAX postback.

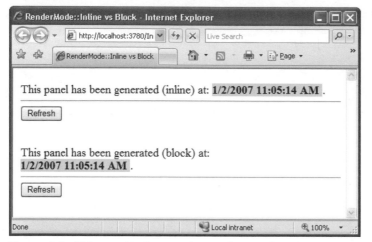

Figure 4-2   Using an *UpdatePanel* control to render inline text

Note that the property is designed for use by control developers only. Marked as a public member, the property can be used from the code-behind class of a page; however, it will always return *false* and is nearly useless at that level. The property is assigned its proper value only at rendering time. If used in the rendering stage of a custom control that inherits from *UpdatePanel*, it has the expected value when you render the markup for the panel.

If used from within the page, the property is set to its expected value only after the page markup has been rendered—for example, in the page *Unload* event or in the override of the *Render* method. This is good for tracing purposes; however, it's too late if you need the property to modify the output.

```
protected override void Render(HtmlTextWriter writer)
{
    // This call assigns the proper value to the
    // IsInPartialRendering property.
    base.Render(writer);

    // From now on, the IsInPartialRendering property
    // has the expected value. It's too late, though,
    // to update the page markup.
    Trace.WriteLine("The update panel {0} partially rendering",
        updatePanel1.IsInPartialRendering ? "is" : "is not");
    ...
}
```

An *UpdatePanel* control can be nested inside other *UpdatePanel* controls. If the parent panel refreshes for whatever reason (a trigger, child postback, or unconditional refresh), the value of *IsInPartialRendering* for the nested panel is nearly always *false*. The property value for the parent is *true* if the panel is truly partially rendering. Nested panels are always refreshed if the parent is.

The value of *IsInPartialRendering* for a nested panel is *true* only if the panel is being refreshed and the parent panel has *UpdateMode* set to *Conditional* (which not the default case). We'll return to conditional updates later in the chapter.

Consider the following code with two nested panels, the output of which is shown in Figure 4-3:

```
<asp:UpdatePanel ID="UpdatePanel1" runat="server">
    <ContentTemplate>
        <b style="background-color:lime">
        <% =DateTime.Now %>
        </b>
        <hr />
        <div>
            <big>The innermost panel has been last updated at:
              <asp:UpdatePanel ID="UpdatePanel2" runat="server">
                <ContentTemplate>
                  <b style="background-color:yellow">
                  <% =DateTime.Now %>
                  </b>
                  <hr />
                  <asp:Button ID="Button2" runat="server" Text="Refresh" />
                </ContentTemplate>
              </asp:UpdatePanel>
            </big>
        </div>
        <asp:Button ID="Button1" runat="server" Text="Refresh" />
    </ContentTemplate>
</asp:UpdatePanel>
```

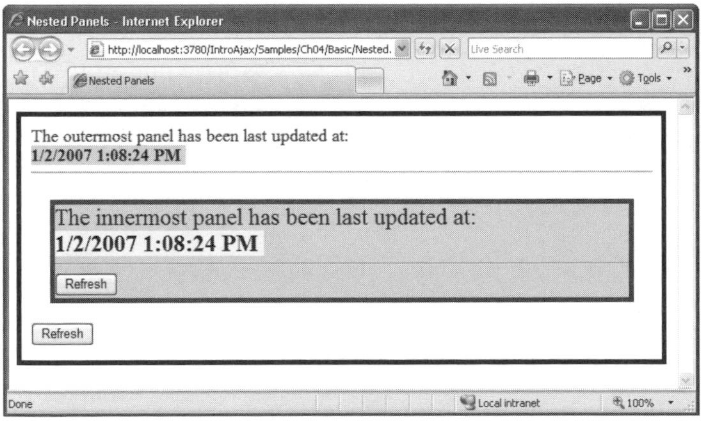

Figure 4-3   Nested *UpdatePanel* controls

If you just need to know whether a portion of a page is being updated as a result of an AJAX postback, you use the *IsInAsyncPostBack* Boolean property on the *ScriptManager* control.

Testing the *UpdatePanel* Control

At this point, you know all the basic facts about updatable panels. Before we take the plunge into more advanced and powerful features, let's consider a couple of data-driven examples.

A First Sample Page

Many ASP.NET controls contain clickable elements such as button and links. As the user interacts with the markup of any of these controls, she clicks and causes the page to post back and refresh entirely. Grid controls such *DataGrid* and *GridView* are the perfect fit. These controls can generate pages of output, and the user needs to click and post back to see the contents of a given page. Is there a way to have grid controls provide a paged, sorted, or filtered view of their contents without fully refreshing the host page?

Let's suppose your page has a grid with some data in it for users to page through. The following listing illustrates this scenario as you would code it for a classic ASP.NET page:

```
<asp:GridView ID="GridView1" runat="server"
    DataSourceID="ObjectDataSource1" AllowPaging="True"
    AutoGenerateColumns="False">
  <Columns>
      <asp:BoundField DataField="ID" HeaderText="ID" />
      <asp:BoundField DataField="CompanyName" HeaderText="Company" />
      <asp:BoundField DataField="Country" HeaderText="Country" />
  </Columns>
</asp:GridView>
<asp:ObjectDataSource ID="ObjectDataSource1" runat="server"
    TypeName="IntroAjax.CustomerManager"
    SelectMethod="LoadAll" />
```

Every time the user clicks to view a new page, the page posts back and gets fully refreshed. For a page that contains a lot of other content, this might be a serious issue. With ASP.NET AJAX, you can isolate the portion of the page that needs updates and wrap it in an *UpdatePanel* control. The net effect is that only the contents of the panel are updated as the user clicks. Here's the AJAX-enabled version of the preceding page:

```
<asp:ScriptManager ID="ScriptManager1" runat="server" />

<asp:UpdatePanel ID="UpdatePanel1" runat="server">
   <ContentTemplate>
      <asp:GridView ID="GridView1" runat="server"
          DataSourceID="ObjectDataSource1" AllowPaging="True"
          AutoGenerateColumns="False">
        <Columns>
          <asp:BoundField DataField="ID" HeaderText="ID" />
          <asp:BoundField DataField="CompanyName" HeaderText="Company" />
          <asp:BoundField DataField="Country" HeaderText="Country" />
        </Columns>
      </asp:GridView>
      <asp:ObjectDataSource ID="ObjectDataSource1" runat="server"
          TypeName="IntroAjax.CustomerManager"
          SelectMethod="LoadAll" />
   </ContentTemplate>
</asp:UpdatePanel>
```

Basically, any updatable contents have been moved to the *<ContentTemplate>* section of the *UpdatePanel* control and a *ScriptManager* control has been added. The changes are limited, but the final effect is significantly better.

The postback is generated as usual and by the usual server controls. As a result, only the page fragment embedded in the *UpdatePanel* control is updated. The markup for the page segment incorporated in the *UpdatePanel* control is regenerated on the server as a result of the AJAX postback. That markup is pasted to an HTTP response and sent back to the client. Next, the AJAX infrastructure takes care of it and updates the page. We'll delve deep into this mechanism in a moment.

Note   In ASP.NET 2.0, the *GridView* and *DetailsView* controls come with a Boolean property named *EnableSortingAndPagingCallbacks*. If set, the property causes the controls to employ a client-side callback for sorting and paging operations. The contents for the host page are retrieved on the server, but the control's markup is updated without fully refreshing the page. The same feature is now replicated by a far larger framework, the ASP.NET AJAX Extensions. It is not recommended, though, that you use sorting and paging callbacks (or any other sort of ASP.NET Script Callback features) along with ASP.NET AJAX Extensions and specifically with updatable panels. The risk is that concurrent calls hit the server resulting in a possibly inconsistent view state for the page.

Using AJAX for Multistep Operations

Wizards and rich controls that support features such as in-place editing, collapse/expand, and multiview facilities are perfect for AJAX pages. By using updatable panels, you only have to wrap the old classic server code in an *UpdatePanel* control. Figure 4-4 shows a sample page obtained by combining a *DetailsView* (for display) and a *SqlDataSource* control (for data editing).

You can navigate through the records and click to edit the various fields. Whatever postback operation is required in this context is limited to the markup around the *DetailsView* control. Everything else in the page is left intact and is not included in the HTTP packets.

Note   All in all, the most interesting trait of this example is not the functionality itself, but rather the fact that you can virtually host any combination of ASP.NET controls in an updatable panel. If any of these controls cause postbacks, you can have the affected segment of the page updated independently from the rest of the page. And no special knowledge of the ASP.NET AJAX framework is required to code this.

Compared to the *EnableSortingAndPagingCallbacks* property, an *UpdatePanel* control might look like its double at first. However, it's much more flexible than that property and addresses a far broader range of scenarios.

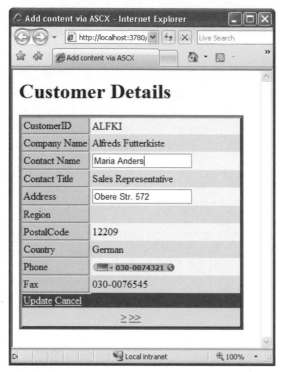

Figure 4-4   Free AJAX-powered in-place editing

Using AJAX for Quicker Data Validation

Input forms of any kind require some sort of data validation. ASP.NET validator controls do a good job both on the client (via JavaScript) and the server side. A client-side validation layer might save you from a number of postbacks, but a server-side validation layer is always necessary if for only for security reasons. If you rely on client script checks only, your entire validation infrastructure might be cut off by disabling JavaScript altogether in the client browser. For this reason, server validation, and subsequently postbacks, are required.

There are also situations in which data can't just be validated on the client. For example, consider the following code:

```
<table>
    <tr>
        <td>User Name</td><td>*</td>
        <td><asp:textbox runat="server" id="userName" />
            <asp:RequiredFieldValidator runat="server"
                id="userReqValidator"
                ControlToValidate="userName"
                Text="!!!"
                ErrorMessage="User name is mandatory" />
            <asp:CustomValidator runat="server" id="userValidator"
```

```
                OnServerValidate="CheckUserName"
                ControlToValidate="userName"
                ErrorMessage="The proposed name already exists or is not
                              valid." /></td></tr>
    <tr>
        <td>Email</td><td>*</td>
        <td><asp:textbox runat="server" id="email" />
            <asp:RequiredFieldValidator runat="server"
                id="emailReqValidator"
                ControlToValidate="email"
                Text="!!!"
                ErrorMessage="Membership is mandatory" />
            <asp:RegularExpressionValidator runat="server"
                id="emailValidator"
                ControlToValidate="email"
                ValidationExpression="[a-zA-Z_0-9.-]+\@[a-zA-Z_0-9.-
                                      ]+\.\w+"
                ErrorMessage="Must be an email address." /></td></tr>
    <tr>
        <td>Membership Level</td><td>*</td>
        <td><asp:textbox runat="server" id="membership" />
            <asp:RequiredFieldValidator runat="server"
                id="membershipReqValidator"
                ControlToValidate="membership"
                Text="!!!"
                ErrorMessage="Membership is mandatory" />
            <asp:CustomValidator runat="server" id="membershipValidator"
                OnServerValidate="CheckMembership"
                ControlToValidate="membership"
                ErrorMessage="Must be Gold or Platinum." /></td></tr>
</table>
```

The form contains three mandatory input fields: user name, e-mail, and membership. The user name must be unique, but the uniqueness of the typed value can't be verified on the client. In contrast, the format of the e-mail address can be easily validated through a regular expression on the client. If you also want to check whether the e-mail address exists, you need server code.

The *CustomValidator* control is an ASP.NET validator control that you use to validate input on the server. You specify the validation code through the *ServerValidate* server event. Here's an example:

```
protected void CheckUserName(object source, ServerValidateEventArgs e)
{
    e.IsValid = false;
    string buf = e.Value.ToLower();

    // Deny all names starting with "dino"
    if (!buf.StartsWith("dino"))
        e.IsValid = true;
}
```

For this code to run, a postback is required. With AJAX, you can go back to the server without a full page refresh. The final effect is similar to client-side validation. (See Figure 4-5.)

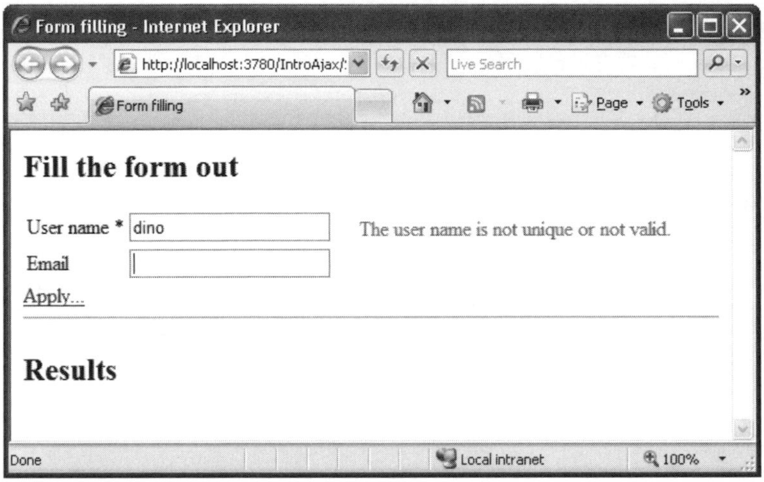

Figure 4-5   Page validation made with AJAX

To trigger the postback, the user needs to click a button unless you turn on the *AutoPostBack* attribute on an input control:

```
<asp:textbox runat="server" id="userName" AutoPostBack="true" />
```

For this example, the validation process is automatically triggered as soon as the user tabs out of the field. In this case, you also need to complete the *Page_Load* event handler with the following code:

```
protected void Page_Load(object sender, EventArgs e)
{
    if (IsPostBack)
        this.Validate();
}
```

> **Note**   A scenario in which it would seemingly be interesting to use AJAX functionality is when uploading files. To do the job, in ASP.NET you either use the *FileUpload* Web control or the *HtmlInputFile* HTML control.
>
> The way in which the control is rendered to HTML is browser specific, but it normally consists of a text box and a *Browse* button. The user selects a file from the local machine and then clicks the button to submit the page to the server. When this occurs, the browser uploads the selected file to the server. The *UpdatePanel* control knows how to capture the submit event of the posting control, but it doesn't upload the file. As a result, on the server there's no uploaded file to save anywhere.
>
> This behavior is by design. A *FileUpload* control can be used in the same page as an *UpdatePanel* control as long as you place it outside of the panel's content template.

Master Pages and Partial Updates

You can safely use *UpdatePanel* controls from within master pages. Most of the time, the use of updatable panels is easy and seamless. There are a few situations, though, that deserve a bit of further explanation.

If you add a *ScriptManager* control to a master page, partial rendering is enabled by default for all content pages. In addition, initial settings on the script manager are inherited by all content pages. As we saw in Chapter 3, "Adding AJAX Capabilities to a Site," you can use the *Script-ManagerProxy* control in the content page to reference the parent manager and change some of its settings. The *ScriptManagerProxy* control, though, is mostly designed to let you edit the list of scripts and services registered with the manager in a declarative manner, and it doesn't let you customize, say, error handling. You can do the same (and indeed much more) by programmatically referencing the script manager in the master page. Here's how:

```
// Reference to the script manager of a content page.
// The script manager is defined on the master page.
ScriptManager sm = ScriptManager.GetCurrent(this);
```

In some cases, a content placeholder on the master page might be wrapped in an updatable region. As the author of the content page, you have no control over that. What if you're going to use in that page a control that doesn't work with *UpdatePanel*, such as with file uploads? In this case, you need to disable partial rendering just for that individual content page. Here's how you can do it:

```
protected void Page_Init(object sender, EventArgs e)
{
    ScriptManager.GetCurrent(this).EnablePartialRendering = false;
}
```

In the content page, you create a handler for the page's *Init* event that sets *EnablePartialRendering* on the script manager property to *false*. You must change the state of the *EnablePartialRendering* property during or before the content page's *Init* event. You can't accomplish this task just by using the *ScriptManagerProxy* control.

Partial Updates from User Controls

User controls provide an easy way to bring self-contained, auto-updatable AJAX components into an ASP.NET page. Because each page can have at most one script manager, you can't reasonably place the script manager in the user control. That would work and make the user control completely self-contained, but it would also limit you to using exactly one instance of the user control per page. On the other hand, the *UpdatePanel* control requires a script manager on the page containing the *UpdatePanel*. Multiple script managers or the lack of at least one script manager cause an exception.

The simplest workaround is that you take the script manager out of the user controls and place it in the host page. User controls assume the presence of a script manager, and they use internally as many updatable panels as needed. Figure 4-6 shows an example.

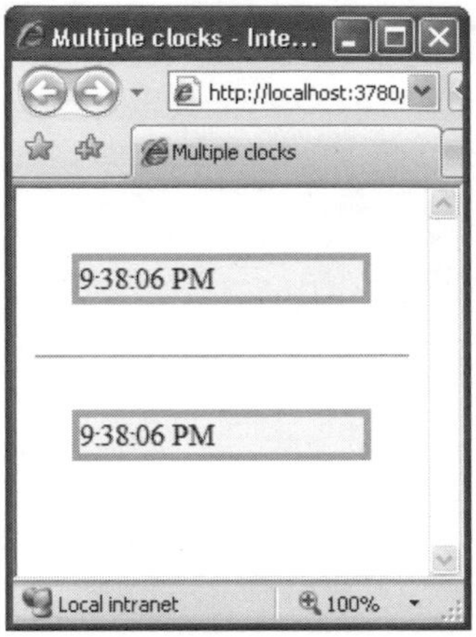

Figure 4-6 Two AJAX-enabled user controls in the same page

```
<asp:ScriptManager runat="server" ID="ScriptManager1" />
<x:Clock runat="server" ID="Clock1" />
<hr />
<x:Clock runat="server" ID="Clock2" />
```

Warning You can't call *Response.Write* from within a postback event handler (for example, *Button1_Click*) that gets called during an asynchronous AJAX postback. If you do so, you'll receive a client exception stating that the message received from the server could not be parsed. In general, calls to *Response.Write*—but also response filters, HTTP modules, or server tracing (*Trace=true*)—modify the stream returned to the client by adding explicit data that alters the expected format.

The Mechanics of Updatable Panels

The magic of updating specific portions of the page springs from the combined efforts of the *UpdatePanel* control and the AJAX script manager component. During the initialization phase, the *UpdatePanel* control gets a reference to the page's script manager and registers with it. In this way, the script manager knows how many updatable panels the host page contains and holds a reference to each of them.

The script manager also emits proper client script code to intercept any postback submit actions started on the client. Such a script code hooks the form's *submit* event and replaces the standard data-submission process with an AJAX asynchronous call that is run through the *XMLHttpRequest* object. Let's step through more details.

Client Script Injection

The following fragment shows the typical script emitted in the client page when partial rendering is enabled:

```
<script type="text/javascript">
//<![CDATA[
```

```
Sys.WebForms.PageRequestManager._initialize(
    'ScriptManager1', document.getElementById('form1'));
Sys.WebForms.PageRequestManager.getInstance()._updateControls(
    ['tUpdatePanel1'], [], [], 90);
//]]>
</script>
```

As you saw in Chapter 2, "The Microsoft AJAX Client Library," *PageRequestManager* is one of the classes that form the client library of ASP.NET AJAX. In particular, the class is in charge of running asynchronous calls through the *XMLHttpRequest* object.

> **Note**   The *_initialize* and *_updateControls* methods are conventionally considered private members of the *PageRequestManager* class; yet they are externally callable. In Chapter 2, we learned that classes in the Microsoft Client Library (MCL) can't really have private members. By convention, private members have their names prefixed with the underscore (_). However, this doesn't prevent code from calling into the underscored methods when necessary.

The *_initialize* method wires up new event handlers for the form's *submit* and *click* events and for the window's *unload* event. The *_updateControls* method takes four parameters: the list of updatable panels in the form; two arrays with the ID of form controls capable of firing AJAX and classic postbacks, respectively; and the time, in seconds, allowed for the update to complete before timing out. (The default is 90 seconds.) You can take a look at the real implementation of the method by scanning the source code contained in the file *MicrosoftAjaxWebForms.js*.

Format of the AJAX Request

So the *_initialize* method prepares a new AJAX request for each classic postback that is going to take place. Manipulated by *PageRequestManager*'s script, the body of an example *GridView* update request sent to the server looks much like this:

```
ScriptManager1=UpdatePanel1|GridView1&
__EVENTTARGET=GridView1&
__EVENTARGUMENT=Page%243&
__VIEWSTATE=%2Fw ... 3D&
__EVENTVALIDATION=%2Fw ... 3D
```

The original request is the one sent over by a *GridView* control named *GridView1* when the user clicks to view page #3. Note that the %24 character is the HTML-encoded format for the dollar symbol ($).

In addition to the view-state and event-validation data (which are specific features of ASP.NET 2.0 postbacks), the request contains the ID of the updatable panel that will serve the call (*UpdatePanel1* in the snippet just shown) and the server control target of the postback (in this case, *GridView1*). The actual format of the request might change a bit depending on the characteristics of the posting control. For example, *GridView* uses the __EVENTTARGET field to pass its name to the server. A *Button* control, on the other hand, uses a new parameter, as shown here:

```
ScriptManager1=UpdatePanel1|Button1&
__EVENTTARGET=&
__EVENTARGUMENT=&
__VIEWSTATE=%2Fw ... 3D&
__EVENTVALIDATION=%2Fw ... 3D&
Button1=Refresh
```

You can look at the bits of the request either by using an ad hoc network monitor tool or by simply adding some debug code to the *Page_Load* event handler:

```
protected void Page_Load(object sender, EventArgs e)
{
    // Need permissions to write
    Request.SaveAs(@"c:\req_details.txt", true);
}
```

In case of anomalies and malfunctions, it's crucial to analyze the response of an AJAX call. For this reason, you need to provide yourself with a tool that monitors HTTP traffic. *Fiddler* is certainly a good one. You can read all about its features at *http://www.fiddlertool.com/fiddler*. It works as a proxy and logs all HTTP traffic so that you can later examine the contents of each request and response. Fiddler supports Internet Explorer as well as other browsers.

Developed by a member of the ASP.NET AJAX team, the Web Development Helper utility is a free tool specifically for Internet Explorer. You can download it from *http://www.nikhilk.net/ Project.WebDevHelper.aspx*. The utility allows viewing information about the current ASP.NET page, such as view state and trace output. In addition, it can also perform some operations on the server, such as restarting the application or managing the *Cache* object. Finally, the utility provides developers with the ability to view the live HTML DOM and allows for monitoring requests and responses for diagnostic scenarios. Most features of the tool work only when the application is hosted by the local host. Installing the tool requires a bit of manual work, as it is implemented as an Internet Explorer browser helper object. Figure 4-7 shows the tool in action. Note that after installing the tool, you display it by using the View|Explorer Bar menu in Internet Explorer.

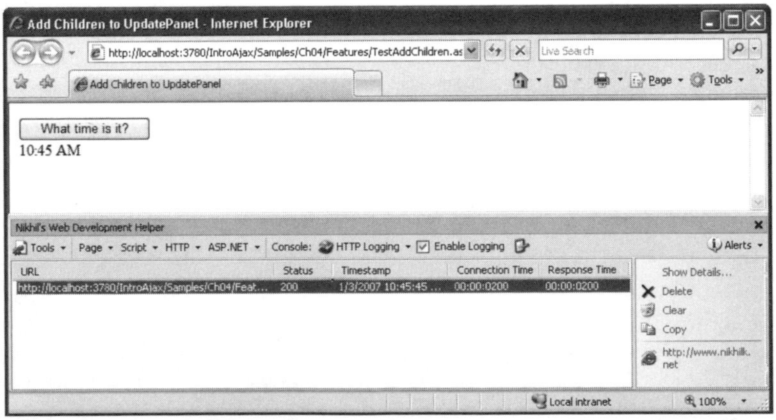

Figure 4-7 The Web Development Helper tool in action

Detecting AJAX Requests at Runtime

On the server, the postback is processed as usual, and indeed there's no way for the ASP.NET runtime to detect it's an AJAX call to refresh only a portion of the original page.

More precisely, each AJAX request contains an extra header that is missing in traditional post-back requests. However, only ad hoc additional runtime components (for example, HTTP modules)—not the default set of runtime components—can take advantage of this. Here are the details of the new request header:

```
x-microsoftajax: Delta=true
```

Figure 4-8 shows the extra header using the user interface of the Web Development Helper tool.

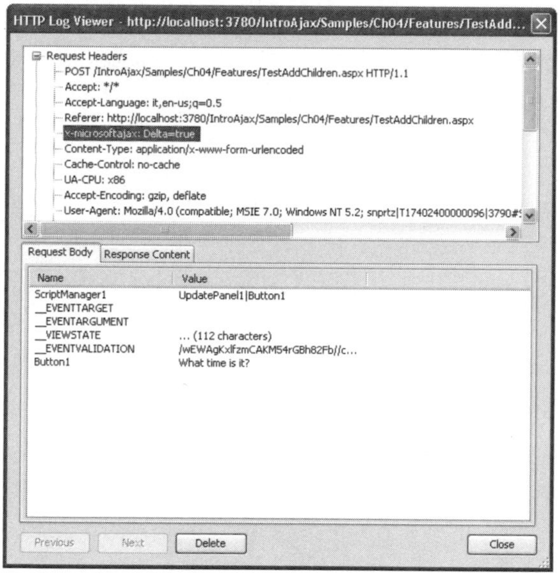

Figure 4-8 The extra request header that decorates ASP.NET AJAX requests sent through the *UpdatePanel* control

The header is added only for requests managed through the *UpdatePanel* control. Other AJAX requests—for example, requests for Web service methods—don't include the header. These requests, though, have a special content type: *application/json*.

To detect an AJAX request from the page life cycle, you just use the *IsInAsyncPostBack* property on the *ScriptManager* control.

Format of the AJAX Response

From within the page life cycle, the script manager hooks up the standard rendering process by registering a render callback method. The modified rendering process loops through all the registered updatable panels and asks each to output its fresh markup.

At the end of the request, the client is returned only contents of updatable regions, and a JavaScript callback function buried in the client library takes care of replacing the current content of regions with any received markup. Here's the typical response of an AJAX *UpdatePanel* response:

```
2735|updatePanel|UpdatePanel1|
...
-- markup for all updated panels goes here --
...
|0|hiddenField|__EVENTTARGET|
|0|hiddenField|__EVENTARGUMENT|
|684|hiddenField|__VIEWSTATE|5A ... /0=
|64|hiddenField|__EVENTVALIDATION|H2 ... /0=
```

The output is made of a sequence of records. Each record contains the overall size, a keyword that identifies the client container of the following information, optionally the name of the container (control, variable), and the actual content. Two consecutive records (and fields inside a single record) are separated with pipe characters (|). In the preceding code snippet, more than 2 KB of information are being returned as the replacement for the contents of *UpdatePanel* control named *UpdatePanel1*. In addition, the response includes empty *__EVENTTARGET* and *__EVENTARGUMENT* hidden fields, plus updated view-state and event-validation data. The response also includes other helper records that cache parameters for the partial update (basically, the input data for the *_initialize* method), the action URL, and the new page title.

The updated markup constitutes the lion's share of the response, followed by the updated view-state and event-validation data. All remaining data rarely adds up to an extra KB of information.

One Partial Update at a Time

From the user perspective, a partial page update is an asynchronous operation, meaning that the user can continue working with the controls page and animation can be displayed to entertain the user during a lengthy task and to provide feedback. Two partial updates, though, can't run together and concurrently.

If you trigger a second partial update when another one is taking place, the first call is aborted to execute the new one. As a result, just one partial update can be executed at a time. This limitation is by design because each partial update updates the view state and event-validation data. To ensure consistency, each AJAX postback must find and return a consistent view state for the next postback to start.

As we'll see later in the chapter, an updatable region can be bound to events fired by the *PageRequestManager* client object that signal key steps in the client life cycle of an update such as begin/end request, page loaded, and the like. By handling these events, you can cancel additional postback requests while another one—with a higher priority—is going on. I'll say more about this later.

Error Handling in Partial Updates

As discussed in Chapter 3, any errors that occur during a partial update are captured by the script manager control and handled in a standard way. The script manager swallows the real exception and sends back to the client a response record similar to the following:

```
53|error|500|Object reference not set to an instance of an object.|
```

The first piece of information is the size of the record, followed by a keyword that qualifies the information. Next, you get the error code and the message for the user. From a pure HTTP perspective, the packet received denotes success—HTTP status code 200. The client-side script, though, knows how to handle an error response and by default pops up a message box with the message received.

As in Chapter 3, you can customize the error handling both on the server and the client. On the server, you can hook up the *AsyncPostBackError* event on the *ScriptManager* control and set a custom error message through the *AsyncPostBackErrorMessage* property:

```
void AsyncPostBackError(object sender, AsyncPostBackErrorEventArgs e)
{
    ScriptManager1.AsyncPostBackErrorMessage = "An error occurred:\n" +
        e.Exception.Message;
}
```

You don't need to write such an event handler if you just want to return a generic and static message whatever the exception raised. In this case, you simply set the property to the desired string in *Page_Load*.

On the client, you can register a handler for the *endRequest* event of the *PageRequestManager* object, do your custom client handling, and then state that you're done with the error:

```
<script type="text/javascript" language="JavaScript">
function pageLoad()
{
    // Handle the endRequest event for partial updates
    var manager = Sys.WebForms.PageRequestManager.getInstance();
    manager.add_endRequest(endRequest);
}
function endRequest(sender, args)
{
    // Do your own error handling here
    $get("Label1").innerHTML = args.get_error().message;

    // State that you're done with the error handling. This statement
    // prevents the standard client-side handling (a message box)
    args.set_errorHandled(true);
}
</script>
```

The *endRequest* client event fires at the end of a partial page refresh operation.

Taking Control of Updatable Regions

So far, I've considered only pages with a single *UpdatePanel* control and silently assumed that any updatable panel had to refresh on every postback. It's more realistic, however, to expect that you'll have pages with multiple panels. In addition, the updating of panels will likely be triggered by controls that are scattered in the page and not necessarily placed inside the panel. Finally, it's common to have each panel logically bound to a well-known set of triggers—button clicks, value changes, or HTML events—and refresh only if any of the assigned triggers are active. Let's see how to take full control of the page update process and assign triggers, conditionally update panels, and use other, more advanced features.

Triggering the Panel Update

In all the examples I've illustrated thus far, the control that causes the asynchronous AJAX postback has always been part of the updatable panel and defined within the *<Content-Template>* section. This arrangement is not what you will see in all cases. In general, a panel update can be triggered by any page controls that have the ability to post back. Furthermore, an updatable panel also can be refreshed programmatically when proper runtime conditions are detected during a partial page update caused by another panel.

By default, an *UpdatePanel* control refreshes its contents whenever a postback occurs within the page. If the control that posts back is placed outside the updatable panel, a full refresh occurs. Otherwise, only the panel that contains the control refreshes. You can programmatically control under which conditions the contents of the panel are refreshed. You have three tools to leverage: the *UpdateMode*, *ChildrenAsTriggers*, and *Triggers* properties.

Updating Modes

Through the *UpdateMode* property, the *UpdatePanel* control supports two update modes: *Always* (the default) and *Conditional*. The values are grouped in the *UpdatePanelUpdateMode* enumeration, listed in Table 4-3.

Table 4-3   The *UpdatePanelUpdateMode* Enumeration

Value	Description
Always	The panel is updated on each postback raised by the page.
Conditional	The panel is updated only when the update is triggered by one of the assigned panel triggers or the update is requested programmatically.

When the *UpdateMode* property is set to *Always*, each postback that originates around the page—from controls inside and out of the panel—triggers the update on the panel. This means that if you have multiple updatable panels in a page, all of them will update even though the event concerns only one of them or even none of them.

When the *UpdateMode* property is set to *Conditional*, the panel is updated only when you call the *Update* method on the control during a postback or when a trigger associated with the

UpdatePanel control is verified. The *ChildrenAsTriggers* Boolean property (which is *true* by default) defines whether children of an updatable panel also trigger a refresh.

We'll also refer to children controls as "implicit triggers" and triggers defined to through the *Triggers* property as "explicit triggers."

Conditional Refresh of an *UpdatePanel* Control

An *UpdatePanel* trigger defines a runtime condition—mostly a control event—that causes an *UpdatePanel* control to be refreshed when the page is working in partial rendering mode. Triggers make sense mostly when the panel is being updated conditionally or when children are not meant to be implicit triggers.

ASP.NET AJAX Extensions supports two types of triggers, both derived from the abstract class *UpdatePanelControlTrigger*. They are *AsyncPostBackTrigger* and *PostBackTrigger*. You associate triggers with an *UpdatePanel* control declaratively through the *<Triggers>* section or programmatically via the *Triggers* collection property. Here's an example of asynchronous triggers in a page with two updatable panels:

```
Query string:<br />
<asp:TextBox ID="TextBox1" runat="server" />
<asp:Button ID="Button1" runat="server" Text="Load ..."
    OnClick="Button1_Click" />

<asp:UpdatePanel runat="server" ID="UpdatePanel1" UpdateMode="Conditional">
    <ContentTemplate>
        <small>Grid contents generated at: <%=DateTime.Now %></small>
        <asp:GridView ID="GridView1" runat="server"
            DataSourceID="ObjectDataSource1">
            ...
        </asp:GridView>
    </ContentTemplate>
    <Triggers>
        <asp:AsyncPostBackTrigger ControlID="Button1" EventName="Click" />
    </Triggers>
</asp:UpdatePanel>

<asp:UpdatePanel ID="UpdatePanel2" runat="server" UpdateMode="Conditional">
    <ContentTemplate>
        <div style="background-color:Lime">
            <big>This panel has been generated at: <%=DateTime.Now %></big>
        </div>
    </ContentTemplate>
    <Triggers>
        <asp:AsyncPostBackTrigger ControlID="Button2" EventName="Click" />
    </Triggers>
</asp:UpdatePanel>

<asp:Button ID="Button2" runat="server" Text="Refresh time"
    OnClick="Button2_Click" />
```

The user types a query string in the text box that will be used to filter the customers in the grid. (See Figure 4-9.)

Figure 4-9   The contents of the grid are refreshed only when the user sets a filter

More precisely, the contents of the grid are refreshed when the user pages through the record and when the user clicks the *Load* button. Paging refreshes the grid as long as *ChildrenAs-Triggers* is set to *true*—the default—because the link buttons used to page are child controls of the *UpdatePanel*. The *Click* event of the *Load* button, conversely, is registered as an asynchronous postback trigger because it is external to the panel.

As you can see in Figure 4-9, the time at which the grid was last refreshed doesn't coincide with the time rendered in the second panel. According to the preceding code, to refresh the bottom panel you have to click the *Refresh time* button—a trigger for the *UpdatePanel2* control.

Programmatic Updates of Panels

What if while refreshing the first panel you realize you need to update a second one? You can programmatically command a panel update by using the following code:

```
protected void Button1_Click(object sender, EventArgs e)
{
   // Do as usual assuming we're refreshing UpdatePanel1
   ...

   // Command an update on an external UpdatePanel control
   UpdatePanel2.Update();
}
```

You should resort to this approach only if some sort of implicit dependency exists between two panels. In this case, when you are in the process of updating one, there might be conditions that require you to update the second one also. Because at this point your code is executing on the server, there's no way for you to do this other than by explicitly invoking the *Update* method on the panel.

Triggers of an *UpdatePanel* Control

As mentioned, there are two types of triggers for an *UpdatePanel* control—*AsyncPostBackTrigger* and *PostBackTrigger*. They have nearly the same syntax; both, when raised, cause the contents of the *UpdatePanel* control to be updated during a postback. Where's the difference between the two? It's indicated by the name, actually.

The event associated with the *AsyncPostBackTrigger* component triggers an asynchronous AJAX postback on the *UpdatePanel* control. As a result, the host page remains intact except for the contents of the referenced panel and its dependencies, if any. Usually, the *AsyncPostBack-Trigger* component points to controls placed outside the *UpdatePanel*. However, if the panel has the *ChildrenAsTriggers* property set to *false*, it could make sense that you define an embedded control as the trigger. In both cases, when a control that is a naming container is used as a trigger, all of its child controls that cause postbacks behave as triggers.

You add an event trigger declaratively using the *<Triggers>* section of the *UpdatePanel* control:

```
<asp:UpdatePanel runat="server" ID="UpdatePanel1">
   <ContentTemplate>
      ...
   </ContentTemplate>
   <Triggers>
      <asp:AsyncPostBackTrigger ControlID="DropDownList1"
          EventName="SelectedIndexChanged" />
   </Triggers>
</asp:UpdatePanel>
```

You need to specify two pieces of information: the ID of the control to monitor, and the name of the event to catch. Note that the *AsyncPostBackTrigger* component can catch only server-side events fired by server controls. Both *ControlID* and *EventName* are string properties. For example, the panel described in the previous code snippet is refreshed when any of the controls in the page post back or when the selection changes on the drop-down list control named *DropDownList1*.

It should be noted that in no way does the panel refresh when a client event (i.e., *onblur*, *onchange*, *click*) fires. If you need to refresh when the selection on a list changes, either you set the *AutoPostBack* property on the control to *true* so that a key client event fires the postback or you wait for something else around the page to trigger the postback. For example, imagine you have *UpdatePanel1* like in the snippet above and *UpdatePanel2* bound to a button. When the user simply changes the selection on the drop-down list nothing happens. However, when another panel is refreshed—say, *UpdatePanel2*, even completely unrelated to the other—then the page places an AJAX postback and the page lifecycle is started for all controls in the page. At this point, the change in the drop-down list is detected and *UpdatePanel1* is refreshed too.

Full Postbacks from Inside Updatable Panels

By default, all child controls of an *UpdatePanel* that post back operate as implicit asynchronous postback triggers. You can prevent all of them from posting by setting *ChildrenAsTriggers* to *false*. Note that when *ChildrenAsTriggers* is *false,* postbacks coming from child controls are just ignored. In no way are such postback events processed as regular form submissions. You can then re-enable only a few child controls to post back by adding them to the *<Triggers>* section of the *UpdatePanel*. These postbacks, though, will only refresh the panel.

There might be situations in which you need to perform full, regular postbacks from inside an *UpdatePanel* control in response to a control event. In this case, you use the *PostBackTrigger* component, as shown here:

```
<asp:UpdatePanel runat="server" ID="UpdatePanel1">
   <ContentTemplate>
     ...
   </ContentTemplate>
   <Triggers>
     <asp:AsyncPostBackTrigger ControlID="DropDownList1"
         EventName="SelectedIndexChanged" />
     <asp:PostBackTrigger ControlID="Button1" />
   </Triggers>
</asp:UpdatePanel>
```

The preceding panel features both synchronous and asynchronous postback triggers. The panel is updated when the user changes the selection on the drop-down list; the whole host page is refreshed when the user clicks the button.

> **Note**   When should you use a *PostBackTrigger* component to fire a full postback from inside an updatable panel? Especially when complex and templated controls are involved, it might not be easy to separate blocks of user interface in distinct panels and single controls. So the easiest, and often the only, solution is wrapping a whole block of user interface in an updatable panel. If a single control in this panel needs to fire a full postback, you need the *PostBackTrigger* component.

A *PostBackTrigger* component causes referenced controls inside an *UpdatePanel* control to perform regular postbacks. These triggers must be children of the affected *UpdatePanel*.

The *PostBackTrigger* object doesn't support the *EventName* property. If a control with that name is causing the form submission, the ASP.NET AJAX client script simply lets the request go as usual. The ASP.NET runtime will then figure out which server postback event has to be raised for the postback control by looking at its implementation of *IPostBackEventHandler*.

Triggering Periodic Partial Updates

ASP.NET pages that require frequent updates can be built to expose clickable elements so that users can order a refresh when they feel it is convenient. What if the update occurs frequently and periodically—that is, every *n* milliseconds? In this case, you can't ask users to stay there and click all the time. Timers exist to help with such situations. And timers have been incorporated in virtually every browser's DOM since the beginning of the Web.

The *setTimeout* method of the DOM *window* object allows you to create a client timer. Once installed, the timer periodically executes a piece of JavaScript code. In turn, this script code can do whatever is needed—for example, it can start an asynchronous call to the server and update the page automatically.

You can use script-based timers with any version of ASP.NET. To do so, though, you need to have some JavaScript skills and be aware of the characteristics of the browser's DOM. ASP.NET AJAX shields you from most of the snags with its *Timer* control.

Generalities of the *Timer* Control

The *Timer* control derives from the *Control* class and implements the *IPostBackEventHandler* and *IScriptControl* interface:

```
public class TimerControl : Control,
            IPostBackEventHandler, IScriptControl
```

Implemented as a server-side control, it actually creates a client-side timer that performs a postback at regular intervals. When the postback occurs, the *Timer* server control raises a server-side event named *Tick*:

```
public event EventHandler Tick
```

The control features only two properties, as described in Table 4-4.

Table 4-4   Properties of the *Timer* Control

Property	Description
Enabled	*True* by default, the property indicates whether the client-side script needed for the timer is generated when the page is first rendered.
Interval	This integer property indicates the interval at which a client timer raises its *Tick* event. The interval is expressed in milliseconds and is set by default to *60,000* milliseconds (one minute).

Basically, the *Timer* control is a server-side interface built around a client timer. It saves you from the burden of creating the timer via script and making it post back when the interval expires.

Using the Timer

The most common use of the *Timer* control is in conjunction with an *UpdatePanel* trigger to refresh the panel at regular intervals. The following script defines a timer that posts back every second:

```
<asp:Timer runat="server" ID="Timer1"
    Interval="1000" OnTick="Timer1_Tick" />
```

It is extremely important that you carefully consider the impact of a too frequent interval on the overall performance and scalability of your application. Setting the interval to a low value (such as one or two seconds) might cause too many postbacks and traffic on the way to the server. As a result, even asynchronous postbacks performed in partial-rendering mode might incur some undesired overhead.

The following page mixes an *UpdatePanel* with a *Timer* control. The timer ticks every second and makes a postback. The *UpdatePanel* control is bound to the *Tick* event of the timer using a trigger:

```
<asp:UpdatePanel runat="server" ID="UpdatePanel1">
    <ContentTemplate>
        <asp:Label runat="server" ID="Label1" />
    </ContentTemplate>
    <Triggers>
        <asp:AsyncPostBackTrigger ControlID="Timer1" EventName="Tick" />
    </Triggers>
</asp:UpdatePanel>

<asp:Timer runat="server" ID="Timer1"
    Interval="1000" OnTick="Timer1_Tick" />
```

As a result, the panel is updated every second. Put another way, the following code is run every second on the server resulting in a sort of Web clock:

```
protected void Timer1_Tick(object sender, EventArgs e)
{
    Label1.Text = DateTime.Now.ToLongTimeString();
}
```

Figure 4-10 shows the sample page in action.

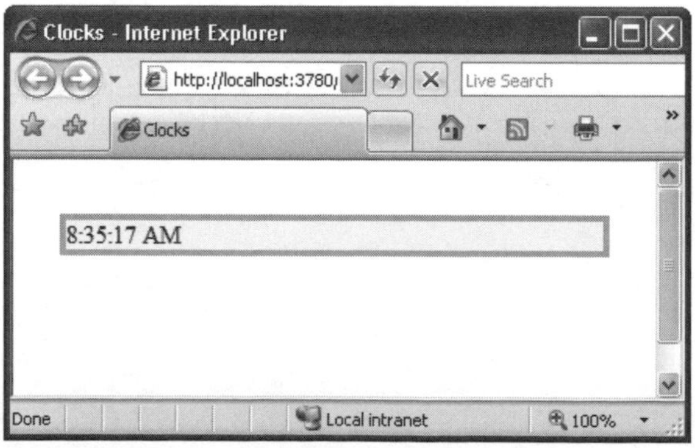

Figure 4-10   An ASP.NET AJAX clock in action in a sample page

Providing User Feedback During Partial Updates

Updating a panel might not be seamless from a user perspective, however. Having the computer engaged in a potentially long task, in fact, might be problematic. Will the user resist the temptation of reclicking that button over and over again? Will the user patiently wait for the results to show up? Finally, will the user be frustrated and annoyed by waiting without any clue of what's going on? After all, if the page is sustaining a full postback, the browser itself normally provides some user feedback that this is happening. Using ASP.NET AJAX, the callback doesn't force a regular full postback and the browser's visual feedback system is not called upon to inform the user things are happening.

Keep in mind that ASP.NET AJAX Extensions is the ASP.NET incarnation of the AJAX paradigm. And in AJAX, the "A" stands for "asynchronous." This implies that ASP.NET AJAX developers should take into careful account ways to explain latency to users and, wherever possible, provide ways for users to cancel pending requests.

Because of the need to keep users informed, ASP.NET AJAX supplies the *UpdateProgress* control to display a templated content while any of the panels in the page are being refreshed.

Generalities of the *UpdateProgress* Control

The *UpdateProgress* control is designed to provide any sort of feedback on the browser while one or more *UpdatePanel* controls are being updated. The *UpdateProgress* control derives from the *Control* class and implements the *IScriptControl* interface—an ASP.NET AJAX-specific interface that qualifies a custom server control as an AJAX control.

```
public class UpdateProgress : Control, IScriptControl
```

If you have multiple panels in the page, you might want to find a convenient location in the page for the progress control or, if possible, move it programmatically to the right place with respect to the panel being updated. You can use cascading style sheets (CSSs) to style and position the control at your leisure.

The *UpdateProgress* control features the properties listed in Table 4-5.

Table 4-5   Properties of the *UpdateProgress* Control

Property	Description
AssociatedUpdatePanelID	Gets and sets the ID of the *UpdatePanel* control that this control is associated with.
DisplayAfter	Gets and sets the time in milliseconds after which the progress template is displayed. This property is set to *500* by default.
DynamicLayout	Indicates whether the progress template is dynamically rendered in the page. This property is set to *true* by default.
ProgressTemplate	Indicates the template displayed during an AJAX postback that is taking longer than the time specified through the *DisplayAfter* property.

An *UpdateProgress* control can be bound to a particular *UpdatePanel* control. You set the binding through the *AssociatedUpdatePanelID* string property. If no updatable panel is specified, the progress control is displayed for any panels in the page. The user interface of the progress bar is inserted in the host page when the page is rendered. However, it is initially hidden from view using the CSS *display* attribute.

When set to *none*, the CSS *display* attribute doesn't display a given HTML element and it reuses its space in the page so that other elements can be shifted up properly. When the value of the *display* attribute is toggled on, existing elements are moved to make room for the new element. If you want to reserve the space for the progress control and leave it blank when no update operation is taking place, you just set the *DynamicLayout* property to *false*.

Composing the Progress Screen

ASP.NET AJAX displays the contents of the *ProgressTemplate* property while waiting for a panel to update. You can specify the template either declaratively or programmatically. In the latter case, you assign the property any object that implements the *ITemplate* interface. For the former situation, you can easily specify the progress control's markup declaratively, as shown in the following code:

```
<asp:UpdateProgress runat="server" ID="UpdateProgress1">
    <ProgressTemplate>
        ...
    </ProgressTemplate>
</asp:UpdateProgress>
```

You can place any combination of controls in the progress template. However, most of the time you'll probably just put some text there and an animated GIF. The lefthand page view shown in Figure 4-11 shows the *ProgressPanel* in action (at the top of the page). Notice the content begins with the letter 'A' while the letter 'F' is to be queried. The righthand view shows the outcome of the postback, which is to say values beginning with the letter 'F' are displayed after the data is asynchronously returned from the server.

Note that the *UpdateProgress* control is not designed to be a gauge component, but rather a user-defined panel that the *ScriptManager* control shows before the panel refresh begins and that it hides immediately after its completion.

> **Note** You can dynamically customize the look and feel of the progress control to some extent. All you have to do is write a handler for the *Load* event of the *UpdateProgress* control and retrieve the controls in the template using the *FindControl* method. In this way, you can change some standard text and make it a bit more context sensitive. Likewise, you can change animated images to make the displayed one better reflect the current context. This is often easier than replacing the template with an entirely new *ITemplate*-based value.

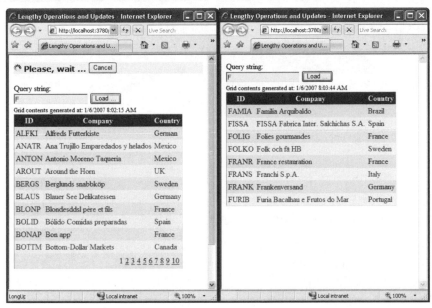

Figure 4-11   A progress template informing users that some work is occurring on the server

Aborting a Pending Update

A really user-friendly system will always let its users cancel a pending operation. How can you obtain this functionality with an *UpdateProgress* control? The progress template is allowed to contain an abort button. The script code injected into the page will monitor the button, and it will stop the ongoing asynchronous call if it's clicked. To specify an abort button, you add the following to the progress template:

```
<input type="button" onclick="abortTask()" value="Cancel" />
```

In the first place, the button has to be a client-side button. So you can express it either through the *<input>* element or the *<button>* element for browsers that support this element. If you opt for the *<input>* element, the *type* attribute must be set to *button*. The script code you wire up to the *onclick* event is up to you, but it will contain at least the following instructions:

```
<script type="text/javascript" >
function abortTask() {
    var obj = Sys.WebForms.PageRequestManager.getInstance();
    if (obj.get_isInAsyncPostBack())
        obj.abortPostBack();
}
</script>
```

You retrieve the instance of the client *PageRequestManager* object active in the client page and check whether an AJAX postback is ongoing. If a postback is in progress, you call the *abortPostBack* method to stop it.

> **Important**   Canceling an ongoing update in this way is equivalent to closing the connection with the server. No results will ever be received and no updates will ever occur on the page. However, canceling the update is a pure client operation and has no effect on what's happening on the server. If the user started a destructive operation, simply clicking the client-side *Cancel* button won't undo the destructive operation on the server.

Associating Progress Screens with Panels

The *AssociatedUpdatePanelID* property allows you to associate a progress screen with a particular *UpdatePanel* control so that when the panel is refreshed the screen is displayed to the user. However, the implementation of this property in the context of the *UpdateProgress* control is not free of issues in spite of the strong sense of simplicity and clearness that name and description suggest.

The property works seamlessly as long as the refresh of an *UpdatePanel* control is caused by a child control. Should the refresh be ordered by an external trigger, no progress screen would ever be displayed for any panels in the page. This weird behavior is due to the code in the *Sys.UI._UpdateProgress* JavaScript class—the client object model of the control. The class is defined in the *MicrosoftAjaxWebForms.js* script file.

Before delving deeper into the reasons for the behavior, let me first address some workarounds. If the page can contain just one *UpdateProgress* to serve any number of updatable panels, then you're just fine. You avoid setting the *AssociatedUpdatePanelID* property for the control and all panels automatically share the same progress screen.

If distinct *UpdatePanel* controls require distinct progress screens, and these panels are bound to external triggers, the only way for you to display the correct progress screen passes through the addition of a bit of JavaScript code that manually displays the right screen. In other words, you bypass the automatic display mechanism of the *UpdateProgress* control that fails if an external trigger fires. I'll show this in a moment after introducing client-side events.

What does cause the script of the *UpdateProgress* control to fail when an external trigger fires an update? The progress screen is displayed just before the request is sent out and only if the request regards the updatable panel referenced by the *AssociatedUpdatePanelID* property. The point is, the ID of the panel being updated is not known to the *UpdateProgress* script. The script attempts to find it out by walking up the hierarchy of the element that caused the postback. Clearly, if the posting element is outside of the *UpdatePanel*'s tree (i.e., an external trigger) the search is unsuccessful and no progress screen is ever displayed.

Client-Side Events for a Partial Update

Each ASP.NET AJAX postback involves the *PageRequestManager* client object, which is responsible for invoking, under the hood, the *XMLHttpRequest* object. What kind of control do developers have on the underlying operation? If you manage *XMLHttpRequest* directly, you have full control over the request and response. But when these key steps are managed for you, there's not much you can do unless the request manager supports an eventing model.

The *PageRequestManager* object provides a few events so that you can customize handling of the request and response.

Events of the Client *PageRequestManager* Object

The client events listed in Table 4-6 are available on the client *PageRequestManager* object. As you can see, these events signal the main steps taken when an AJAX postback partially updates a page. The events are listed in the order in which they fire to the client page.

Table 4-6   Events of *PageRequestManager* Object

Event	Event Argument	Description
initializeRequest	*InitializeRequestEventArgs*	Occurs before the AJAX request is prepared for sending.
beginRequest	*BeginRequestEventArgs*	Occurs before the request is sent.
pageLoading	*PageLoadingEventArgs*	Occurs when the response has been acquired but before any content on the page is updated.
pageLoaded	*PageLoadedEventArgs*	Occurs after all content on the page is refreshed as a result of an asynchronous postback.
endRequest	*EndRequestEventArgs*	Occurs after an asynchronous postback is finished and control has been returned to the browser.

To register an event handler, you use the following JavaScript code:

```
var manager = Sys.WebForms.PageRequestManager.getInstance();
manager.add_beginRequest(OnBeginRequest);
```

The prototype of the event handler method—*OnBeginRequest* in this case—is shown here:

```
function beginRequest(sender, args)
```

The real type of the *args* object, though, depends on the event data structure. The other events have similar function prototypes.

Kick In before the Request Starts

The *initializeRequest* event is the first event in the client life cycle of an AJAX request. The life cycle begins at the moment in which a postback is made that is captured by the *UpdatePanel*'s client infrastructure. You can use the *initializeRequest* event to evaluate the postback source and do any additional required work. The event data structure is the *InitializeRequestEventArgs* class. The class features three properties: *postBackElement*, *request*, and *cancel*.

The *postBackElement* property is read-only and evaluates to a *DomElement* object. It indicates the DOM element that is responsible for the postback. The *request* property (read-only) is an object of type *Sys.Net.WebRequest* and represents the ongoing request. Finally, *cancel* is a read-write Boolean property that can be used to abort the request before it is sent.

Immediately after calling the *initializeRequest* handler, if any, the *PageRequestManager* object aborts any pending asynchronous requests. Next, it proceeds with the *beginRequest* event and then sends the packet.

A typical scenario for many Web applications is that the user clicks to start a potentially lengthy operation, no (or not enough) feedback is displayed, and the user keeps on clicking over and over again. Given the implementation of *PageRequestManager*, any new request kills the current request that is still active. Note that the abort has no effect on the server-side operation; rather, it simply closes the connection and returns an empty response. This potentially results in multiple actions on the server, one for each button click, yet the user will only see the results of the final button click (if they're patient enough).

By handling the *initializeRequest* event, though, you can assign a higher priority to the current event and abort any successive requests until the other has terminated. Let's see how to implement this sort of click-only-once functionality:

```
<script type="text/javascript">
function pageLoad()
{
    var manager = Sys.WebForms.PageRequestManager.getInstance();
    manager.add_initializeRequest(OnInitializeRequest);
}
function OnInitializeRequest(sender, args)
{
    var manager = Sys.WebForms.PageRequestManager.getInstance();

    // Check if we're posting back because of Button1
    if (manager.get_isInAsyncPostBack() &&
        args.get_postBackElement().id.toLowerCase() == "button1")
    {
        $get("Label1").innerHTML = "Still working on previous request.
                                    Please, be patient ...";
        args.set_cancel(true);
    }
}
</script>
```

The preceding script aborts any requests originated by the *Button1* element if another request from the same element is still being processed. In this way, when the user clicks several times on the same button, no other requests will be accepted as long as there's one being processed. (See Figure 4-12.)

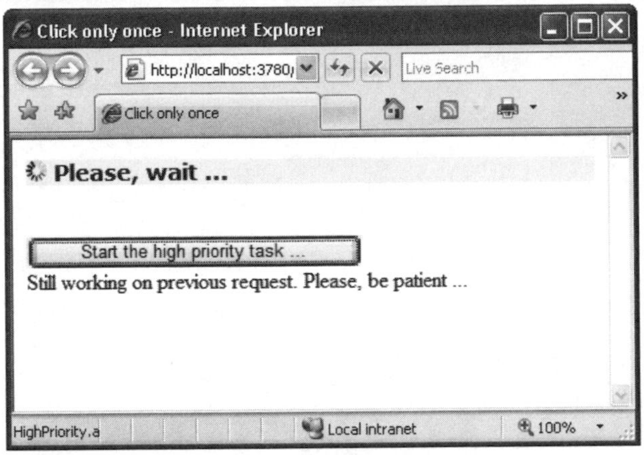

Figure 4-12   Users are allowed to start only one high-priority task at a time

Disabling Visual Elements during Updates

If you want to prevent users from generating more input while a partial page update is being processed, you can also consider disabling the user interface—all or in part. To do so, you write handlers for *beginRequest* and *endRequest* events:

```
<script type="text/javascript">
function pageLoad()
{
    var manager = Sys.WebForms.PageRequestManager.getInstance();
    manager.add_beginRequest(OnBeginRequest);
    manager.add_endRequest(OnEndRequest);
}
</script>
```

The *beginRequest* event is raised before the processing of an asynchronous postback starts and the postback is sent to the server. You typically use this event to call custom script to animate the user interface and notify the user that the postback is being processed. You can also use the *beginRequest* event to set a custom request header that identifies your request uniquely.

```
// Globals
var currentPostBackElem;
var oldStyleString = "";

function OnBeginRequest(sender, args)
{
    currentPostBackElem = args.get_postBackElement();
    if (typeof(currentPostBackElem) === "undefined")
        return;
    if (currentPostBackElem.id.toLowerCase() == "button1")
    {
```

```
        // Disable the Load button
        $get("Button1").disabled = true;

        // Optionally, highlight the grid
        oldStyleString = $get("GridView1").style.border;
        $get("GridView1").style.border = "solid red 5px";
    }
}
```

The *beginRequest* handler receives event data through the *BeginRequestEventArgs* data structure—the *args* formal parameter. The class features only two properties: *request* and *postBackElement*. The properties have the same characteristics as the analogous properties on the aforementioned *InitializeRequestEventArgs* class.

In the preceding code snippet, I disable the clicked button to prevent users from repeatedly clicking the same button. In addition, I draw a thick border around the grid to call the user's attention to the portion of the user interface being updated. (See Figure 4-13.)

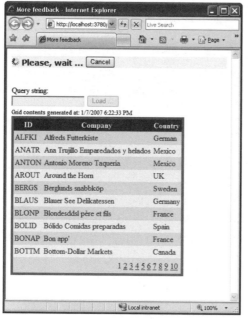

Figure 4-13   The *Load* button, disabled and grid-framed during the server processing

At the end of the request, any temporary modification to the user interface must be removed. So animations must be stopped, altered styles must be restored, and disabled controls re-enabled. The ideal place for all these operations is the *endRequest* event. The event passes an *EndRequestEventArgs* object to handlers. The class has a few properties, as described in Table 4-7.

As you can see, when the *endRequest* event occurs there's no information available about the client element that fired the postback. If you need to restore some user-interface settings from inside the *endRequest* event handler, you might need a global variable to track which element caused the postback. In the following code, you need to track the postback trigger as well as the original style of the grid that is shown in Figure 4-13:

Table 4-7   Properties of the *EndRequestEventArgs* Class

Property	Description
dataItems	Returns the client-side dictionary packed with server-defined data items for the page or the control that handles this event. (I'll say more about registering data items later.)
error	Returns an object of type *Error* that describes the error (if any) that occurred on the server during the request.
errorHandled	Gets and sets a Boolean value that indicates whether the error has been completely handled by user code. If this property is set to *true* in the event handler, no default error handling will be executed by the Microsoft AJAX client library. We saw an example of this property in Chapter 3.
response	Returns an object of type *Sys.Net.WebRequestExecutor* that represents the executor of the current request. Most of the time, this object will be an instance of *Sys.Net.XMLHttpExecutor*. For more information, refer to Chapter 2.

```
function OnEndRequest(sender, args)
{
    if (typeof(currentPostBackElem) === "undefined")
        return;
    if (currentPostBackElem.id.toLowerCase() == "button1")
    {
        $get("Button1").disabled = false;
        $get("GridView1").style.border = oldStyleString;
    }
}
```

Managing Progress Screens

To display the progress screen, you wait for the *beginRequest* event, then apply your own logic to decide which screen is appropriate and go. Here's a quick example:

```
<script type="text/javascript">
function pageLoad()
{
    var manager = Sys.WebForms.PageRequestManager.getInstance();
    manager.add_beginRequest(OnBeginRequest);
}
function OnBeginRequest(sender, args)
{
    var postBackElement = args.get_postBackElement();
    if (postBackElement.id == 'ButtonTrigger')
      $get('UpdateProgress2').style.display = "block";
}
</script>
```

You first check the ID of the postback element. Next, based on that information you figure out the update progress block to turn on. You display or hide a block of markup by acting on its *display* CSS attribute. Additional progress screens would be handled in the same way (i.e., by adding code to display them in *OnBeginRequest*).

Page Loading Events

In an asynchronous postback, there are two distinct and nested phases: begin/end of the request, and begin/end of the partial page update. After the request has been sent to the server, the client waits for any response to become available.

> **Note** If you're curious about the real sequence of steps accomplished to execute an asyn-chronous AJAX request, take a look at the *_onFormSubmit* method on the *Sys.WebForms. PageRequestManager* class. The class is defined in the *MicrosoftAjaxWebForms.js* script file.

When the response arrives, the *PageRequestManager* object first processes any returned data and separates hidden fields, updatable panels, data items, and whatever pieces of information are returned from the server. Once the response data is ready for processing, the object fires the *pageLoading* client event. The event is raised after the server response is received but before any content on the page is updated. You can use this event to provide a custom transition effect for updated content or to run any clean-up code that prepares the panels for the next update.

The event data is packed in an instance of the class *PageLoadingEventArgs*. The class has three properties: *panelsUpdating*, *panelsDeleting*, and *dataItems*. The first two are arrays and list the updatable panels to be updated and deleted, respectively. The *dataItems* property is the same as described in Table 4-7. From within a *pageLoading* event handler, you can't cancel the page update. Immediately after the *pageLoading* event, the page request manager starts its render-ing engine and updates all involved panels.

The *pageLoaded* event is raised after all content on the page is refreshed. You can use this event to provide a custom transition effect for updated content, such as flashing or highlighting updated contents. The event data is packed in the class *PageLoadedEventArgs*, which has three properties: *panelsUpdated*, *panelsDeleted*, and *dataItems*. The first two are arrays and list the updatable panels that were just updated and deleted, respectively. The *dataItems* property is the same as described in Table 4-7.

You can use this event as well as *endRequest* to provide notification to users or to log errors.

Passing Data Items during Partial Updates

The *UpdatePanel* control allows you to wrap groups of controls that need to be updated over a postback. There might be pages, though, in which grouping all controls involved in an oper-ation inside a single panel is too challenging or impractical. What if, therefore, you need to update controls outside the *UpdatePanel* that fired the call? If the control lives inside another *UpdatePanel*, you can programmatically order a refresh of the whole panel. What if, instead, just one control needs update? And what if the update on the client must be done with data generated during the asynchronous postback? The *RegisterDataItem* method of the *Script-Manager* control addresses exactly this issue.

The *RegisterDataItem* method specifies a server-generated string that will be added to the response of the asynchronous postback along with the updated markup of the panel or panels. This string is then passed to the client infrastructure of ASP.NET AJAX through the *dataItems* property of the event data for *pageLoading*, *pageLoaded*, and *endRequest* events.

The *RegisterDataItem* is used when the page, or a server control, needs to pass additional data to the client that requires explicit processing on the client that is beyond the capabilities of updatable panels. Let's arrange an example that illustrates the usefulness of data items.

Motivation for Using Data Items

Imagine a page that incorporates a kind of clock. It is made by a timer control that updates a label every second. The panel also contains a couple of buttons to increase and decrease the clock interval.

```
<asp:UpdatePanel runat="server" ID="UpdatePanel1">
    <ContentTemplate>
        <asp:Label runat="server" ID="Label1" />
    </ContentTemplate>
    <Triggers>
        <asp:AsyncPostBackTrigger ControlID="Timer1" EventName="Tick" />
        <asp:AsyncPostBackTrigger ControlID="Button1" EventName="Click" />
        <asp:AsyncPostBackTrigger ControlID="Button2" EventName="Click" />
    </Triggers>
</asp:UpdatePanel>
<asp:Timer ID="Timer1" runat="server" OnTick="Timer1_Tick"
    Interval="1000" />
<hr />
<asp:Button runat="server" ID="Button1" Text="Increase Interval"
    OnClick="Button1_Click" />
<asp:Button runat="server" ID="Button2" Text="Decrease Interval"
    OnClick="Button2_Click" />
```

As you can see, the timer is not part of the updatable panel. As such, no markup for the *Timer* control will be sent over during an AJAX postback. In light of this, what about the following code?

```
protected void Button1_Click(object sender, EventArgs e)
{
    Timer1.Interval += 1000;
}
```

This code is certainly executed during the postback. There's no visible mechanism, though, that ensures that the new interval is passed to the client. Without this key information, how can the client timer update its interval and tick the server properly? However, such code works just fine. You click the button and the clock is updated every two seconds. What's up with that?

The *Timer* control internally registers a data item and, through it, passes its server state to the client also over an AJAX postback. Here's a brief excerpt from the source code of the *Timer* control:

```
protected override void OnPreRender(EventArgs e)
{
    base.OnPreRender(e);
    if (ScriptManager.IsInAsyncPostBack)
    {
        ScriptManager.RegisterDataItem(this, GetJsonState(), true);
    }
    ...
}
protected string GetJsonState()
{
    ...
}
```

The internal *GetJsonState* function returns a JSON string that renders out as a key/value dictionary object. In particular, the *Timer* control saves the value of the *Enabled* and *Interval* properties—the only two properties that can affect the behavior of the timer on the client.

Preparing Data Items

Let's see how to proceed to make an ASP.NET AJAX page pass a message for a client label that can't be included directly in an updatable panel. The data to pass is related to events that occur on the server. For example, imagine you want to display the current interval of the timer and the increment/decrement it underwent on the server. Here's the code-behind class for page *DataItems.aspx*:

```
public partial class Samples_Ch04_Advanced_DataItems : System.Web.UI.Page
{
    private const int OneSecond = 1000;
    private int oldInterval;
    private static bool isDirty = false;

    protected void Page_Load(object sender, EventArgs e) {
        oldInterval = Timer1.Interval;
    }
    protected void Timer1_Tick(object sender, EventArgs e) {
        Label1.Text = DateTime.Now.ToLongTimeString();
    }
    protected void Button1_Click(object sender, EventArgs e) {
        Timer1.Interval += OneSecond;
        isDirty = true;
    }
    protected void Button2_Click(object sender, EventArgs e) {
        if (Timer1.Interval > OneSecond)
        {
            Timer1.Interval -= OneSecond;
```

```
                isDirty = true;
            }
    }
    private string GetJsonState() {
        return ("[" + Timer1.Interval.ToString() + "," +
                (Timer1.Interval - oldInterval).ToString() + "]");
    }
    private void Page_PreRender(object sender, EventArgs e) {
        if (isDirty && ScriptManager1.IsInAsyncPostBack)
        {
            isDirty = false;
            ScriptManager1.RegisterDataItem(this, GetJsonState(), true);
        }
    }
}
```

The AJAX-sensitive state of the page is tracked down and, if dirty, saved as a JSON string during the *PreRender* event through a call to *RegisterDataItem*. The state to send to the client is a comma-separated JSON value string that includes the *Interval* of the timer as modified by *Increase* and *Decrease* buttons in the page. *RegisterDataItem* takes up to three parameters: the object for which the data is registered (page or control), the string to pass, and *true* if the string is a JSON string.

Note   You get an exception if you call *RegisterDataItem* in a non-AJAX postback. Tracking the dirtiness of the object's state is not mandatory but helps in two ways: it reduces the bandwidth and makes it easier for you to manage data items on the client. In fact, the client will receive data only if there's some data to consume and some user interface to update.

Data Items as JSON Strings

You use the *RegisterDataItem* method to send data from the server to the client during asynchronous postbacks, regardless of whether the control receiving the data is inside an *UpdatePanel* control. The data you send is a string and is associated with a particular server control or the page itself. The internal format of the string is up to you. It can be a single value string or a string that represents multiple values—for example, a comma-separated list of values. Needless to say, if you opt for a custom format inside the string, any deserialization is up to you and must be accomplished in the event handler where you get to process sent data items.

Data items are available with the *pageLoading* event and the following *pageLoaded* and *endRequest* events. All event data structures for these events, in fact, feature a *dataItems* property. The *dataItems* property is a key/value dictionary where the key is the ID of the control that references the data or *__Page* if the referrer is the ASP.NET page. The value is the string you passed to *RegisterDataItem* on the server for that control or page.

When you need to pass multiple values to the client, you can use a JSON-serialized array of values. In JavaScript, an array can be expressed as a comma-separated list of values wrapped by square brackets, as shown in the following code:

```
var x = [1,2,3];
```

Returned as a string, the expression must be pre-processed by the *eval* function to become a valid array:

```
var x = eval("[1,2,3]");
```

This is exactly what happens in the code-behind class described earlier, where the *GetJsonState* method returns an array of strings:

```
private string GetJsonState()
{
    return ("[" + Timer1.Interval.ToString() + "," +
        (Timer1.Interval-oldInterval).ToString() + "]");
}
```

On the client, the *dataItems* object for the page points to an array with interval and last change information.

> **Note** When data items are expressed in a format that requires a call to *eval* for them to be transformed into usable client objects, you must turn on the JSON flag on the *Register-DataItem* method. When the data item is JSON-enabled, the *eval* JavaScript function is called to evaluate the returned string. You should only use JSON serialization if you're passing multiple data values to the client. To learn more about JSON, visit http://json.org/.

Retrieving Data Items on the Client

The dictionary with data items is sent to the client and, as mentioned earlier, is available in the *pageLoading*, *pageLoaded*, and *endRequest* events through the *dataItems* property on the event argument data object. For a sample page that contains a timer and is bound to the code-behind class considered earlier, the following is an excerpt from the postback response:

```
11|dataItemJson|__Page|[3000,1000]|
11|dataItemJson|Timer1|[true,3000]|
```

This text is appended to the response along with the updated markup and new values for hidden fields. The text should be read as follows. It contains two JSON-serialized data items, which is to say they both require *eval* to evaluate the returned 11 bytes of data each. The first data item is bound to the page and contains an array of two values: *3000* and *1000*. The second data item refers to the *Timer1* control in the page and contains an array of two values: *true* and *3000*. Let's see how to retrieve and consume this information programmatically:

```
function pageLoad()
{
    var manager = Sys.WebForms.PageRequestManager.getInstance();
    manager.add_endRequest(OnEndRequest);
}
```

```
function OnEndRequest(sender, args)
{
   var dataItem = args.get_dataItems()["__Page"];
   if (dataItem)
   {
      var text = String.format("Interval set to {0}ms;
                  last change {1}ms.", dataItem[0], dataItem[1]);
      $get("Msg").innerHTML = text;
   }
}
```

The *endRequest* handler retrieves the data item record for the page (or any control you're interested in) and then uses the returned object as an array. In particular, it refreshes the innermost HTML of a label in the page. (See Figure 4-14.)

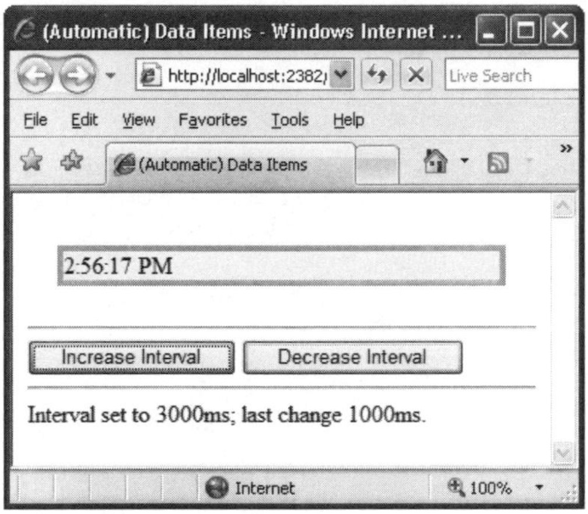

Figure 4-14   Refreshing some text in the page that is outside any *UpdatePanel* controls

The *__Page* ID used in the preceding example indicates that data items are related to the page. The string is emitted as a generic ID for the page and depends on the object you specify as the first argument of *RegisterDataItem*. You can also associate data items to a specific control in the page; in that case, the ID to use in the *endRequest* client-side event handler is the ID of the referenced server control.

Animating Panels during Partial Updates

Most users of the first ASP.NET AJAX applications reported that for them it was a problem not being able to find a visual clue of the changes in the various portions of the page. An *UpdatePanel* control allows you to partially refresh a page; the operation, though, might pass unnoticed to users, especially when it turns out to be particularly quick or when it serves only a slightly different markup. Animating panels to call a user's attention to the changes has therefore become the next challenge for ASP.NET AJAX developers.

Visual Feedback during the Partial Update

A primary and quite effective form of animation consists of wiring up the *beginRequest* and *endRequest* events of the page request manager and changing the style of controls in the page for the time it takes to complete the server operation. In Figure 4-13 (shown earlier), you see a button that is disabled during the partial update. At the same time, the grid that will receive the new data is framed. Of course, you can choose any combination of style settings to reflect your idea of visual feedback.

For example, in the *beginRequest* event handler you can disable all controls involved with a postback, change their background color, modify borders, collapse tables, and so on. In the *endRequest* or *pageLoaded* handler, you then restore the original settings. As a result, the style of the user interface is altered for the duration of the server request and then restored when the new markup is available.

Visual Feedback after the Page Refresh

Another option is to call the user's attention only when the modified page is up and running. In this case, nothing happens while the request is processed on the server; as soon as the *page-Loaded* event is fired, though, the animation starts to notify the user of changes. As a first step, let's arrange a JavaScript class that implements the animation:

```
Type.registerNamespace('IntroAjax');

IntroAjax.BorderAnimation = function IntroAjax$BorderAnimation(
    color, thickness, duration)
{
    this._color = color;
    this._thickness = thickness;
    this._duration = duration;
}

// Method to start the animation on the specified panel
function IntroAjax$BorderAnimation$animatePanel(panelElement)
{
    if (arguments.length !== 1) throw Error.parameterCount();

    var style = panelElement.style;
    style.borderWidth = this._thickness;
    style.borderColor = this._color;
    style.borderStyle = 'solid';

    window.setTimeout( function() {{style.borderWidth = 0;}},
                       this._duration);
}

IntroAjax.BorderAnimation.prototype = {
    animatePanel: IntroAjax$BorderAnimation$animatePanel
}

IntroAjax.BorderAnimation.registerClass('IntroAjax.BorderAnimation');
```

The *BorderAnimation* class features an *animatePanel* method that renders out a solid border of the specified thickness, color, and duration around all the panels updated during the postback.

For the script to be executed, you must first register the *.js* file with script manager:

```
<asp:ScriptManager ID="ScriptManager1" runat="server">
    <Scripts>
        <asp:ScriptReference Path="animation.js" />
    </Scripts>
</asp:ScriptManager>
```

Then you need to add some script to the page to trigger it:

```
<script type="text/javascript">
var postbackElement;
var animation;

function pageLoad() {
    var manager = Sys.WebForms.PageRequestManager.getInstance();
    manager.add_beginRequest(OnBeginRequest);
    manager.add_pageLoaded(OnPageLoaded);
}

function OnBeginRequest(sender, args) {
    postbackElement = args.get_postBackElement();
}

function OnPageLoaded(sender, args) {
    animation = new IntroAjax.BorderAnimation('red', '5px', 2000);

    var updatedPanels = args.get_panelsUpdated();
    if (typeof(postbackElement) === "undefined")
        return;
    else if (postbackElement.id.toLowerCase().indexOf('button1') > -1)
    {
        for (i=0; i < updatedPanels.length; i++)
            animation.animatePanel(updatedPanels[i]);
    }
}
</script>
```

As the page loads up, you register handlers for the *beginRequest* and *pageLoaded* events. The *beginRequest* handler doesn't do anything related to the user interface; it simply tracks the DOM element that caused the asynchronous postback. The handler for the *pageLoaded* event creates an instance of the animation class and uses it to animate all panels that have been updated. It does that only if the ID of the postback element matches the ID stored in the *postbackElement* element variable, indicating it is the same element that triggered the postback (in this case "button1"). In this way, you can animate based on the specific action commanded. (See Figure 4-15.)

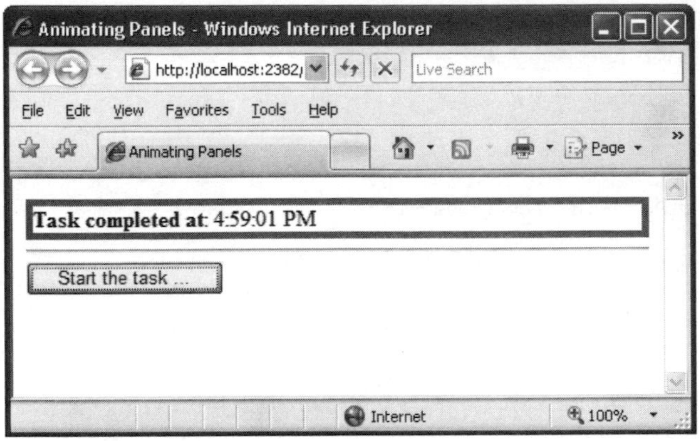

Figure 4-15   Updated panels are framed for a few seconds to get the user's attention

> **Note**   The definitive solution for animating updatable panels is not in the ASP.NET AJAX Extensions platform but just outside of it, in the AJAX Control Toolkit. (See *http://ajax.asp.net/ ajaxtoolkit*.)
>
> As we'll see in Chapter 5,"The AJAX Control Toolkit", the AJAX Control Toolkit is a joint project between the developer community and Microsoft. It extends the ASP.NET AJAX Extensions platform with a collection of Web client components, including controls and control extenders. One of coolest extenders is the *UpdatePanelAnimation* component. Attached to an *UpdatePanel*, the component automatically injects client script to animate the panel during the postback operation.

Conclusion

The *UpdatePanel* control and other similar server controls provide an excellent compromise between the need to implement asynchronous and out-of-band functionality and the desire to use the same familiar ASP.NET application model. As you've seen in this chapter, any ASP.NET page can be easily transformed into an ASP.NET AJAX page. You divide the original page into regions and assign each markup region to a distinct *UpdatePanel* control. From that point on, each updatable region can be refreshed individually through independent and asynchronous calls that do not affect the rest of the page. The current page remains up and active while regions are updated. This feature is known as *partial rendering*.

If required, you can define one or more triggers for each updatable region so that the update of each region occurs under specified and well-known conditions. The *UpdatePanel* and other server controls covered in this chapter represent the first, and certainly the easiest, path to using ASP.NET AJAX. With minimal effort, you can transform an ordinary ASP.NET page into an AJAX page and start practicing with the new framework until you feel the need to use braveheart JavaScript code.

In the next chapter, we'll look at another key category of ASP.NET AJAX server controls—the extenders. A *control extender* is a server-side component that adds a new behavior and extra capabilities to a bunch of existing ASP.NET controls.

The AJAX Control Toolkit

Although ASP.NET AJAX is a framework designed to bring more programming power to the Web client, it happens to be mostly used by server developers—for example, ASP.NET developers or, at least, Web developers with strong server-side skills. Unfortunately, for the time being, there's no way to add rich capabilities and functionalities to the Web client other than by crafting good and tricky JavaScript code.

ASP.NET AJAX takes up the challenge and provides two ways for developers to build rich Web applications using a server-centric development approach. As we discussed in Chapter 4, "Partial Page Rendering," developers can refresh specific regions of the page using partial rendering instead of normal ASP.NET postbacks. To create such regions, you just use a particular set of server controls—the most important of which is the *UpdatePanel* control.

In addition to partial rendering, developers can use *control extenders* to add a predefined client-side behavior to new and existing ASP.NET controls. A client-side behavior is a block of JavaScript code that adds a new capability to the markup generated by a given ASP.NET control. An extender is basically a server control that emits proper script code—the client behavior—to enhance how a given ASP.NET control behaves on the client. An extender is not simply a custom control derived from an existing control. Rather, it represents a general behavior—such as auto-completion, focus management, generation of popups, and draggability—that can be declaratively applied to various target control types. For example, a special behavior can be applied to any focused control—be it a *TextBox*, *Button*, or *CheckBox* control.

ASP.NET AJAX Extensions 1.0 simply delivers the base class for extender controls. No concrete extender controls are provided with the binaries. The online documentation provides some good tutorials on how to build extenders. You can find one at *http:// ajax.asp.net/docs/tutorials/ExtenderControlTutorial1.aspx*. A fair number of sample extenders and additional rich client controls are provided through a separate download—the AJAX Control Toolkit (ACT).

In this chapter, I'll first review the syntax and semantics of control extenders and then take you on a tour of the major components in the ACT.

Extender Controls

ASP.NET pages are made of server controls. ASP.NET comes with a fairly rich collection of built-in controls. In addition, plenty of custom controls are available for developers from third-party vendors, from community projects, and even from contributions by volunteers. If you need a text box with a set of features that the ASP.NET control can't provide (for example, a numeric text box), you typically write one yourself or buy a new specialized control that extends the original control and adds the desired behavior. Object orientation, of course, encourages this approach.

However, it's rare that you need to write a completely new control yourself. More often, your control will derive from an existing ASP.NET control base class. Blindly using inheritance for building specialized versions of controls might not be a wise choice, though. Even in relatively small projects, in fact, it can lead straight to a proliferation of controls. For example, you can end up with a regular text box, plus a numeric text box, a filtered text box, a text box that changes its style when focused, a text box that displays a prompt when left empty, and so on. On the other hand, merging all these behaviors into a single super *TextBox* control might not be wise either. In this case, the resulting code will be literally full of branches, logical conditions, and properties to check. For just a simple extra feature, you would load a huge control. There has to be a different approach. Enter extender controls.

What Is an Extender, Anyway?

First and foremost, an extender control is a server control itself. It represents a logical behavior that can be attached to one or more control types to extend their base capabilities.

Formalizing the Concept of a "Behavior"

Imagine you want only the text boxes in a given input form to change their style when focused. If you create a new control, say *FocusedTextBox*, you're fine. What if, instead, you want the same behavior from buttons, check boxes, and drop-down lists? You should create a bunch of new controls—all of which will extend the target controls with the same logical behavior. Extender controls are just a formal way to define such a behavior.

> **Note**   Virtually all behaviors require the injection of some script code in the client page. For this reason, extenders are naturally associated with ASP.NET AJAX. From a technology standpoint, on the other hand, ASP.NET AJAX and extenders are independent concepts. You could

develop extenders for ASP.NET 1.1 and ASP.NET 2.0 that work without ASP.NET AJAX Extensions. However, ASP.NET AJAX Extensions provides some interesting facilities for writers of extender controls—specifically, base classes and, more importantly, the Microsoft AJAX library for developing JavaScript functionalities more comfortably.

A typical extender control is made of a set of properties and one or more JavaScript files that, all together, define the expected behavior of the target control in the browser. The ASP.NET developer adds extenders declaratively to a server page and configures properties to obtain the desired behavior.

Next, when the extender renders out, it emits proper script code in the client page. This script code typically registers handlers for client-side events and modifies the Document Object Model (DOM) of the markup elements it is associated with. As a result, the original control looks and behaves in a slightly different manner while its programming interface remains intact.

To some extent, the concept of a "behavior" is similar to a theme. The theme is used to change the control's look and feel. Where the behavior and theme differ, however, is that the behavior might change some visual aspects of the control, but it is not limited to graphical attributes. It can alter the structure of the control by accessing the client DOM, add event handlers, and even expose a true object model with properties and methods.

Examining a Sample Extender

To better understand the goals and characteristics of AJAX extenders, let's briefly consider the behavior encapsulated by one of the extenders contained in the ACT—the *TextBoxWatermark* extender.

A text box watermark is a string of text that is displayed in an empty text box as a guide to the user. This help text is stripped off when the text box is submitted and is automatically removed as the user starts typing in the field. Likewise, it is automatically re-inserted when the user wipes out any text in the text box.

The watermark behavior hooks up three HTML events: *onfocus*, *onblur*, and *onkeypress*. In its initialization stage, it also sets a new style and default text for the target text box if the body of the field is empty. When the text box gets the input focus, the event handler promptly removes the watermark text and restores the original style. As the user types, the handler for *onkeypress* ensures that the current text box is watermarked. Finally, when the input field loses the focus—the *onblur* event—the handler sets the watermark back if the content of the field is the empty string.

To associate this behavior with an ASP.NET *TextBox*, you use the extender. Alternatively, if you feel comfortable with ASP.NET control development and JavaScript, you can use a client-side code fragment to achieve the same results.

Note   The concept of AJAX extenders closely resembles Dynamic HTML (DHTML) behavior. Introduced with Internet Explorer 5.0, DHTML behaviors were nothing more than a script file (or a compiled COM object) that hooked up HTML events and modified the DOM of a given HTML tag to implement a given behavior. DHTML behaviors were used to extend the capabilities of individual HTML tags. ASP.NET AJAX behaviors are used to extend the capabilities of the markup block generated by individual ASP.NET controls.

Target Properties

Extender controls are characterized by a set of properties that determine the resulting behavior. The values of these properties are passed on to the client and incorporated in the client script.

Obviously, a made-to-measure framework is required both on the server and the client to make the implementation of behaviors effective and, more importantly, affordable. This framework is exactly the benefit that ASP.NET AJAX Extensions provides. We'll examine the internals of extenders in a moment while going through some sample code. Meanwhile, let's take a quick look at how you actually use extenders in ASP.NET pages.

In a page, you have one extender instance for each control you want to enhance. The extender is decorated with a set of properties, as shown here:

```
<act:TextBoxWatermarkExtender ID="Watermark1" runat="server"
    TargetControlID="TextBox1"
    WatermarkText=" ... "
    WatermarkCssClass=" ... " />
</act:TextBoxWatermarkExtender>
<act:TextBoxWatermarkExtender ID="Watermark2" runat="server"
    TargetControlID="TextBox2"
    WatermarkText=" ... "
    WatermarkCssClass=" ... " />
</act:TextBoxWatermarkExtender>
```

The *TargetControlID* property is common to all extenders and indicates the control in the page that is the target of the extender. Other properties specific to the extender tailor its individual behavior. The *WatermarkText* and *WatermarkCssClass* properties are implemented only by the Watermark Extender, for example, and serve to assign the text and style the watermarked text should exhibit.

Armed with this background information, let's take the plunge into the programming interface of extender controls.

The *ExtenderControl* Class

As mentioned, ASP.NET AJAX Extensions doesn't include any concrete implementation of an extender. However, it defines the base class from which all custom extenders, as well as all extenders in the ACT, derive. This class is named *ExtenderControl*.

Generalities of Extender Controls

The *ExtenderControl* class derives from *Control* and implements the *IExtenderControl* interface. The class defines one specific property—*TargetControlID*. The property is a string and represents the ID of the server control being extended. The *Visible* property, common to all server controls is overridden and made virtually read-only. More precisely, you can't override a read/write property to remove the set modifier, but you can just make it throw an exception if invoked. Here's the pseudocode of the property:

```
public override bool Visible
{
    get { return base.Visible; }
    set { throw new NotImplementedException(); }
}
```

An extender requires a script manager control in the page, just as any ASP.NET AJAX server controls do. Note that extenders are mostly used declaratively and are never modified programmatically. For this reason, an extender doesn't need (and doesn't use) view state.

The *IExtenderControl* Interface

The *IExtenderControl* interface defines the contract of an extender control. It comprises two methods: *GetScriptDescriptors* and *GetScriptReferences*. Here's the definition of the interface:

```
public interface IExtenderControl
{
    IEnumerable<ScriptDescriptor> GetScriptDescriptors(
        Control targetControl);
    IEnumerable<ScriptReference> GetScriptReferences();
}
```

Both methods return a collection of specific objects—script descriptors and script references, respectively.

A script descriptor is represented by an instance of the *ScriptDescriptor* class, whereas the *ScriptReference* class represents a linked script file. What is a script descriptor, anyway? It describes the JavaScript class that provides the expected client behavior. A script descriptor indicates the client type to create, the properties to set, and the client events for which handlers are required.

Actually, *ScriptDescriptor* is just a base class that you use only as a reference. The real class you work with is *ScriptBehaviorDescriptor*. Here's some code that demonstrates the typical implementation of a *GetScriptDescriptors* method in a sample extender control:

```
protected IEnumerable<ScriptDescriptor> GetScriptDescriptors(
    Control targetControl)
{
    ScriptBehaviorDescriptor descriptor;
    descriptor = new ScriptBehaviorDescriptor(className, id);
```

```
    descriptor.AddProperty(propertyName1, value1);
    ...
    return new ScriptDescriptor[] { descriptor };
}
```

The *ScriptBehaviorDescriptor* class doesn't feature public properties, but it does expose a cargo collection property that is filled with property descriptions—typically, name and value.

As discussed in Chapter 3, "The Pulsing Heart of ASP.NET AJAX," a *ScriptReference* object describes a piece of JavaScript code. In particular, in this context it represents the client script included with the behavior. All referenced scripts define client types and any other auxiliary JavaScript code that is required. We'll return to this method in a moment.

The *ExtenderControl* base class implements the *IExtenderControl* interface by falling back into internal members that are declared as *protected* and *abstract* (or as must-override in Microsoft Visual Basic .NET):

```
IEnumerable<ScriptDescriptor> IExtenderControl.GetScriptDescriptors(
        Control targetControl)
{
    return this.GetScriptDescriptors(targetControl);
}
IEnumerable<ScriptReference> IExtenderControl.GetScriptReferences()
{
    return this.GetScriptReferences();
}
```

The internal members must be overridden in any derived classes.

Creating a Sample Extender

Let's apply the previously exposed concepts to a practical scenario and create a sample extender control. The new extender adds a highlighting behavior that changes the appearance of the control when this gets focused. This extender, named *FocusExtender*, is not specific to just one control but can be applied to virtually any ASP.NET control.

The *FocusExtender* Control

The focus extender is implemented as a control type that derives from *ExtenderControl* and overrides the two abstract members on the base class:

```
[TargetControlType(typeof(Control))]
public class FocusExtender : ExtenderControl
{
    protected override IEnumerable<ScriptReference> GetScriptReferences()
    {
        ...
    }
```

```
protected override IEnumerable<ScriptDescriptor> GetScriptDescriptors(
    Control targetControl)
{
    ...
}
...
}
```

The *TargetControlType* attribute defines the base class of controls that can be extended. In this case, all Web controls can be extended. As you can see, if multiple control types must be extended, it is required that they all derive from the same base class.

The skeleton of the extender is pretty much done. You only have to add some properties to make the extender configurable and flesh out the body of abstract methods.

The focus extender is designed to change the appearance of the target control when this gets the focus. At a minimum, you need two sets of visual properties: one for the highlighted state and one for the normal state. However, these attributes will be processed and applied on the client. On the client browser, though, there's a better way to set the appearance of elements than by using individual properties—cascading styles. To assign these styles, the extender has two properties—*HighlightCssClass* and *NormalCssClass*:

```
public class FocusExtender : ExtenderControl
{
    private string _highlightCssClass;
    private string _normalCssClass;

    public string HighlightCssClass
    {
        get { return _highlightCssClass; }
        set { _highlightCssClass = value; }
    }

    public string NormalCssClass
    {
        get { return _normalCssClass; }
        set { _normalCssClass = value; }
    }
    ...
}
```

As mentioned, an extender class doesn't need a view state and implements storage for properties through private fields. This requires that an extender be either used declaratively (and not modified programmatically during postbacks) or fully configured in the page initialization phase regardless of postbacks.

Defining the Client Behavior

The *GetScriptDescriptors* method instantiates a descriptor class and it uses that class to bind the *IntroAjax.FocusBehavior* JavaScript class to the HTML subtree rooted in the client ID of the specified control. The descriptor registers bindings between properties on the JavaScript class and properties on the extender control. The *AddProperty* method is called upon to link, say, the *highlightCssClass* on the JavaScript's *FocusBehavior* class and the *HighlightCssClass* on the extender.

```
protected override IEnumerable<ScriptDescriptor> GetScriptDescriptors(
        Control targetControl)
{
    ScriptBehaviorDescriptor descriptor;
    descriptor = new ScriptBehaviorDescriptor("IntroAjax.FocusBehavior",
        targetControl.ClientID);
    descriptor.AddProperty("highlightCssClass", this.HighlightCssClass);
    descriptor.AddProperty("normalCssClass", this.NormalCssClass);

    return new ScriptDescriptor[] { descriptor };
}
```

The binding between client and server properties serves to have the client property set with the value specified on the server. An extender should be seen as a pair of classes—one server control class, and a JavaScript class that exposes the extender's object model on the client.

You save the JavaScript class in one or more *.js* files and then register all of them with the ASP.NET AJAX infrastructure through the *ScriptReference* class. Here's a typical implementation of the *GetScriptReferences* method:

```
protected override IEnumerable<ScriptReference> GetScriptReferences()
{
    ScriptReference reference = new ScriptReference();
    reference.Path = ResolveClientUrl("FocusBehavior.js");

    return new ScriptReference[] { reference };
}
```

The *ResolveClientUrl* method is defined on the *Control* class, and it resolves a relative URL in the context of the application. Used as in the preceding code snippet, the method looks for a *FocusBehavior.js* file in the same folder as the host page. (However, that's not the place where reasonably most developers would put it.)

The Extender's Client Object Model

The *FocusBehavior.js* file defines a behavior class with properties that reflect the properties of the server-side extender control—*highlightCssClass* and *normalCssClass*. In addition, the behavior registers a couple of handlers for *blur* and *focus* client events. When the *focus* event fires, the behavior sets the highlighted cascading style sheet (CSS) style. It sets the normal CSS style when the *blur* event occurs. Here's the full source code:

```
Type.registerNamespace('IntroAjax');

// Constructor
IntroAjax.FocusBehavior = function(element)
```

```
{
    IntroAjax.FocusBehavior.initializeBase(this, [element]);
    this._highlightCssClass = null;
    this._normalCssClass = null;
}

// Create the prototype for the behavior
IntroAjax.FocusBehavior.prototype =
{
    initialize : IntroAjax$FocusBehavior$initialize,
    dispose : IntroAjax$FocusBehavior$dispose,
    _onFocus : IntroAjax$FocusBehavior$_onFocus,
    _onBlur : IntroAjax$FocusBehavior$_onBlur,
    get_highlightCssClass : IntroAjax$FocusBehavior$get_highlightCssClass,
    set_highlightCssClass : IntroAjax$FocusBehavior$set_highlightCssClass,
    get_normalCssClass : IntroAjax$FocusBehavior$get_normalCssClass,
    set_normalCssClass : IntroAjax$FocusBehavior$set_normalCssClass
}

// Internal methods
function IntroAjax$FocusBehavior$initialize()
{
    IntroAjax.FocusBehavior.callBaseMethod(this, 'initialize');

    this._onfocusHandler = Function.createDelegate(this, this._onFocus);
    this._onblurHandler = Function.createDelegate(this, this._onBlur);

    $addHandlers(this.get_element(),
                    { 'focus' : this._onFocus,
                      'blur' : this._onBlur },
                    this);

    this.get_element().className = this._normalCssClass;
}

function IntroAjax$FocusBehavior$dispose()
{
    $clearHandlers(this.get_element());
    IntroAjax.FocusBehavior.callBaseMethod(this, 'dispose');
}

function IntroAjax$FocusBehavior$_onFocus(e)
{
    if (this.get_element() && !this.get_element().disabled)
        this.get_element().className = this._highlightCssClass;
}

function IntroAjax$FocusBehavior$_onBlur(e)
{
    if (this.get_element() && !this.get_element().disabled)
        this.get_element().className = this._normalCssClass;
}

function IntroAjax$FocusBehavior$get_highlightCssClass()
```

```
{
    return this._highlightCssClass;
}

function IntroAjax$FocusBehavior$set_highlightCssClass(value)
{
    if (this._highlightCssClass !== value)
    {
        this._highlightCssClass = value;
        this.raisePropertyChanged('highlightCssClass');
    }
}

function IntroAjax$FocusBehavior$get_normalCssClass()
{
    return this._normalCssClass;
}

function IntroAjax$FocusBehavior$set_normalCssClass(value)
{
    if (this._normalCssClass !== value)
    {
        this._normalCssClass = value;
        this.raisePropertyChanged('normalCssClass');
    }
}

// Register the class
IntroAjax.FocusBehavior.registerClass('IntroAjax.FocusBehavior',
        Sys.UI.Behavior);

Sys.Application.notifyScriptLoaded();
```

The *IntroAjax.FocusBehavior* class derives from *Sys.UI.Behavior*—a Microsoft AJAX library provided class that sets the baseline for behaviors. Note the final call to the *notifyScriptLoaded* method on the *Sys.Application* class. It serves to notify the ASP.NET AJAX client infrastructure that a required script has been loaded.

Note When writing a JavaScript class, you can optionally define a JSON serializer to be used when an instance of the class is serialized—for example, if the instance of the class is used as an argument to a remote method call. (We'll cover remote scripting in Chapter 7, "Remote Method Calls with ASP.NET AJAX.")

```
IntroAjax.FocusBehavior.descriptor = {
    properties: [   {name: 'highlightCssClass', type: String},
                    {name: 'normalCssClass', type: String} ]
```

To support JSON serialization, you add a *descriptor* member defined as in the preceding code snippet. The *properties* member refers to an array of pairs made by property name and type.

Using the Focus Extender Control

To use the sample extender in an ASP.NET page, you first register the control using the @*Register* directive:

```
<%@ Register Namespace="IntroAjax.Controls" TagPrefix="x" %>
```

The host page must also have a script manager just as any other ASP.NET AJAX page. Imagine a sample page with three text boxes and a button that you want to change style when focused. Here is what the code looks like:

```
<asp:ScriptManager ID="ScriptManager1" runat="server" />
<table>
   <tr>
      <td><asp:Label runat="server" ID="Label1">Name</asp:Label></td>
      <td><asp:TextBox ID="TextBox1" runat="server" /></td>
   </tr>
   <tr>
      <td><asp:Label runat="server" ID="Label2">Phone</asp:Label></td>
      <td><asp:TextBox ID="TextBox2" runat="server" /></td>
   </tr>
   <tr>
      <td><asp:Label runat="server" ID="Label3">E-mail</asp:Label></td>
      <td><asp:TextBox ID="TextBox3" runat="server" /></td>
   </tr>
</table>
<asp:Button runat="server" ID="Button1" Text="Submit Form" />
```

You extend these controls through the focus extender using the following ASP.NET markup:

```
<x:FocusExtender ID="FocusExtender1" runat="server"
        NormalCssClass="Normal"
        HighlightCssClass="HighLight"
        TargetControlID="TextBox1" />
<x:FocusExtender ID="FocusExtender2" runat="server"
        NormalCssClass="Normal"
        HighlightCssClass="HighLight"
        TargetControlID="TextBox2" />
<x:FocusExtender ID="FocusExtender3" runat="server"
        NormalCssClass="Normal"
        HighlightCssClass="HighLight"
        TargetControlID="TextBox3" />
<x:FocusExtender ID="FocusExtender4" runat="server"
        NormalCssClass="NormalButton"
        HighlightCssClass="HighLightButton"
        TargetControlID="Button1" />
```

As you can see, each instance of the extender is bound to a particular target control and sets properties. In particular, all text boxes share the same normal and highlighted CSS styles. Figure 5-1 shows the sample page in action.

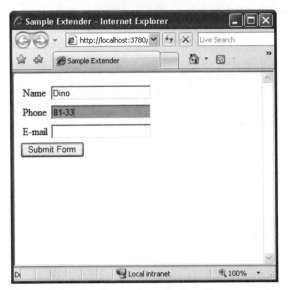

Figure 5-1   The focus extender in action

In the code snippet, *Normal* and *HighLight* are just CSS classes. Here's a possible definition:

```
<style type="text/css">
.Normal {
    background-color:#FFFFEE;
}
.HighLight {
    background-color:Orange;
}
.NormalButton {
    font-weight:normal;
    width:100px;
}
.HighLightButton {
    font-weight:bold;
    width:100px;
}
</style>
```

CSS classes are the preferred way to define visual properties for behaviors and client controls because they let you group multiple visual attributes in a single object and, subsequently, a single class property of type *string*.

Introducing the AJAX Control Toolkit

As mentioned, currently the vast majority of control extenders are compiled into an assembly known as the AJAX Control Toolkit. This assembly is a separate download and must be registered with any applications in which you plan to use it. The ACT project is an open-source project that results from a joint effort of Microsoft and the ASP.NET community. You can learn more about the project by visiting the home page of the project on the CodePlex Web site. The exact URL is *http://www.codeplex.com/AtlasControlToolkit*.

If interested, you can become a contributor to the project and have your work highlighted. The main purpose of the ACT is to provide a collection of controls and extenders that fully benefit from the ASP.NET AJAX programming model and provide free and effective Web components to developers. The ACT is expected to remain and evolve separately from ASP.NET AJAX. However, chances are that, in the future, part of the contents of the ACT assembly will be merged with the ASP.NET core binaries. Time will tell.

As of today, you have two main options for using ACT controls. You can link the full assembly to your application, or you can incorporate some of the controls as source code in your project. Before you do this, though, make sure you read the license page at *http://www.codeplex.com/AtlasControlToolkit/Project/License.aspx*.

Get Ready for the Toolkit

To download the latest bits of the ACT, visit the project's home page on CodePlex: *http://www.codeplex.com/AtlasControlToolkit*. Once it is downloaded, the Toolkit looks like a ZIP file that you click to unpack and install any contained files.

The ACT Project

At the end of the setup, you have a Microsoft Visual Studio 2005 ASP.NET project on your hard disk. If you run the project, you should see something like the screen shown in Figure 5-2.

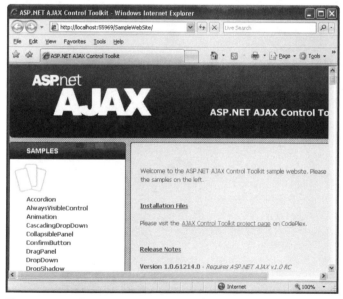

Figure 5-2   The sample Web site built to illustrate the facilities in the ACT

If you take a tour of the project files, you'll see that the ACT is a collection of ASP.NET AJAX controls and extenders plus many examples that illustrate their functionality and tests. In addition, the ACT contains a development kit to simplify the creation and re-use of your own custom controls and extenders. The development kit includes Visual Studio 2005 templates for Visual Basic and Visual C# to let developers write their own controls and extenders. In addition, it features a library of helper classes to speed up the creation of controls and extenders.

Adding ACT Components to the Toolbox

So the ACT contains a number of controls and extenders that you might want to compose and combine in your ASP.NET pages. The Visual Studio 2005 toolbox appears to be the perfect place to list all these components so that developers can pick up exactly the one they need and paste it to the current page. To add ACT components to the toolbox, you first create a new tab in the toolbox. You right-click on the toolbox surface and select Add Tab from the context menu. Once the new tab is added, you can give it any name you want—for example, AJAX Control Toolkit.

Next, you populate the tab with all components in the ACT assembly. To do this, you right-click the toolbox area below the newly added tab and select Choose Items. The standard dialog box that lists .NET assemblies and COM components will show up. Browse to the location where you installed the ACT, and select the *AjaxControlToolkit* assembly from the *Bin* folder of the SampleWebsite folder. That's all there is to it. When you're done, your toolbox will magically look like the one shown in Figure 5-3.

Figure 5-3   Creating a new tab in the Visual Studio 2005 toolbox to host the ACT components

Note   In the ACT, you find a few server controls (such as *TabContainer*) and many more extenders (such as *RoundedCorners*, *DropShadow*, and *TextBoxWatermark*). What's the difference between controls and extenders? A *control* provides a closed set of functionalities and a well-known, fixed behavior that you can rule only through properties and events. An *extender* is a (mostly) client-side behavior that can be attached to a variety of controls. For example, you can attach the *DropShadow* extender to a *TextBox* as well as to a *Panel* and, in both cases, the target control renders out with a shadow. In spite of such logical differences, both server controls and extenders are implemented in the same way—both are, in the end, ASP.NET server controls.

Registering ACT Components with the Page

Although the ACT is a native part of the ASP.NET AJAX framework and a constituent part of the next ASP.NET platform, as of today it is simply an external library. For this reason, you need to explicitly register the ACT with each and every page where you happen to use any of its controls or extenders. You use the *@Register* directive, as shown here:

```
<%@ Register Assembly="AjaxControlToolkit"
            Namespace="AjaxControlToolkit"
            TagPrefix="act" %>
```

If you don't like the idea of repeating the same code for all the pages of a given application, you can take the same shortcut that the ASP.NET team took for avoiding the same burden with ASP.NET AJAX controls.

In fact, the same ASP.NET AJAX core library discussed here is also an external library to the ASP.NET platform and would need explicit registration with each page. In ASP.NET 2.0, you can use the following configuration script to enable a *@Register* directive for all pages of the application:

```
<pages>
   <controls>
      <add tagPrefix="asp"
           namespace="System.Web.UI"
           assembly="System.Web.Extensions, ..." />
   </controls>
</pages>
```

For example, all controls in the *System.Web.UI* namespace are associated with the *asp* tag prefix and don't need an explicit *@Register* directive in the pages where they're used. You can add a similar block to the *web.config* file for ACT controls as well:

```
<pages>
   <controls>
      <add namespace="AjaxControlToolkit"
           assembly="AjaxControlToolkit, ..."
           tagPrefix="act" />
      ...
   </controls>
</pages>
```

As you may already know, the string you choose as the tag prefix is arbitrary. For the sake of clarity, though, it is not recommended that you choose the *asp* prefix as well. The *asp* prefix should be reserved for system controls.

What's in the AJAX Control Toolkit

The ACT is a library designed to extend the capabilities of the ASP.NET AJAX framework. Its control set might change in the future and could be further extended or cut down. You can check the progress of the project from the aforementioned CodePlex site. At the time of this writing, the ACT contains a fair number of extenders and controls, but they certainly don't address every possible development scenario.

Extenders in the ACT

Table 5-1 lists the components currently available in the ACT. Note that the full name of the extender class contains an "Extender" suffix that I omitted in the table for brevity. So, for example, there will be no *CollapsiblePanel* component in the ACT assembly, but you will find a *CollapsiblePanelExtender* control instead.

Table 5-1   Extenders in the ACT

Component	Description
AlwaysVisibleControl	Pins a control to a corner of the page, and keeps it floating over the page background as the user scrolls or resizes the page. You use this extender to make sure that, say, a given panel shows up at the top-left corner of the page regardless of the scroll position or the size of the browser window.
Animation	Provides a specialized framework for adding animation effects to controls hosted in ASP.NET pages. You associate client-side events of the target control with one or more of the predefined animation effects.
AutoComplete	Associated with a text box, provides a list of suggestions for the text to type in the field.
Calendar	Attached to a text box, the extender provides client-side date-picking functionality with customizable date format and pop-up control.
CascadingDropDown	Associated with a *DropDownList* control. This extender automatically populates the list with data retrieved from a Web service method. The nice thing about this extender is that you can create a hierarchy of drop-down lists and have the extender automatically populate child drop-down lists based on the current selections in any of the previous lists in the heirarchy, if any.
CollapsiblePanel	Adds collapsible sections to a Web page. This extender can be used only with panel controls—that is, with the ASP.NET *Panel* control or any class derived from it. You let the extender know which panel in the page acts as the header and which panel provides the contents that collapse and expand.

Table 5-1   Extenders in the ACT (Continued)

Component	Description
ConfirmButton	Associated with a button control. This extender adds a confirmation JavaScript dialog box to the click event of the button. The extender is supported on any class that implements the *IButtonControl* interface, including *Button*, *LinkButton*, and *ImageButton*.
DragPanel	Associated with panel controls. This extender adds drag-and-drop capabilities so that you can move the panel around the page. You can specify the contents to move as well as the handle that, if pressed, triggers the dragging operation.
DropDown	The extender provides a mouse-over link to open a drop-down panel.
DropShadow	Adds drop shadows to any control available on the page. With this extender, you can specify the opacity and width of the shadow.
DynamicPopulate	Updates the contents of a control with the result of a Web service or page method call.
FilteredTextBox	Lets users enter text in a *TextBox* control that matches a given set of valid characters.
HoverMenu	Displays the contents of an associated panel control when the mouse hovers next to a given control. You can associate this extender with any ASP.NET control. The extender works as a kind of specialized and extremely flexible ToolTip.
MaskedEdit	Lets users enter text in a *TextBox* control according to a given input layout.
ModalPopup	Associated with a control that can fire a client-side *onclick* event (typically, buttons and hyperlinks), this extender implements a classic modal dialog box without using HTML dialog boxes. Basically, it displays the contents of a given panel and prevents the user from interacting with the rest of the page.
MutuallyExclusiveCheckBox	Associated with *CheckBox* controls, this extender lets you define logical groups of check boxes so that users can check only one in each group.
NoBot	Applies some *anti-bot* techniques to input forms. Bots, or robot applications, are software applications that run automated tasks over the Internet. For example, bots are used to fill input forms and submit ad hoc values.
NumericUpDown	Associated with text box controls, this extender allows you to click automatically displayed buttons to enter the next/previous value in the field. It works with numbers, custom lists, and Web service methods.
PagingBulletedList	Associated with *BulletedList* controls, this extender groups all items bound to the list and organizes them in client-side sorted pages.
PasswordStrength	Associated with text box controls used to type a password, this extender provides visual feedback on the strength of the password being typed.

Table 5-1   Extenders in the ACT   (Continued)

Component	Description
PopupControl	Transforms the contents of a given panel into a pop-up window without using HTML dialog boxes. You can associate this extender with any control that can fire any of the following client-side events: onfocus, onclick, and onkeydown.
ResizableControl	Attaches to any page element, and allows the user to resize the element using a handle placed at the lower-right corner of the control.
RoundedCorners	Adds a background panel to any ASP.NET control so that the control appears with rounded corners. The overall height of the original control changes slightly.
Slider	Extends a TextBox control with a slider user interface.
TextBoxWatermark	Associated with TextBox controls. This extender adds sample or prompt text, called a "watermark," that illustrates the type of text the user is expected to enter in the field. For example, the watermark might say, "Type your name here." The watermark text disappears as soon as the user starts typing and reappears as the text box becomes empty.
ToggleButton	Associated with CheckBox controls. This extender enables you to use custom images to render the check buttons. You can use different images to indicate the selected and cleared states.
UpdatePanelAnimation	Plays animations during key steps of a partial update. You can use the extender to animate the page both while the panel is being updating and when the update has completed.
ValidatorCallout	Works on top of ASP.NET validators, and improves their user interface. In particular, the extender displays a yellow callout with the error message.

As you can probably guess, some extenders listed in the table require rich browser capabilities, whereas others are just a smart piece of JavaScript code attached to a block of markup elements. Note that all these features work in a cross-browser way. I'll return to each of the aforementioned extenders with code samples and more details in a moment.

Controls in the ACT

Along with all the extenders listed in Table 5-1, the ACT also supplies a few traditional server controls with rich capabilities: the *Accordion*, *Rating*, *ReorderList* and *TabContainer* controls.

The *Accordion* control allows you to provide multiple collapsible panes and display only one at a time. When the user clicks a new pane, the currently displayed pane is collapsed to leave room for the new one.

The *Rating* control provides an intuitive user interface to let users select the number of stars that represents their rating of a given subject. The control is the wrapped-up version of the user interface that several Web sites provide to let users rate published items.

A data-bound control, *ReorderList*, allows its child elements to be reordered on the client using drag-and-drop functionality. To move an item in the list, the user drags the item's handle up to its new position. At the end of the operation, the control posts back so that the new status of the data source can be recorded.

Finally, the *TabContainer* control is a purely client-side container of tabbed forms.

Let's first get to know more about these controls and then move on to discuss extenders.

The *Accordion* Control

Collapsible panels are a frequent feature in modern and cutting-edge Web sites. They allow you to display a short highlight—the header—and keep more text hidden and available on demand. The *CollapsiblePanel* extender (discussed later) allows you to hide and display any block of markup. But what if you need to build a sort of hierarchy of panels?

The *Accordion* control allows you to group multiple collapsible panels in a single control, and it manages the collapsed/expanded state of each panel so that only one can be expanded at a time.

Generalities of the *Accordion* Control

The *Accordion* control contains a collection of child *AccordionPane* controls, each of which features a template property to define header and content. Each pane can include any HTML, ASP.NET, or ASP.NET AJAX markup you want.

Properties of the Control

Table 5-2 lists the key properties of the *Accordion* control.

Table 5-2   Properties of the *Accordion* Control

Property	Description
AutoSize	The value assigned to this property indicates how the control will determine its actual size.
ContentCssClass	Gets and sets the CSS class used to style the content of child panes.
FadeTransitions	Indicates whether to use a fade-out transition effect while hiding the current pane. This property is set to *false* by default.
FramesPerSecond	Gets and sets the number of frames per second used in the transition animation for the newly selected pane. This property is set to *30* frames by default.
HeaderCssClass	Gets and sets the CSS class used to style the header of child panes.
Panes	Returns the collection of child panes.
SelectedIndex	Gets and sets the currently expanded pane.
TransitionDuration	Gets and sets the number of milliseconds to animate the transition. This property is set to *250* by default.

As you can see, the control has no visual properties except for the ASP.NET base properties defined on the parent *WebControl* class (such as *BackColor*, *ForeColor*, and so on). In particular, there's no style property for child panes. To style the header and content of child panes, you use CSS classes. Note that if the control worked through regular postbacks, you would probably have had *Style* objects instead of CSS class properties, as in many other classic ASP.NET controls.

Animating the Control

The *Accordion* control supports animation in two different contexts. First, it might optionally fade out the content of the current pane when a new one is selected. This effect is controlled by the *FadeTransitions* Boolean property. The effect is not very visible on small-sized content panes. Note also that the fade animation is tightly coupled with the transition animation that slowly rolls down the content of the new pane.

This second form of animation is controlled by the *TransitionDuration* and *FramesPerSecond* properties. If this latter effect is disabled, you won't see any fade-out effect regardless of the setting of the *FadeTransitions* property.

To skip transition animation completely and obtain a quick swap of panes, you set both *FramesPerSecond* and *TransitionDuration* to 0. If you do so, also set *FadeTransitions* to *false* to save the control unnecessary tasks that will produce no observable effects.

Sizing the Control

The size of the *Accordion* control is clearly determined by any container element as well as the content of the various panes. This means that the overall size of the accordion might vary with the selected pane. In this case, other elements in the page might be pushed up or down. The *AutoSize* property helps to keep the overall size of accordion under control.

The *AutoSize* property takes its values from the *AutoSize* enumeration, whose values are *None* (default), *Limit*, and *Fill*. When the *AutoSize* property is set to *None*, the accordion modifies its size freely following the size of the selected pane.

When you set *AutoSize* to *Limit*, the accordion never grows larger than the value specified by its *Width* and *Height* properties. The *Accordion* control inherits these properties from its base class. The *Height* and *Width* properties are both ignored if *None* is set. If the content to display is larger than the designated size of the accordion, scrollbars are employed to let users see all of it.

With the *Fill* value set, the accordion stays exactly within the bounding box delimited by the *Width* and *Height* properties. In this case, the content will be expanded or made scrollable if it isn't the right size. Expanding the contents just means making the pane larger.

Using the *Accordion* Control

The accordion consists of a number of child panes, each of which is an instance of the *AccordionPane* class. You add panes using markup and retrieve the collection of panes programmatically using the *Panes* collection property.

The *Accordion* Control in Action

The following code demonstrates the usage of the *Accordion* control:

```
<div style="width:300px;">
   <act:Accordion ID="Accordion1" runat="server" Height="400px"
       SelectedIndex="0"
       ContentCssClass="accordionContent"
       HeaderCssClass="accordionHeader"
       FadeTransitions="true"
       AutoSize="Fill">
     <Panes>
        <act:AccordionPane ID="AccordionPane1" runat="server">
           <Header>One</Header>
           <Content>This is the first pane</Content>
        </act:AccordionPane>
        <act:AccordionPane ID="AccordionPane2" runat="server">
           <Header>Two</Header>
           <Content>
              <div style="height:400px">
              This is the second pane</div>
           </Content>
        </act:AccordionPane>
        <act:AccordionPane ID="AccordionPane3" runat="server">
           <Header>Three</Header>
           <Content>This is the third pane</Content>
        </act:AccordionPane>
        <act:AccordionPane ID="AccordionPane4" runat="server">
           <Header>Four</Header>
           <Content>This is the fourth pane</Content>
        </act:AccordionPane>
     </Panes>
   </act:Accordion>
</div>
```

You add an *<act:AccordionPane>* element for each collapsible panel you want to display. Each pane consists of a *<header>* and *<content>* template.

The sample accordion is embedded in a fixed-width *<div>* tag. The outermost container determines the width and height of the accordion. The *AutoSize* property set to *Fill* forces the accordion to cover and fill the whole bounding box. Figure 5-4 shows the results.

Note that the content of the second pane is set to a height of 400 pixels; the accordion itself, though, can't be taller than 400 pixels and can't grow uncontrolled because of the *AutoSize* setting. As a result, the second pane displays a scrollbar to let you see the content that exceeds that limit.

Figure 5-4   The *Accordion* control in action

Accordion Panes

An accordion pane is a simple Web control named *AccordionPane*. It has a *Header* template property that you use to define the highlighting of the panel—that is, the portion of the panel that is visible also when it is collapsed. You can style the header using the settings in the CSS class defined by the *HeaderCssClass* property.

Likewise, the content of the pane is defined by the *Content* template property and styled using the settings in the CSS class referenced by the *ContentCssClass* property.

The *Rating* Control

The satisfaction of users is one of the key metrics used to determine the success of a Web site. And how do you recognize the satisfaction level of a user? Many Web sites kindly ask users to provide their feedback through ad hoc panels scattered through the pages. The most common user-interface pattern for user feedback is a ratings system. The Web site shows a fixed number of stars and lets users click those stars to rate a given feature (usually, more stars clicked indicates a higher level of satisfaction).

Most ASP.NET developers can easily arrange a rating mechanism that works through classic postbacks. The ACT *Rating* control, on the other hand, provides a standard rating mechanism that works over callbacks.

Generalities of the *Rating* Control

The output of the control consists of a repeated *<span>* tag that is decorated through a set of CSS classes. Each *<span>* tag represents a "star" in the rating system and is styled according to the status it represents. Figure 5-5 gives you an idea of the *Rating* control.

Figure 5-5   The *Rating* control in action

Properties of the Control

Table 5-3 lists the key properties of the *Rating* control.

Table 5-3   Properties of the *Rating* Control

Property	Description
AutoPostBack	Indicates whether the control will post back whenever the user rates a given associated content.
CurrentRating	Gets and sets the current value rendered by the control. The default value is *3*.
EmptyStarCssClass	Gets and sets the CSS class to render an unselected star.
FilledStarCssClass	Gets and sets the CSS class to render a selected star.
MaxRating	Gets and sets the maximum value that can be rated through the control. The default value is *5*.
RatingAlign	Indicates the alignment of the stars. The default is *horizontal*.
RatingDirection	Indicates the orientation of the stars. The default is left to right if the *RatingAlign* value is horizontal and top to bottom if *RatingAlign* is vertical.
ReadOnly	Indicates whether the control accepts user input.

Table 5-3   Properties of the *Rating* Control (Continued)

Property	Description
StarCssClass	Gets and sets the CSS class to style the whole control.
Tag	A string to pass to the server-side code that handles the user's click.
WaitingStarCssClass	Gets and sets the CSS class to render selected stars during a server post-back following a user update.

The markup generated by the *Rating* control looks like the following code:

```
<div id="Rating1" style="float: left;">
    <span id="Rating1_Star_1" class="ratingStar filledRatingStar"
        style="float:left;"> </span>
    <span id="Rating1_Star_2" class="ratingStar filledRatingStar"
        style="float:left;"> </span>
    ...
</div>
```

As you can see, each "star" is characterized by a unique ID and is represented with a *<span>* tag set to the empty string. In Figure 5-5, though, each star is clearly an image. How is that possible?

Styling the Control

The *Rating* control supports four different CSS classes. *StarCssClass* defines the style for the entire control. *WaitingStarCssClass* defines the style to be used when the control is posting back. *EmptyStarCssClass* and *FilledStarCssClass* define the style for the *<span>* tag. You can use either an image to fill the tag or a contrasting background color. Let's consider the following CSS classes:

```
.filledRatingStar
{
    background-color: #2E4d7B;
}
.emptyRatingStar
{
    background-image: url(images/NotSelected.png);
}
```

These classes produce an effect like the second rating object shown in Figure 5-5. The selected part is rendered as a gauge bar; the unselected part is rendered using empty stars. By editing the CSS classes, you can choose the "star" images to meet the expectations of the users of your application.

Using the *Rating* Control

The *Rating* control is relatively simple to use. It only requires you to set a few properties—the CSS classes—and it has no child elements or templates.

The *Rating* Control in Action

The following code demonstrates the usage of the *Rating* control:

```
<h2>Rate this item:</h2>
<div>
    <act:Rating ID="Rating1" runat="server"
        CurrentRating="3"
        MaxRating="10"
        StarCssClass="ratingStar"
        WaitingStarCssClass="savedRatingStar"
        FilledStarCssClass="filledRatingStar"
        EmptyStarCssClass="emptyRatingStar"
        OnChanged="Rating_Changed" />
</div>
```

The *MaxRating* property determines the number of stars to render. Of these, the first stars (or the last ones, depending on the direction) up to the value specified by *CurrentRating* are styled using the class name specified by *FilledStarCssClass*. The remaining stars are styled using the attributes set by *EmptyStarCssClass*.

Specifying valid CSS class names is key. If you omit, say, the empty-star style, the corresponding *<span>* tag will be rendered as is, without any graphical adjustments. Because the *<span>* tag is set to the empty string, no visible output will be generated.

The Eventing Model

The *Rating* control injects into the client browser a piece of script code that does two main things. First, it captures mouse movements over the bounding box of the control. Second, it handles the user's clicking.

As the user moves the mouse over the unselected stars, the script code automatically toggles the class name of the underlying *<span>* tag to give you an idea of the interface if you select the given number of stars.

To change the current value, you just click on the star that represents the new value. For example, in an rating system with five stars, you click on the fourth star to set a rating of 4. When this happens, the *Rating* control makes an out-of-band call to the server and raises the *Changed* event:

```
protected void Rating_Changed(object sender, RatingEventArgs e)
{
    // Perform any significant server-side action
    // such as storing the new value to a database
}
```

The *RatingEventArgs* class contains three main properties: *Tag*, *Value*, and *CallbackResult*. *Tag* is a cargo property used to carry any custom string from the client to the server. *Value* indicates the currently selected value in the control. *CallbackResult*, on the other hand, is a string property you can set on the server with any information you want to bring back to the client. For example, you can use the *Changed* event to store the rating value to a database and use the *CallbackResult* string to return an error message if the operation fails.

The *ReorderList* Control

Data-bound lists of data are commonly displayed to Web users and, most of the time, are read-only, immutable lists. There might be situations, though, in which the end user might want to reorder a displayed list of items. A good example is a page on which the user can select multiple cities in the world to be informed about the current weather. The cities appear in a given order on the page, but the user might want to change the order at some point.

As a developer, you can add a *Move Up* button to the page and have the user click three times to bring the last city to the top of a list with four cities. Although this approach is functionally effective, it is certainly not very user friendly. A more natural approach would be to enable the user to simply select the item of a given city and drop it to the desired new location.

This is exactly what the *ReorderList* control allows you to do. Let's learn more about this new ASP.NET AJAX control.

Generalities of the *ReorderList* Control

The contents of the *ReorderList* control are expressed through a series of templates that you use to indicate the structure of each data-bound item, the user interface for the drag handle, and the user interface for the insertion point where the dragged item is being moved. More properties and events, though, interact to form the programming interface of the control.

Properties of the Control

Table 5-4 lists the key properties of the *ReorderList* control. In particular, the list describes the properties that can be set through attributes in an ASP.NET Web page. The control, in fact, derives from *DataBoundControl* and implements the *IRepeatInfoUser* interface—the typical interface for controls that support a variety of alignments and layouts, such as *CheckBoxList*. The base class and the interface include a bunch of additional properties that relate to data binding and control layout.

Table 5-4   Properties of the *ReorderList* Control

Property	Description
AllowReorder	Indicates whether the control supports drag-and-drop reordering. This property is automatically set to *true* if a reorder template is specified.
DataKeyField	Indicates the name of the data-bound source that operates as the primary key field.
DataSourceID	Indicates the ID of the data source control used to populate the control.
DragHandleAlignment	Indicates the position of the drag handle with respect to the item to drag. It can have any of the following values: *Top*, *Left*, *Bottom*, or *Right*.

Table 5-4   Properties of the *ReorderList* Control   (Continued)

Property	Description
DragHandleTemplate	The template for the drag handle that the user clicks to drag and reorder items.
EditItemTemplate	The template used to show that a row is in edit mode.
EmptyListTemplate	The template used to show that the list has no data. This item is not data bindable.
InsertItemTemplate	The template used to add new items to the list.
ItemInsertLocation	When the *InsertItemTemplate* property is used to add a new item to the displayed list, this property indicates where the item has to be inserted. Feasible values are *Beginning* and *End*.
ItemTemplate	The template for any items in the list.
PostBackOnReorder	Indicates whether the control has to post back at the end of a reorder operation.
ReorderTemplate	The template used to show the drop location during a reorder operation. This template is not data bindable.
SortOrderField	The field, if any, that represents the sort order of the items.

The key properties are *ItemTemplate*, *DragHandleTemplate*, and *ReorderTemplate*. *ItemTemplate* allows you to populate the list control with any information and layout you need. *DragHandleTemplate* defines the graphical elements that users need to identify when they want to reorder the list. Finally, the *ReorderTemplate* defines the template of the visual feedback that is shown to the user while the operation is occurring.

Events of the Control

The *ReorderList* control is primarily a data-bound control with a rich user interface largely made up of templates. This means that the control can include a number of child controls that might trigger postbacks and cause the contents of the control to change.

It is not surprising, then, to find a long list of events associated with this control. These events are detailed in Table 5-5.

Table 5-5   Events of the *ReorderList* Control

Event	Description
CancelCommand	Occurs when a button with the *CommandName* of "Cancel" is clicked from within the control.
DeleteCommand	Occurs when a button with the *CommandName* of "Delete" is clicked from within the control.
EditCommand	Occurs when a button with the *CommandName* of "Edit" is clicked from within the control.
InsertCommand	Occurs when a button with the *CommandName* of "Insert" is clicked from within the control.
ItemCommand	Occurs when a button is clicked from within the item template of a row.

Table 5-5   Events of the *ReorderList* Control (Continued)

Event	Description
ItemCreated	Occurs when an item row is created.
ItemDataBound	Occurs when an item row is bound to its data.
ItemReorder	Occurs when an item row is moved to a new location at the end of a reorder operation.
UpdateCommand	Occurs when a button with the *CommandName* of "Update" is clicked from within the control.

Most command events are related to the capabilities of the bound data source. For example, the *InsertCommand* event occurs if the control features a proper template with controls to capture data and invoke an *Insert* command on the bound data source control. Here's a quick example:

```
<act:ReorderList ...>
    ...
    <InsertItemTemplate>
        <div>
            <asp:TextBox ID="TextBox1" runat="server"
                Text='<%# Bind("Title") %>'></asp:TextBox>
            <asp:LinkButton ID="LinkButton1" runat="server"
                CommandName="Insert">Add</asp:LinkButton>
        </div>
    </InsertItemTemplate>
</act:ReorderList>
```

By clicking on the link button, you cause the *ReorderList* control to invoke the *Insert* command on the bound data source, if there is any. The new item, which will have a *Title* property, is added at the top or bottom of the data source based on the value of the *ItemInsertLocation* property.

The *ItemReorder* event is fired on the server before the new control is rendered back to the client with the new order of items. The event carries a *ReorderListItemReorderEventArgs* object with the following structure:

```
public class ReorderListItemReorderEventArgs : EventArgs
{
    public ReorderListItem Item { get; set; }
    public int NewIndex { get; set; }
    public int OldIndex { get; set; }
}
```

The *Item* property indicates the item being moved, whereas *NewIndex* and *OldIndex* specify the new and old positions (a 0-based index), respectively.

Using the *ReorderList* Control

Let's consider a sample page that makes use of the *ReorderList* control. As you'll see in a moment, the *ReorderList* control must be bound to a data source and embedded in an *UpdatePanel* control.

Configuring the *ReorderList* Control

The following code snippet demonstrates a sample reorder list control bound to an *ObjectDataSource* control:

```
<act:ReorderList runat="server" ID="list"
    DataSourceID="ObjectDataSource1">
    <ItemTemplate>
        <asp:Label ID="Label1" runat="server"
            Text='<%# Eval("lastname") %>' />
    </ItemTemplate>
    <ReorderTemplate>
        <asp:Panel ID="Panel2" runat="server" CssClass="reorderCue" />
    </ReorderTemplate>
</act:ReorderList>
<asp:ObjectDataSource ID="ObjectDataSource1" runat="server"
    TypeName="IntroAtlas.EmployeeManager"
    SelectMethod="LoadAll">
</asp:ObjectDataSource>
```

The sample control has no *DragHandleTemplate* set, which means that its user interface has no visible element to start dragging. In this case, the output looks like a bulleted list, and to start reordering you simply click and drag the text beside the bullet point, as shown in Figure 5-6.

Figure 5-6   Reordering the items in a *ReorderList* control

Generally, the item being moved is rendered through a template that you specify via the *ReorderTemplate* property. In this case, the reorder template consists of the sole text of the item plus a cascading style. If you omit the template but still enable reordering through the *AllowReorder* Boolean property, the text of the item, rendered with a gray color, is used to give feedback to users about the ongoing operation.

Building a reorder list that allows items to be moved around is a breeze. However, a couple of essential issues still need to be properly addressed.

Reordering and Postback Events

The *ReorderList* control can be configured to post back at the end of each drag-and-drop operation. To avoid a full page refresh, you need to wrap the *ReorderList* control in an *UpdatePanel* control. As explained in Chapter 4, in this way you guarantee that only the user interface of the list control is refreshed rather than the entire page being updated with a complete postback. The following few lines of markup can accomplish this for us:

```
<asp:UpdatePanel runat="server" ID="UpdatePanel1">
    <ContentTemplate>
        ...
        <!-- ReorderList goes here -->
        ...
    </ContentTemplate>
</asp:UpdatePanel>
```

Why does the control do a postback of its own? The *ReorderList* control attempts to persist the changes the user made so that if any postback occurs from within the page—say, a postback caused by the user clicking on another button in the page—the contents of the *ReorderList*, as modified via a drag-and-drop operation, are maintained. Note, in fact, that any changes made on the client should be persisted on the server; otherwise, they will be lost in the first subsequent page postback.

Persisting Reordered Items

If you run a page that contains a *ReorderList* control, you notice that invariably after a postback, any moved element is restored to its original location. Why is that so? At the end of the drop operation, the *ReorderList* control posts back, fires the *ItemReorder* event on the server, and rebuilds the list. The list is data bound, so unless you change something in the binding process, the list will be bound back to the same record set in the same old order.

Subsequently, a page that hosts a *ReorderList* control should wire up the *ItemReorder* event and make sure that the data source bound to the control properly reflects the changes generated on the client. The *ItemReorder* event has the following signature:

```
void OnItemReorder(object sender, ReorderListItemReorderEventArgs e)
```

In this event handler, you should do the real work of the reorder—that is, move the item from the old position to the new position in the data source used to populate the list. How you do this depends on the binding mechanism. If you opted for a data source control (for example, *ObjectDataSource*), you can try sorting on a given field, if any, that reflects the new order. If you set the data source assigning an *IEnumerable* object to the *DataSource* property, you can retrieve and modify this object to reflect the new order. For a *DataTable*, for example, this means swapping two rows.

Note   The *ReorderList* can automatically perform server-side reorders if its *SortOrderField* property is set and if the data source can be sorted on that field. In addition, the type of the sort field must be *integer*.

The *TabContainer* Control

Multiple views are a common feature in most pages. They group information in tabs and let users click to display only a portion of the information available. In ASP.NET 2.0, the *MultiView* control provides an effective shortcut to this feature. But it requires a postback to update the page when the user selects a new tab. In the ACT, the *TabContainer* control provides an AJAX version of the multiview control.

Generalities of the *TabContainer* Control

The *TabContainer* control is made of a collection of tabs, each of which is represented by an instance of the *TabPanel* class. You can add and remove panels programmatically, as well as define them declaratively.

Properties of the Control

Table 5-6 lists the properties supported by the control.

Table 5-6   Properties of the *TabContainer* Control

Property	Description
ActiveTab	Returns a reference to the currently selected tab.
ActiveTabIndex	Gets and sets the 0-based index of the selected tab.
CssClass	Gets and sets the CSS class to use to style the control.
Height	Gets and sets the height of the tabs. The value of the property is expressed as a *Unit* value. This value doesn't include headers.
OnClientActiveTabChanged	Gets and sets the JavaScript code to be executed on the client when the user changes the selection.
Scrollbars	Gets and sets the desired support for scrollbars. This property is set to *Auto* by default. Feasible values come from the ASP.NET 2.0 *Scrollbars* type.
Tabs	Returns the collection of *TabPanel* objects that defines the user interface of the control.
Width	Gets and sets the width of the tabs. The value of the property is expressed as a *Unit* value.

In addition, the control fires the *ActiveTabChanged* event when the selected tab changes. The event is a mere notification, and the required delegate is *EventHandler*. No additional information is passed along with the event.

Properties of Tab Panels

The *TabPanel* class represents an individual tab in the container. Each tab defines its header either as plain text or as a template. Likewise, a tab features a template to let developers specify its content. The most recent tab should remain selected after a postback. Table 5-7 lists the properties of the *TabPanel* class.

Table 5-7   Properties of the *TabPanel* Class

Property	Description
ContentTemplate	Sets the contents of the tab.
Enabled	Indicates whether the tab should be displayed. The value of the property can be changed on the client.
HeaderTemplate	Gets and sets the template to use to define the header of the tab.
HeaderText	Gets and sets the text to display in the tab's header.
OnClientClick	JavaScript code to attach to the client-side *click* event of the tab.
OnClientPopulated	JavaScript code to run on the client when the tab has been fully populated.
OnClientPopulating	JavaScript code to run on the client when the tab is going to be populated.
Scrollbars	Gets and sets the desired support for scrollbars. This property is set to *Auto* by default. Feasible values come from the ASP.NET 2.0 *Scrollbars* type.

The JavaScript code you can attach to some client events can be either the name of function embedded in the host page or a string of JavaScript executable code.

Using the *TabContainer* Control

Let's consider a sample page that makes use of the *TabContainer* control. As you'll see in a moment, the markup required for a tab container is straightforward.

Configuring the *TabContainer* Control

The *TabContainer* tag maps its child tags to the *Tabs* collection of *TabPanel* objects. You add one <*TabPanel*> tag for each desired tab and configure it at will. Here's an example:

```
<act:TabContainer runat="server" ID="TabContainer1">
    <act:TabPanel runat="server" ID="TabPanel1" HeaderText="Your Tab">
        <ContentTemplate>
            <h3>Some text here</h3>
        </ContentTemplate>
    </act:TabPanel>
    ...
</act:TabContainer>
```

All tabs are given the same size, and you can control the size designation through the *Width* and *Height* properties of the container. The height you set refers to the body of tags and doesn't include the header.

Changing the Selected Tab

You can add some script code to run when the user selects a new tab. You can wrap up all the code in a page-level JavaScript function and bind the name of the function to the *OnClientActive-TabChanged* property of the tab container. The following code writes the name of the currently selected tab to a page element (originally, an ASP.NET *Label* control) named *CurrentTab*:

```
<script type="text/javascript">
    function ActiveTabChanged(sender, e)
    {
        var tab = $get('<%=CurrentTab.ClientID%>');
        tab.innerHTML = sender.get_activeTab().get_headerText();
    }
</script>
```

Note the usage of code blocks in JavaScript. In this way, the client ID of the label is merged in the script regardless of whether the page is a regular page or a content page (with a hierarchy of parent controls and naming containers). Figure 5-7 shows the control in action.

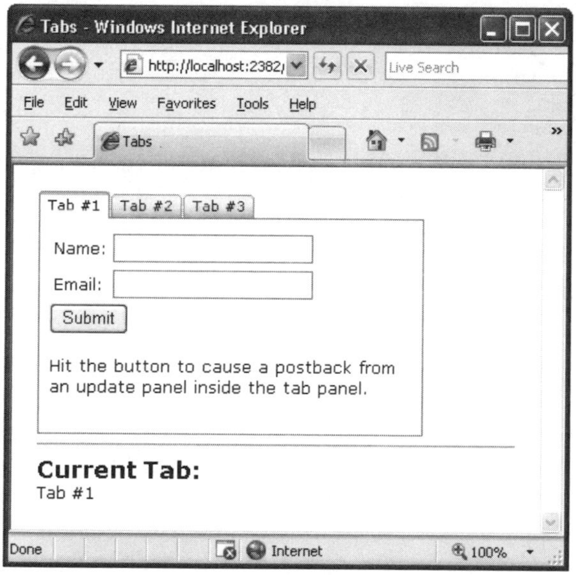

Figure 5-7   The *TabContainer* control in action

The Client-Side Object Model

As a full-fledged ASP.NET AJAX control, the *TabContainer* control exposes a client-side object model. In particular, there's a set of properties that represents the programming interface of the container and another set of properties for each tab panel.

The container features read/write properties—such as *activeTabIndex*, *activeTab*, *tabs*, and *scrollBars*—plus the *activeTabChanged* event.

The tab panel exposes read/write properties such as *enabled*, *headerText*, and *scrollBars* along with a read-only *tabIndex* property and a few events—*click*, *populating*, and *populated*.

AJAX Control Toolkit Extenders

In addition to finding full-fledged server controls such as *ReorderList* and *Accordion* in the ACT, you find a bunch of other server controls designed to extend existing controls on the page and provide them with new and additional behaviors. Existing extenders can be categorized into a few groups: panel, input, popup, user interface, animation, and button. Let's dig deeper into these groupings.

Panel Extenders

ASP.NET pages are full of blocks of markup that, ideally, users would love to move around, collapse if too large, and expand on demand. The perfect panel control in ASP.NET is, therefore, both draggable and expandable. Purposely, ASP.NET AJAX defines a few server-side behaviors that allow you to easily create collapsible sections and drag panels around the page.

The *CollapsiblePanel* Extender

The extender builds up a collapsible section in your pages by combining two panels—one acting as the content panel, and one being the expand/collapse controller. In its simplest form, the *CollapsiblePanel* extender looks like the following code sample:

```
<act:CollapsiblePanelExtender ID="CollPanel" runat="server"
      TargetControlID="ContentPanel"
      ExpandControlID="HeaderPanel"
      CollapseControlID="HeaderPanel" />
```

As usual, the *TargetControlID* property sets the target panel to expand or collapse. *ExpandControlID* and *CollapseControlID* indicate the panel to use to expand and collapse the content panel. Note the extreme flexibility of the component design—it might not make sense in all cases, but you can use different panels to control the expansion and collapsing of the content panel. In most cases, though, you'll be using the same header panel with an image button that changes according to the state of the content panel. The following code snippet shows a more complete usage for the extender:

```
<act:CollapsiblePanelExtender ID="cpe" runat="server"
      TargetControlID="CollapsibleCustomersPanelContent"
      ExpandControlID="CollapsibleCustomersPanel"
      CollapseControlID="CollapsibleCustomersPanel"
      Collapsed="true"
      ExpandDirection="Vertical"
      ImageControlID="ToggleImage"
      ExpandedImage="~/images/collapse.jpg"
      ExpandedText="Collapse"
      CollapsedImage="~/images/expand.jpg"
      CollapsedText="Expand" />
```

The *ImageControlID* indicates the *Image* control, if any, that if clicked causes the panel to expand or collapse. The *ExpandedImage* and *CollapsedImage* properties set the URL of the images to use to expand and collapse. Likewise, *CollapsedText* and *ExpandedText* set the Tool-Tip text for the image. *Collapsed* sets the state of the panel, whereas *ExpandDirection* indicates whether the panel expands horizontally or vertically. Figure 5-8 provides a view of the control in action.

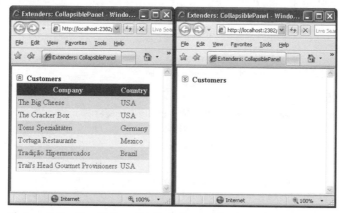

Figure 5-8   The *CollapsiblePanel* extender in action

The following code demonstrates a typical pair of *Panel* controls used with the extender:

```
<asp:Panel ID="CollapsibleCustomersPanel" runat="server">
    <asp:Image ID="ToggleImage" runat="server"
               ImageUrl="~/images/collapse.jpg" />
    <b>Customers</b>
</asp:Panel>
<asp:Panel ID="CollapsibleCustomersPanelContent" runat="server"
    Height="0" CssClass="collapsePanel">
    ...
</asp:Panel>
```

Unlike draggable panels, the header and content panels are distinct and are typically placed one after the next in the page layout. The extender panel is also *postback aware*, meaning that, on a client postback, it automatically records and restores its collapsed/expanded client state.

> **Note**   To avoid the initial flickering when a collapsible panel is displayed, make sure you properly style the panel that is going to be collapsed and expanded. This panel needs to have *Height=0* and the CSS *overflow* style set to *hidden*.

The *DragPanel* Extender

The *DragPanel* extender is one of the simplest extenders in the ACT. It has only two properties—one to indicate the panel to drag, and one to indicate the panel to use as the drag handle:

```
<act:DragPanelExtender ID="DragPanelExtender1" runat="server"
        TargetControlID="CustomerPanel"
        DragHandleID="CustomersDragHandle" />
```

As the name suggests, the *TargetControlID* property refers to the ID of the panel control in the page that is going to be moved. The *DragHandleID*, on the other hand, indicates the ID of the panel control that is used as the handle of the drag. In other words, to drag the target panel users drag and drop the handle panel. Although functionally distinct, the two panels are, in effect, logically correlated and rendered through nested tags:

```
<asp:Panel ID="CustomersPanel" runat="server" >
    <asp:Panel ID="CustomersDragHandle" runat="server">
        <div style="background-color:yellow">Customers</div>
    </asp:Panel>
    <asp:Panel runat="server">
        <asp:gridview runat="server" DataSourceID="ObjectDataSource1">
            <Columns>
                ...
            </Columns>
        </asp:gridview>
        <asp:ObjectDataSource ID="ObjectDataSource2" runat="server"
            TypeName="IntroAjax.CustomerManager"
            SelectMethod="LoadAll">
        </asp:ObjectDataSource>
    </asp:Panel>
</asp:Panel>
```

The target panel usually contains as a child the drag handle panel. In this way, you obtain the effect of moving the whole panel as if it were a Microsoft Windows window. (See Figure 5-9.)

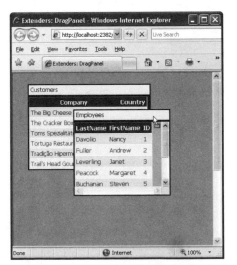

Figure 5-9 The *DragPanel* extender in action

The *DropDown* Extender

The *DropDown* extender can be attached to virtually any ASP.NET control. Once attached to a control, the extender provides a mouse-over link to open a drop-down panel. The contents of the panel are entirely up to you—typically, arranged as a menu. The drop-down is activated by clicking the extended control with any mouse buttons.

```
<asp:Label ID="Label1" runat="server" Text="Move the mouse here" />
<asp:Panel ID="Panel1" runat="server" CssClass="ContextMenuPanel"
    Style="display:none;visibility:hidden;">
    <asp:LinkButton runat="server" ID="Option1" Text="I'm the first"
        CssClass="ContextMenuItem" OnClick="LinkButton1_Click" />
    <asp:LinkButton runat="server" ID="Option2" Text="I'm the second"
        CssClass="ContextMenuItem" OnClick="LinkButton1_Click" />
    <asp:LinkButton runat="server" ID="Option3" Text="I'm the third"
        CssClass="ContextMenuItem" OnClick="LinkButton1_Click" />
</asp:Panel>

<act:DropDownExtender runat="server" ID="DropDownExtender1"
    TargetControlID="Label1" DropDownControlID="Panel1" />
```

In the sample just shown, the drop-down user interface is a *Panel* that contains a list of link buttons. Link buttons are styled to look like menu items. Link and push buttons, and indeed embedded controls in general, operate normally. (See Figure 5-10.)

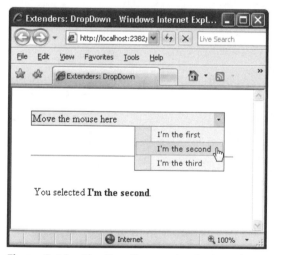

Figure 5-10   The *DropDown* extender in action

Button Extenders

Buttons are by far one of the most common elements in ASP.NET pages. However, as pages become functionally richer, additional features are required for buttons to stay in sync with users' expectations. ASP.NET AJAX provides a few extenders that apply to submit buttons and to the pseudo-buttons that form a *CheckBox* element.

The *ConfirmButton* Extender

Many times, a safe approach to responding to a user clicking a button is to ask the user for a confirmation for the operation she's going to start. A common solution for implementing this behavior entails that the ASP.NET page attach some script code to the button to pop up a JavaScript message box with a confirmation message. The *ConfirmButton* extender greatly simplifies this common task by making it declarative:

```
<asp:Button runat="server" ID="Button1" Text="Click me" />

<act:ConfirmButtonExtender ID="ConfirmButtonExtender1" runat="server"
      TargetControlID="Button1"
      ConfirmText="Are you sure you want to click this?\nReally sure?" />
```

The *ConfirmText* property specifies the text of the message box being displayed as the user clicks the button. Note that HTML entities can be used in the text, but by design no HTML formatting, such as *<b>* or *<i>*, can be used. You can, however, use entitized special characters. For example, you can use *
* to break the line and continue the text on the next line. The reason for this lies in the JavaScript code for the *ConfirmButton*—it's using JavaScript's *window.confirm*. Providing HTML formatting makes no sense because the confirmation dialog box is basically a non-HTML Windows *MessageBox* call.

Internally, the *ConfirmButton* extender sets a handler for the *onsubmit* event of the form and swallows the event if the user doesn't confirm the operation. Only controls that implement the *IButtonControl* interface can be used with the extender, including *LinkButton* and *ImageButton* controls. (See Figure 5-11.)

Figure 5-11   The *ConfirmButton* extender in action

The *MutuallyExclusiveCheckBox* Extender

The *MutuallyExclusiveCheckBox* extender can be attached to any ASP.NET *CheckBox* control to make it part of a group of logically related options. The extender implements a behavior that looks a lot like a list of radio buttons—multiple options are available but only one can be chosen. So what's the point of having a mutually exclusive set of check boxes rather than a radio button list?

A list of radio buttons can be initially unselected, but once one option has been selected there's no way for the user to return to the initial state of having all options unselected. Returning to the original, completely unselected state is possible with the *MutuallyExclusiveCheckBox* extender.

The idea is that you group a number of check boxes under the same key. The extender then ensures that only one check box with the specified key can be selected at a time:

```
<h2>What Kind of Experience Do You Have with ASP.NET?</h2>
<asp:CheckBox runat="server" ID="chkBeginner" Text="Beginner" />
<asp:CheckBox runat="server" ID="chkIntermediate" Text="Intermediate" />
<asp:CheckBox runat="server" ID="chkExpert" Text="Expert" />

<act:MutuallyExclusiveCheckBoxExtender runat="server" ID="Mutual1"
    TargetControlID="chkBeginner"
    Key="AspNetExpertise" />
<act:MutuallyExclusiveCheckBoxExtender runat="server" ID="Mutual2"
    TargetControlID="chkIntermediate"
    Key="AspNetExpertise" />
<act:MutuallyExclusiveCheckBoxExtender runat="server" ID="Mutual3"
    TargetControlID="chkExpert"
    Key="AspNetExpertise" />
```

It can be argued that the same functionality could have been applied to radio buttons instead of check boxes. Using check boxes was the choice of developers, and it also provides a more consistent and expected user interface. However, you can re-implement the behavior to use JavaScript to allow the deselection of a radio button item.

The *ToggleButton* Extender

Check boxes are graphical HTML elements visually represented by a pair of little bitmaps (selected and unselected) plus companion text. Each browser can use its own pair of bitmaps, thus resulting in the check boxes having a slightly different look and feel. Most browsers, though, tend to represent check-box buttons as square embossed buttons.

The *ToggleButton* extender provides a way to simulate a check-box element that uses custom bitmaps. The extender is applied to a *CheckBox* control, and it replaces the control with a completely new markup block that uses custom images and provides the same behavior as a standard check box:

```
<act:ToggleButtonExtender ID="ToggleButtonExtender1" runat="server"
        TargetControlID="CheckBox1"
        ImageWidth="19"
        ImageHeight="19"
        UncheckedImageUrl="DontLike.gif"
        CheckedImageUrl="Like.gif" />
```

ImageWidth and *ImageHeight* properties indicate the desired size of the images. Note that these attributes are required. *UncheckedImageUrl* and *CheckedImageUrl* specify the images to use when the check box is selected or not selected.

Pop-up Extenders

Virtually every Web developer has a sort of love/hate relationship with pop-up windows. As a matter of fact, pop-up windows often greatly simplify a number of tasks—especially modal dialog boxes. One of the nasty things about HTML pop-up windows is that they are browser windows and require a page to navigate. The pop-up extenders that ASP.NET AJAX Extensions has to offer, on the other hand, do not require a new browser instance. Instead, they are limited to popping up the content of any panel you indicate, with or without modality.

The *HoverMenu* Extender

The *HoverMenu* extender is similar to the *PopupControl* extender and can be associated with any ASP.NET control. Both extenders display a pop-up panel to display additional content, but they do it for different events. The *HoverMenu*, in particular, pops up its panel when the user moves the mouse cursor over the target control. The panel can be displayed at a position specified by the developer. It can be at the left, right, top, or bottom of the target control. In addition, the control can be given an optional CSS style so that it looks like it is in a highlighted state. (See Figure 5-12.)

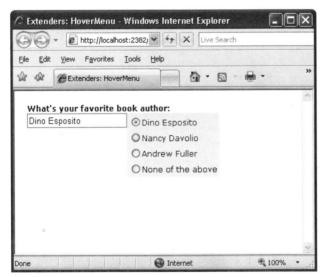

Figure 5-12   The *HoverMenu* extender in action

The *HoverMenu* extender is good for implementing an auto-display context menu for virtually every ASP.NET control instance and for providing tips to fill in some input fields. In Figure 5-12, for example, when the user hovers the cursor over the text box, a list of suggestions appears to simplify the work.

```
<asp:TextBox ID="TextBox1" runat="server" />

<asp:Panel ID="Panel1" runat="server" CssClass="popupMenu">
    <asp:RadioButtonList ID="RadioButtonList1" runat="server"
        AutoPostBack="true"
        OnSelectedIndexChanged="RadioButtonList1_SelectedIndexChanged">
        <asp:ListItem Text="Dino Esposito"></asp:ListItem>
        <asp:ListItem Text="Nancy Davolio"></asp:ListItem>
        <asp:ListItem Text="Andrew Fuller"></asp:ListItem>
        <asp:ListItem Value="" Text="None of the above"></asp:ListItem>
    </asp:RadioButtonList>
</asp:Panel>

<act:HoverMenuExtender ID="HoverMenu1" runat="server"
    TargetControlID="TextBox1"
    HoverCssClass="hoverPopupMenu"
    PopupControlID="Panel1"
    PopupPosition="Right" />
```

The *Panel1* control defines a list of radio buttons, each containing a suggestion for filling the text box. The *HoverMenu* extender targets the text box control and defines *Panel1* as its dynamic pop-up panel. The *PopupPosition* property indicates the position of the panel with respect to the target control. Likewise, other properties not shown in the previous example code, such as *OffsetX* and *OffsetY*, define the desired offset of the panel. The *PopDelay* sets the time (in milliseconds) to pass between the mouse movement and the display of the panel. The *HoverCssClass* can optionally be used to give the text box a different style when the hover menu is on. It is interesting to look at the CSS class associated with the panel:

```
.popupMenu
{
    position:absolute;
    visibility:hidden;
    background-color:#F5F7F8;
}
.hoverPopupMenu
{
    background-color:yellow;
}
```

It is key that the *visibility* attribute of the panel is set to *hidden* just as with *CollapsiblePanel* control; otherwise, the panel will display upon page loading and hidden immediately afterwards.

Just as for the *PopupControl* extender, to take full advantage of the *HoverMenu* extender you need to place extended controls inside of an *UpdatePanel* control. In this way, whenever the user clicks a radio button, the panel posts back asynchronously and fires the *SelectedIndexChanged* event on the server.

```
void RadioButtonList1_SelectedIndexChanged(object sender, EventArgs e)
{
    TextBox1.Text = RadioButtonList1.SelectedValue;
}
```

The server-side event handler will then just update the text in the text box., as shown in Figure 5-12.

The *ModalPopup* Extender

The *ModalPopup* extender displays in a modal way any content associated with the control identified by the *PopupControlID* property. The *TargetControlID* property in this case refers to a clickable control:

```
<act:ModalPopupExtender ID="ModalPopupExtender1" runat="server"
        TargetControlID="LinkButton1"
        PopupControlID="PopupContent"
        OkControlID="Button1"
        CancelControlID="Button2">
```

Notice that the *ModalPopup* extender is fired by the *onclick* event on the target control. It turns out, therefore, that the target control can only be a control that supports clicking. The pop-up control doesn't have to be a *Panel* control; generally, it can be any control. However, it will normally be a control that contains a bunch of other controls—typically, a *Panel*.

In the pop-up panel you can optionally identify an *OK* control and a *Cancel* control. You set the ID of such controls (commonly, buttons) through the *OkControlID* and *CancelControlID* properties. The pop-up behavior is clearly a client-side action, so some JavaScript code might be required in response to the user's clicking the *OK* or *Cancel* control. You use the *OnOkScript* property to specify the JavaScript function to run in case the user clicks the OK button; you use *OnCancelScript* otherwise.

The following markup shows the content of a sample modal panel. Note that the *Panel* control should set its CSS *display* attribute to *none* to make any contents invisible at first.

```
<asp:LinkButton ID="LinkButton1" runat="server" text="Click me" />
<asp:Panel runat="server" ID="PopupContent" BackColor="Yellow">
        <div style="margin:10px">
        Take note of this message and tell us if you strongly agree.
        <br /><br />
        <asp:Button ID="Button1" runat="server" Text="Yes" width="40px"  />
        <asp:Button ID="Button2" runat="server" Text="No"  width="40px" />
        </div>
</asp:Panel>
```

Figure 5-13 shows the modal dialog box in action.

A couple of graphical properties—*DropShadow* and *BackgroundCssClass*—complete the extender. A Boolean property, *DropShadow* indicates whether a drop shadow—as shown in Figure 5-13—should be rendered. *BackgroundCssClass*, on the other hand, determines the style that is temporarily applied to the underlying page:

Figure 5-13   The *ModalPopup* extender in action

```
modalBackground {
    background-color:Gray;
    filter:alpha(opacity=70);
    opacity:0.7;
}
```

The preceding style grays out the page and makes it partially opaque for a nicer effect.

The *PopupControl* Extender

The *PopupControl* extender can be attached to any HTML element that fires the *onclick*, *onfocus*, or *onkeydown* events. The ultimate goal of the extender is to display a pop-up window that shows additional content, such as a calendar on a text box in which the user is expected to enter a date. The contents of the pop-up panel are expressed through a *Panel* control, and they can contain ASP.NET server controls as well as static text and HTML elements:

```
<asp:textbox runat="server" ID="InvoiceDateTextBox" />
<asp:panel runat="server" ID="Panel1">
    ...
</asp:panel>

<act:PopupControlExtender ID="PopupExtender1" runat="server"
        TargetControlID="InvoiceDateTextBox"
        PopupControlID="Panel1"
        Position="Bottom" />
```

The *TargetControlID* property points to the control that triggers the popup, whereas *PopupControlID* indicates the panel to display. The *Position* property sets the position of the panel—either at the top, left, right, or bottom of the parent control. (See Figure 5-14.)

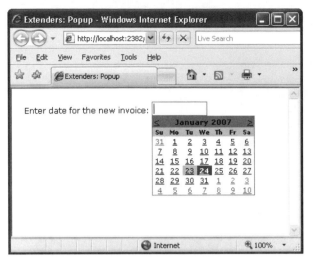

Figure 5-14   The *PopupControl* extender in action

Additional properties are *OffsetX* and *OffsetY*, which indicate the number of pixels to offset the popup from its position, as well as *CommitProperty* and *CommitScript*, which can be used to assign values to the target control.

The pop-up window will probably contain some interactive controls and post back. For this reason, you might want to insert it within an *UpdatePanel* control so that it can perform server-side tasks without refreshing the whole page. Typically, the popup will be dismissed after a postback—for example, the popup shown in Figure 5-14 is configured to be dismissed after the user has selected a date. The calendar in this case fires the *SelectionChanged* event on the server:

```
protected void Calendar1_SelectionChanged(object sender, EventArgs e)
{
    PopupExtender1.Commit(
          Calendar1.SelectedDate.ToShortDateString());
}
```

The *Commit* method sets the default property of the associated control to the specified value. If you want to control which (nondefault) property is set on the target when the popup is dismissed, use the *CommitProperty* property. Likewise, you use the *CommitScript* property to indicate the Javascript function to execute on the client after setting the result of the popup.

Warning   Note that an extender can't be placed in a different *UpdatePanel* than the control it extends. If the extended control is incorporated in an *UpdatePanel*, the extender should also be placed in the updatable panel. If you miss this, you get a runtime exception.

User-Interface Extenders

In the family of ASP.NET AJAX extenders, the biggest group is user-interface extenders—that is, special components that help in the implementation of rich and user-friendly features.

The *AlwaysVisibleControl* Extender

The *AlwaysVisibleControl* extender allows you to pin a given control, or panel of controls, to one of the page corners so that it appears to float over the background body as the page is scrolled or resized. You can use the extender with virtually any ASP.NET control.

```
<span style="background-color:yellow;" runat="server" id="Msg">
    Need a bit of dummy text? Look at
    <b>http://www.loremipsum.net</b></span>

<act:AlwaysVisibleControlExtender ID="av1" runat="server"
    TargetControlID="Msg"
    HorizontalSide="Left"
    VerticalSide="Top" />
```

You set the target position for the bound control using the *HorizontalSide* and *VerticalSide* properties to define the corner of the page where the content should be docked. The *HorizontalSide* property accepts *Left* and *Right* as values, whereas *Top* and *Bottom* are feasible values for the *VerticalSide* property. You can also control the offset from each border using the *VerticalOffset* and *HorizontalOffset* properties. Finally, *ScrollEffectDuration* indicates how many seconds the scrolling effect will last when the target control is repositioned. (See Figure 5-15.)

Figure 5-15   The *AlwaysVisible* extender in action

Note that you can't add the extender to a plain HTML element. If you have an HTML block to keep always visible (for example, the *<span>* tag in the previous example), add the *runat=server* attribute and give it a unique ID.

The *CascadingDropDown* Extender

The *CascadingDropDown* extender can be attached to a *DropDownList* control to automatically populate it based on the current selection of one or more parent *DropDownList* controls.

The *CascadingDropDown* extender is designed to fit in a relatively common scenario in which the contents of one drop-down list depend on the selection of another list. With this arrangement, you don't need to transfer to the client the entire data set from which a child list can select a subset of items to display in accordance with the selection on its parent. For example, suppose you want the user to select a country and a city in that country. To minimize data transfer and provide a friendlier user interface, you might want to keep the city list empty until a selection is made on the country list. When a country is selected, you get back to the server to download the list of cities available for that country. The *CascadingDropDown* extender simplifies this scenario by injecting some glue code into the client page and also making some assumptions on the structure of your page code.

All the logic about the contents of the set of *DropDownList* controls is expected to reside on a Web service. The Web service, in turn, can use any suitable method for storing and looking up any relevant data. The Web service, though, is somewhat forced to use a contracted schema. In particular, it needs to have a method with the following signature:

```
[WebMethod]
public CascadingDropDownNameValue[] GetDropDownContents(
    string knownCategoryValues, string category)
{
    ...
}
```

The name of the method can vary, of course. The *CascadingDropDownNameValue* type is an internal collection type that is designed to contain the name/value items to show in the drop-down list. Each drop-down list bound to the extender belongs to a category:

```
<act:CascadingDropDown ID="CascadingDropDown1" runat="server"
    TargetControlID="DropDownList1"
    Category="Country"
    PromptText="Please select a country"
    ServiceMethod="GetDropDownContentsPageMethod" />
<act:CascadingDropDown ID="CascadingDropDown2" runat="server"
    TargetControlID="DropDownList2"
    Category="City"
    PromptText="Please select a city"
    LoadingText="Please, wait ..."
    ServicePath="CityFinderService.asmx"
```

```
                ServiceMethod="GetDropDownContents"
                ParentControlID="DropDownList1" />
```

The content of the *Category* property is any name that helps the Web service method to understand what kind of data should be retrieved and the meaning of the input arguments. The *PromptText* property sets any text that you want to display in the drop-down list when no selection is currently made and the control is typically disabled. The *LoadingText* property indicates any text that has to be displayed while the drop-down list is being populated. The *ServiceMethod* property indicates the method to call to fill in the list control. If no *ServicePath* is specified, the method is assumed to be a page method. Finally, *ParentControlID* creates a hierarchy and designates a list to be the child of another list.

Each time the selection changes in a parent *DropDownList* control, the extender makes a call to the Web service and retrieves the list of values for the next *DropDownList* in the hierarchy. If no selection is currently made, the extender automatically disables the control. (See Figure 5-16.)

Figure 5-16   The *CascadingDropDown* extender in action on two drop-down lists

The *DropShadow* Extender

The *DropShadow* extender is designed to add a drop shadow to panel controls to make them look more professional. You can also set the opacity and width of the shadow:

```
<asp:Panel runat="server" ID="Panel1">
    <div style="padding:8px">
        <asp:TextBox ID="TextBox1" runat="server" />
    </div>
</asp:Panel>

<act:DropShadowExtender ID="DropShadowExtender1" runat="server"
    TargetControlID="Panel1" Opacity=".65" Width="5" Rounded="true" />
```

The *TargetControlID* property sets the control that will be rendered with a drop shadow. This control should generally be a *Panel*; however, as long as you don't set rounded corners, it can also be any other ASP.NET control, such as a *TextBox*. You control the opacity of the shadow through the *Opacity* property. Values for the property range from *0.0* to *1.0*, where *0* (or *0.0*) means total transparency. Hence, the closer the value is to *1* (or *1.0*) the darker the shadow will be.

The *Rounded* Boolean property indicates whether the surrounding panel and the shadow should have rounded corners. The default is *false*. Figure 5-17 shows the extender in action.

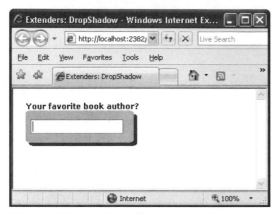

Figure 5-17   The *DropShadow* extender in action

The *DynamicPopulate* Extender

The *DynamicPopulate* extender is a sort of binder component that replaces the markup of a given control with the markup returned by a Web service method call. The extender can be seen as a shrink-wrapped and simplified version of the *UpdatePanel* control that we discussed in Chapter 4. It captures a client event and fires a remote call. The returned string is inserted in the page DOM as the child of the target element. Here's an example:

```
<input type="button" id="Button1" runat="server" value="Refresh ..." />
<hr />
<b>Last updated: </b>
<asp:Panel runat="server" ID="Msg" Style="padding:2px;height:2em;" />

<act:DynamicPopulateExtender ID="DynamicPopulateExtender1" runat="server"
    TargetControlID="Msg"
    ClearContentsDuringUpdate="true"
    PopulateTriggerControlID="Button1"
    ServiceMethod="GetTimeOnServer"
    UpdatingCssClass="updating" />
```

When the user clicks on the specified item—in this case, the button named *Button1*—the extender starts working. It invokes the method *GetTimeOnServer* and replaces the subtree rooted in the *Msg* control with its output. The method *GetTimeOnServer* is a Web service method. You specify the URL to the service using the *ServicePath* property. If this property is not set, the method is assumed to be a page method defined either in the code file of the page or inline through a server *<script>* tag:

```
[WebMethod]
public string GetTimeOnServer(string contextKey)
{
    // Use contextKey to receive data from the client
```

```
    // Get the output—it can be HTML markup
    return DateTime.UtcNow.ToString();
}
```

ClearContentsDuringUpdate is a Boolean property that clears the contents of the target control during the update. If you want to display a special style or a bitmap during the operation, you set a CSS style through the *UpdatingCssClass* property. When creating such a CSS class, bear in mind that you should ensure the target control has a minimum height. (It must be explicitly set on panels.) You use the *background-image* CSS attribute to set the image to display.

Note that you can use any HTML element to trigger the dynamic population of the target control. It doesn't have to be a button control; and it doesn't have to be a submit button such as *LinkButton* or *Button*. In this case, in fact, the page will post back and you'll lose the benefit of the ASP.NET AJAX platform.

> **Note**   You can also use a piece of JavaScript code to dynamically populate a given DOM element. In this case, you set the *CustomScript* property to the name of a JavaScript global function. Whether you use a custom script or a server method, you can use the *ContextKey* property of the extender to pass an arbitrary string to the code.

The *PagingBulletedList* Extender

Imagine a page that has to present a long list of items to users—say, a list of customers. A common solution entails using a pageable grid control. ASP.NET grids do a postback for each new page, but by wrapping the grid in an *UpdatePanel* control you can brilliantly fix the issue. What if you figure that a grid is far too heavy a control and that you need to list items using a bullet-list control?

The ASP.NET *BulletedList* control lists the contents of a data source using a variety of bullet-point user interfaces. It doesn't provide paging, though. The *PagingBulletedList* extender is a surprisingly simple and effective extender to page through the contents of a *BulletedList* control. Let's consider the following code that populates a bulleted list with no paging:

```
<asp:BulletedList ID="BulletedList1" runat="server" DisplayMode="Text"
    DataSourceID="ObjectDataSource1" DataTextField="CompanyName" />

<asp:ObjectDataSource ID="ObjectDataSource1" runat="server"
        TypeName="IntroAjax.CustomerManager"
        SelectMethod="LoadAll">
</asp:ObjectDataSource>
```

Such a page will generate more than 80 bullet-point items—one for each customer in the Northwind database. By extending the *BulletedList* control with the extender, you get output like that shown in Figure 5-18.

Figure 5-18   The *PagingBulletedList* extender in action

But then add the code for the extender:

```
<act:PagingBulletedListExtender ID="PagingBulletedList1" runat="server"
    TargetControlID="BulletedList1"
    ClientSort="true"
    IndexSize="2"
    Separator=" - "
    SelectIndexCssClass="selectIndex" />
```

The extender organizes all bound items in pages and displays links to each of them. Pages can contain a fixed number of items or all the items that match an initial string. The *IndexSize* property indicates how many letters in the displayed text should be used to create a page. If you set it to *1*, you will have a pure alphabetical menu. If you set it to *2*, you obtain a more granular view, as each page contains only the items whose name matches the two-letter initial. As an alternative to using *IndexSize*, you can use *MaxItemsPerPage*. In this case, each page (except perhaps the last one) will have exactly the specified number of items.

The *Separator* property indicates the character used to separate menu items. *SelectIndexCssClass* and *UnselectIndexCssClass* set the CSS classes for selected and unselected menu items. Finally, if *ClientSort* is set to *true*, items are alphabetically sorted on the client before display.

The *ResizableControl* Extender

Most users would welcome pages where they can dynamically resize certain HTML elements, such as panels of text or images. The *ResizableControl* extender attaches to an element of a Web page and provides a graphical handle for users to resize that element. Placed at the lower-right corner of the element, the handle lets the user resize the element as if it were a window. Let's consider the following markup:

```
<asp:Panel ID="Panel1" runat="server" Style="overflow:hidden"
        Width="130px" Height="65px">
    <asp:Image ID="Image1" runat="server" ImageUrl="~/images/ajax.gif"
            Style="width:100%; height:100%;" />
</asp:Panel>

<asp:Panel ID="Panel2" runat="server" Style="overflow:auto"
        Width="130px" height="100px">
    This text resizes itself to be as large as possible
    within its container.
</asp:Panel>
```

As you can see, the first panel contains an image; the second includes plain text. Some CSS attributes are necessary for the extender to work properly. In particular, you might want to set the overflow attribute to *hidden* for images and to *auto* for text. The *overflow* attribute controls the appearance of scrollbars when the contents of the element exceeds the reserved space. In the example, I stretch or shrink the image and scroll the text.

It is important to give panels an initial correct size. In particular, for images you should give the surrounding panel the same size of the image. Panels surrounding a block of text should be given an explicit size too.

```
<act:ResizableControlExtender ID="Resizable1" runat="server"
    TargetControlID="Panel1"
    ResizableCssClass="resizingStyle"
    HandleCssClass="handleStyle" />
<act:ResizableControlExtender ID="Resizable2" runat="server"
    TargetControlID="Panel2"
    ResizableCssClass="resizingStyle"
    HandleCssClass="handleStyle" />
```

The *ResizableControl* extender features two mandatory properties: *TargetControlID* and *HandleCssClass*. The former indicates the control to resize; the latter sets the name of the CSS class to apply to the resize handle. In addition, *ResizableCssClass* is the CSS class to apply to the element when resizing. You might want to use this class to change or thicken the color of the border to emphasize the operation. Here's a typical handle CSS class:

```
. handleStyle
{
    width:16px;
    height:16px;
    background-image:url(~/images/HandleGrip.gif);
    overflow:hidden;
    cursor:se-resize;
}
```

Figure 5-19 shows the extender in action.

Figure 5-19 The *ResizableControl* extender in action

The *ResizableControl* extender also features two client events (*onresizing* and *onresize*) that can trigger some JavaScript code to do more complex things, such as increasing the font size to fit a larger area. The extender allows you to define a minimum and maximum size for the elements being resized. Any changes resulting from control resizing are automatically persisted across postbacks.

The *RoundedCorners* Extender

The *RoundedCorners* extender is a subset of the *DropShadow* extender, as it is limited to rounding the corners of child panels:

```
<asp:Panel runat="server" ID="Panel1" BackColor="LightBlue" Width="170px">
    <div style="margin-left:2px">
        <asp:TextBox ID="TextBox1" runat="server"
                    BackColor="LightBlue"
                    BorderWidth="0px" />
    </div>
</asp:Panel>

<act:RoundedCornersExtender ID="RoundedCornerExtender1" runat="server"
    TargetControlID="Panel1" Radius="6" Color="LightBlue" />
```

The extender accepts arguments to set the target control and define the desired radius of the rounded corner and the color of the surrounding border. The rounded corner, in fact, is obtained by rendering an additional border all around the target control. By removing all borders around the text box and using the same background color for the panel and the text box, you can obtain the nice effect shown in Figure 5-20–a rounded text box control.

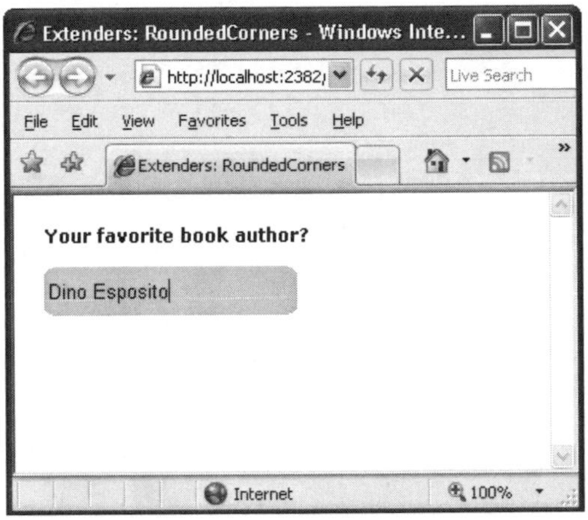

Figure 5-20   The *RoundedCorners* extender in action

Input Extenders

Web pages still rely on the facilities built into the HTML markup language to let users enter data into forms and input fields. But HTML input elements are sometimes too limited and simple for today's applications and users. For this reason, the plain old *<input type="text">* element, and its *TextBox* ASP.NET counterpart, need some extra features. The ACT supplies a couple of extenders that transform the classic input field into a more interactive and user-friendly text box.

The *AutoComplete* Extender

Typing data into a text box might be boring at times, and even more so when you type the same chunk of text over and over again. For this reason, Web browsers began supporting auto-completion features a while ago. A Web browser's auto-completion feature consists of the code's ability to track any URL that the user ever types in. In this way, the browser can quickly prompt you with a suggestion when you're typing a possibly long and hard-to-remember URL.

Auto-completion is also a feature that some browsers, such as Internet Explorer 5 and newer versions, support for any custom text box you use in HTML forms. The browser saves on the local machine any data ever typed into an input field with a given name, and it makes that information available to all pages in the site that feature an HTML element with the same name. The feature is integrated with the browser and is transparent to users and developers. The list of suggestions builds up incrementally and is entirely beyond the control of page authors.

The *AutoComplete* extender extends the auto-completion to any ASP.NET *TextBox* control; more importantly, it gives page authors the means to define programmatically the list of suggestions (as retrieved via a Web Service).

```
<asp:TextBox ID="CustomerName" runat="server" />

<act:AutoCompleteExtender runat="server" ID="AutoCompleteExtender1"
    TargetControlID="CustomerName"
    Enabled="true"
    MinimumPrefixLength="1"
    ServicePath="Suggestions.asmx"
    ServiceMethod="GetSuggestions" />
```

In the code snippet, the text box is auto-completed using the data returned by the *Get-Suggestions* method of the specified Web service. The *ServicePath* and *ServiceMethod* extender properties identify the service to provide auto-completion data; the *MinimumPrefixLength* property sets how many characters the user has to type to trigger the auto-completion feature. In the preceding code, auto-completion begins with the first typed character.

> **Note**   The Web service has to be a local Web service that is installed on the same server machine and application as the page that is using it. Note that this consideration holds true for all Web services used by ASP.NET AJAX extenders.

The Web service method you use to provide suggestions must have a known signature:

```
[WebMethod]
public string[] GetSuggestions(string prefixText, int count)
{
    ...
}
```

The *prefixText* argument indicates the text the user has typed so far; the *count* argument sets the desired number of suggestions. The result is displayed in a drop-down panel underneath the text box. The user can use either the mouse or the keyboard to select one of the suggested items. The following code shows a Web service method that returns a subset of customer names that match the provided prefix. (See Figure 5-21.)

```
public class SuggestionService : System.Web.Services.WebService
{
    [WebMethod]
    public string[] GetSuggestions(string prefixText, int count)
    {
        int i=0;
        DataView data = GetData();
        data = FilterData(data, prefixText);
        string [] suggestions = new string[data.Count];

        foreach (DataRowView row in data)
            suggestions[i++] = row["companyname"].ToString();

        return suggestions;
    }

    private DataView GetData()
```

```
    {
        DataView view = (DataView)HttpContext.Current.Cache["Suggestions"];
        if (view == null)
        {
            SqlDataAdapter adapter = new SqlDataAdapter(
                "SELECT * FROM customers", "...");
            DataTable table = new DataTable();
            adapter.Fill(table);
            view = table.DefaultView;

            // Store the entire data set to the ASP.NET Cache for
            // further reuse
            HttpContext.Current.Cache["Suggestions"] = view;
        }

        return view;
    }

    private DataView FilterData(DataView view, string prefix)
    {
        // Filter out undesired strings
        view.RowFilter = String.Format("companyname LIKE '{0}%'", prefix);
        return view;
    }
}
```

Figure 5-21   The *AutoComplete* extender in action

The *Calendar* Extender

Plenty of input forms require users to specify a date. As an ASP.NET developer, you know how frustrating it can be for a user to cope with separators, formats, cultures, and all sorts of things that affect the representation of a date. The most natural way of choosing a date in an input form is through a calendar; and ASP.NET 2.0 does indeed provide such a control. The original

ASP.NET 2.0 *Calendar* control requires full-page postbacks, although you can find a number of good workarounds for it—from wrapping it up in an updatable panel to using the hover-menu extender we considered earlier.

The *Calendar* extender is the ultimate and, I believe, definitive solution. Attached to a text box, it provides client-side date-picking functionality with customizable date format and pop-up control. You can interact with the calendar by clicking on a day, navigating to a month, or selecting a particular link to set the current date. (See Figure 5-22.)

Figure 5-22   The *Calendar* extender in action

```
<asp:TextBox runat="server" ID="TextBox1" />

<act:CalendarExtender runat="server" ID="CalendarExtender1"
    TargetControlID="TextBox1"
    CssClass="MyCalendar"
    Format="dd/MM/yyyy" />
```

By clicking on the title of the calendar, you can change the view from days-per-month to months-per-year, and even years-per-decade. The *Format* property allows you to select the final format of the date, which will be inserted in the bound text box. Normally, the calendar pops up when the companion text box gets the input focus. However, you can associate the display of the calendar with the clicking of an element—for example, an image. The *PopupButtonID* property gets and sets the ID of a control to show the calendar popup when clicked.

The *FilteredTextBox* Extender

The *FilteredTextBox* extender filters out some characters from the buffer of a given text box control. It differs from a validation control in that it just prevents users from entering invalid characters, whereas a validation control operates at a later time when the user tabs out of the input field.

```
<strong>How old are you?</strong>
<asp:TextBox ID="TextBox1" runat="server" />

<act:FilteredTextBoxExtender ID="Filtered1" runat="server"
    TargetControlID="TextBox1"
    FilterType="Numbers" />
```

The preceding text box is expected to accept a number indicating the age of the user. Clearly, it can accept only numbers. The extender ensures that only numbers can be typed in the input field. It does that by adding a piece of JavaScript code to the text box to filter out undesired characters.

The extender supports a few properties, including *FilterType*, which determine the filter applied to the input. The property can take any of the following values: *Numbers*, *UppercaseLetters*, *LowercaseLetters*, and *Custom*. The effect of the filter is obvious for the first three cases. When *Custom* is specified, though, you also set the *ValidChars* property to a comma-separated string where each item denotes a valid character. For example, the following code allows users to enter only A and B characters regardless of the case:

```
<act:FilteredTextBoxExtender ID="Filtered1" runat="server"
    TargetControlID="TextBox1"
    FilterType="Custom"
    ValidChars="A,a,B,b" />
```

You can't combine multiple filters on the same text box. If you want to filter all but letters, you can't add two *FilteredTextBox* extenders to the same control. Instead, you resort to a custom filter where you specify in the *ValidChars* property all acceptable characters.

> **Important**   Client-side filtering, as well as validation, is subject to the action of some Java-Script code. This means that by deactivating JavaScript on the client browser, any filtering or validation is subsequently disabled. In any case, you should not blindly trust what's typed by a user in a text box and, instead, apply proper filtering and validation on the server before you use that data for critical operations.

The *MaskedEdit* Extender

Added to a *TextBox* control, the *MaskedEdit* extender forces users to enter input according to the specified mask. In addition, data is validated on the client according to the data type chosen. To achieve the validation, a new validator control is introduced—*MaskedEditValidator*—that verifies the input. The masked edit validator is, in turn, associated with an instance of the masked edit extender:

```
<asp:TextBox runat="server" ID="TextBox1" />

<act:MaskedEditValidator ID="MaskedEditValidator1" runat="server"
    ControlExtender="MaskedEditExtender1"
    ControlToValidate="TextBox1"
    IsValidEmpty="False"
```

```
    EmptyValueMessage="Date is required"
    InvalidValueMessage="Date is invalid"
    TooltipMessage="Input a Date" />
<act:MaskedEditExtender runat="server" ID="MaskedEditExtender1"
    TargetControlID="TextBox1"
    Mask="99/99/9999"
    MessageValidatorTip="true"
    OnFocusCssClass="MaskedEditFocus"
    OnInvalidCssClass="MaskedEditError"
    MaskType="Date" />
```

Figure 5-23 shows the extender at work with date and monetary values.

Figure 5-23   The *MaskedEdit* extender in action

The extender supports three different masks for most common and specialized types: date, number, and time. The *MaskType* property sets the type of the final data; the *Mask* property defines the required input mask.

The *NoBot* Extender

Web applications such as blogs, forums, and portals are subject to having their input forms automatically filled by robot applications (also known as *bots*). For example, a bot can register as a user of the mail service and use the portal to send spam. The techniques employed to ensure that humans are filling an input form instead of a piece of smart software go under the name of CAPTCHA, an acronym for *Completely Automated Public Turing test to tell Computers and Humans Apart*. In practice, CAPTCHA is a challenge-response test that requires the provision of additional information that must be figured out on the fly. Figuring this out is nothing special for humans, but virtually impossible for automated programs. The most popular example of CAPTCHA technique is a distorted image that represents a number. In a variety of blog systems, users encounter an additional input field to specify a number depicted within a figure before their posts will be accepted.

The *NoBot* extender is a control that attempts to apply anti-bot techniques to input forms. The extender might not be as powerful as a distorted image with a number inside, but it has the advantage of being completely invisible and hard to detect. All in all, the *NoBot* extender's usefulness is probably limited to sites with low traffic where the main goal is stopping spam, and where it's not a big deal if it doesn't achieve 100-percent effectiveness.

The *NumericUpDown* Extender

Added to a *TextBox* control, the *NumericUpDown* extender adds a couple of arrow buttons next to the control to let users increment and decrement the displayed value. Note that increment and decrement apply to numeric input as well as any user-defined enumeration.

```
<strong>How old are you?</strong>
<asp:TextBox ID="TextBox1" runat="server" Width="100px" />

<act:NumericUpDownExtender ID="UpDown1" runat="server"
    Width="100"
    TargetControlID="TextBox1" />
```

You should set the *Width* property on both the text box and the extender to control the size of the input field. Note that the *Width* property on the extender indicates the total width of the control including the arrow buttons. (See Figure 5-24.)

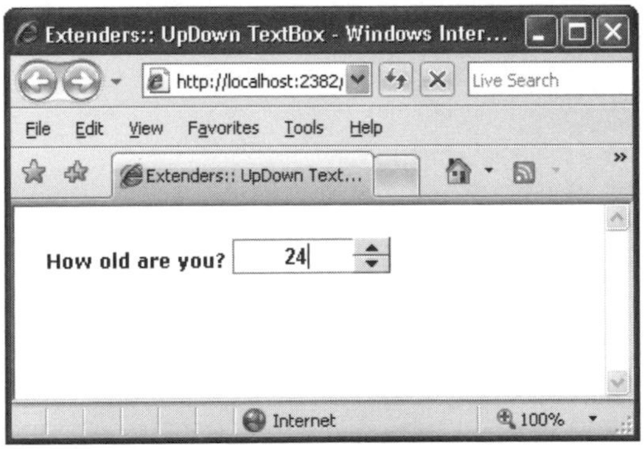

Figure 5-24   The *NumericUpDown* extender in action

The default increment is a numeric +1 or -1. However, the *RefValues* property lets you define a sequence of values to cycle through. The property accepts a string where each value is separated by a semicolon (;) symbol.

```
<act:NumericUpDownExtender ID="UpDown1" runat="server"
    Width="100"
    RefValues="Sun;Mon;Tue;Wed;Thu;Fri;Sat"
    TargetControlID="TextBox1"  />
```

The extender can also use a Web service to calculate the next or the previous value. In this case, you use *ServiceUpPath* and *ServiceUpMethod* to locate the service and method for the *up* operation. Likewise, you use *ServiceDownPath* and *ServiceDownMethod* for the *down* operation. The service methods can receive an arbitrary value from the client through the *Tag* property.

> **Note**   The sole use of the up-down extender is usually not enough to guarantee a pleasant experience. The up-down extender, in fact, doesn't force the text box to accept "only" the values generated by the up-down process. So you could type words in a numeric text box with an associated up-down extender. To avoid that, you might want to combine the up-down extender with a filter extender and use the *TextBox*'s *MaxLength* property to set the maximum number of characters.

The *PasswordStrength* Extender

Even the most secure system can't do much to protect your server if authorized users employ weak and easy-to-guess passwords. A number of best practices have been developed lately that characterize a strong password. The *PasswordStrength* extender attaches to a *TextBox* control and measures the strength of the current text if it's being used as a password.

From a syntax point of view, the extender can be attached to any *TextBox* control; from a semantic perspective instead, it makes sense only if applied to a *TextBox* control that is used for the entry of a password. The scenario in which the *PasswordStrength* extender proves useful is not a login page where the user enters his password to access a given functionality. Rather, it is helpful in forms where users registers their credentials to access a system feature.

```
<h2>Choose your password</h2>
<asp:TextBox ID="TextBox1" runat="server" />
<act:PasswordStrength runat="server" TargetControlID="TextBox1" />
```

The extender validates the current text against a set of requirements set by the page author. The result of the validation process is output through either a text message or a bar indicator to let users know about the level of complexity of the chosen password. With all default settings, the extender works as shown in Figure 5-25.

The feedback is displayed as plain text and dynamically as the user types in the buffer. The properties of the extender can be divided into two groups: appearance and behavior.

Appearance properties include *DisplayPosition* to set the position of the feedback text (above, below, left side, or right side), and *StrengthIndicatorType* to choose the type of visual feedback. It can be *Text* or *BarIndicator*. When the indicator type is *Text*, the *PrefixText* property sets some text to use in the composition of the feedback message. The *TextCssClass* defines the CSS class to style the feedback message.

Figure 5-25   The *PasswordStrength* extender in action

When the indicator type is *BarIndicator*, the feedback appears as a gauge bar in a framed area. *BarBorderCssClass* and *BarIndicatorCssClass* properties let you style the bar.

The following properties allow you to set the password requirements to check: *RequiresUpperAndLowerCaseCharacters*, *PreferredPasswordLength*, *MinimumNumericCharacters*, and *MinimumSymbolCharacters*. By default, the password length is set to *10* and no other check is enabled on the contents.

The extender ranks the password text based on the requirements set. The score is rendered as a gauge bar or through a text message, as you saw in Figure 5-25. Text messages can be customized by assigning a list of semicolon-separated descriptions to the *TextStrengthDescriptions* property. You can specify a minimum of *2* and a maximum of *10* strings ordered from the weakest to the strongest.

The feedback you get from the extender is split in two parts: score and status message. The score is used to update the indicator or display a strength description. The status message is a help message displayed on a companion control identified by the *HelpStatusLabelID* property:

```
<asp:TextBox ID="TextBox1" runat="server" /> <br />
<asp:Label runat="server" ID="Label1" />

<act:PasswordStrength runat="server"
    TargetControlID="TextBox1"
    DisplayPosition="RightSide"
    PreferredPasswordLength="12"
    HelpStatusLabelID="Label1" />
</act:PasswordStrength>
```

The *Label1* control receives a message that suggests what to do to meet password requirements. You can also keep this message hidden all the time and display it on demand by clicking a button. In this case, you set two new properties: *HelpHandlePosition* and *HelpHandleCssClass*. The former sets the display position for the help icon; the latter styles the icon.

```
<act:PasswordStrength runat="server">
    <act:PasswordStrengthExtenderProperties TargetControlID="TextBox1"
        DisplayPosition="BelowRight"
        PreferredPasswordLength="12"
        HelpHandlePosition="RightSide"
        HelpHandleCssClass="helpHandle" />
</act:PasswordStrength>
```

To be precise, you set the icon to display using the CSS style:

```
.helpHandle
{
    width:16px;
    height:14px;
    background-image:url(images/Question.png);
    overflow:hidden;
    cursor:help;
}
```

Figure 5-26 shows the final page.

Figure 5-26   The *PasswordStrength* extender in action with a help button

The *Slider* Extender

The *Slider* extender allows you to morph a classic *TextBox* into a graphical slider so that users can pick up a numeric value from a finite range. You can set the orientation of the slider (horizontal or vertical) and also make it accept a discrete interval of values—that is, only a specified number of values within a given range. By default, the slider accepts values in the 0 through 100 range.

```
<h2>Your age</h2>
<asp:TextBox ID="TextBox1" runat="server" />
<hr />
<asp:Label runat="server" ID="Label1" />
```

```
<act:SliderExtender runat="server" ID="SliderExtender1"
    TargetControlID="TextBox1"
    BoundControlID="Label1" />
```

A value chosen using the slider is automatically persisted via a full or partial postback. You can reference the value using the *TextBox* programming interface. (See Figure 5-27.)

Figure 5-27   The *Slider* extender in action

The *TextBoxWatermark* Extender

The *TextBoxWatermark* extender allows you to define default text to display when the text box is empty. The extender takes care of showing and hiding the text as required.

```
<h2>Watermark</h2>
<br/>
<asp:TextBox ID="TextBox1" runat="server" />
 
<asp:TextBox ID="TextBox2" runat="server" />

<act:TextBoxWatermarkExtender runat="server" ID="TextBoxWatermark1"
    TargetControlID="TextBox1"
    WatermarkText="Type First Name Here"
    WatermarkCssClass="watermarked" />
<act:TextBoxWatermarkExtender runat="server" ID="TextBoxWatermark2"
    TargetControlID="TextBox2"
    WatermarkText="Type Last Name Here"
    WatermarkCssClass="watermarked" />
```

The extender uses the *TargetControlID* property to designate the target text box. The *WatermarkText* property defines the text to display, whereas *WatermarkCssClass* indicates the CSS style to apply to the watermark text. (See Figure 5-28.)

Figure 5-28   The *TextBoxWatermark* extender in action

The *ValidatorCallout* Extender

The *ValidatorCallout* extender enhances the graphical capabilities of existing ASP.NET valida-
tors. It displays the error message of a validator using the balloon-style ToolTips of Windows
XP. (See Figure 5-29.)

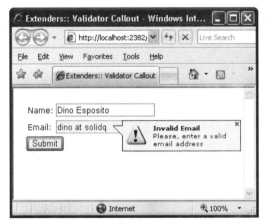

Figure 5-29   The *ValidatorCallout* extender in action

Here's how to use the extender:

```
<table>
<tr>
    <td>Name:</td>
    <td><asp:TextBox runat="server" ID="txtName" /></td>
</tr>
<tr>
    <td>Email:</td>
    <td><asp:TextBox runat="server" ID="txtEmail" /></td>
</tr>
</table>
```

```
<asp:Button runat="server" ID="Button1" Text="Submit" />
<asp:RequiredFieldValidator runat="server" ID="requiredName"
    ControlToValidate="txtName"
    Display="None"
    ErrorMessage="Required Field Missing<br />A name is required." />
<asp:RequiredFieldValidator runat="server" ID="requiredEmail"
    ControlToValidate="txtEmail"
    Display="None"
    ErrorMessage="Required Field Missing<br />Email address required." />
<asp:RegularExpressionValidator runat="server" ID="regularEmail"
    ControlToValidate="txtEmail"
    Display="None"
    ValidationExpression="[a-zA-Z_0-9.-]+\@[a-zA-Z_0-9.-]+\.\w+"
    ErrorMessage="<b>Invalid Email</b><br />Please, enter a valid email
                address" />
<act:ValidatorCalloutExtender runat="server" ID="CalloutExtender1"
    TargetControlID="requiredName" HighlightCssClass="highlight" />
<act:ValidatorCalloutExtender runat="server" ID="CalloutExtender2"
    TargetControlID="requiredEmail" HighlightCssClass="highlight" />
<act:ValidatorCalloutExtender runat="server" ID="CalloutExtender3"
    TargetControlID="regularEmail" HighlightCssClass="highlight" />
```

Animation Extenders

The ACT comes with a full-fledged framework for building animations over the Web, leveraging the capabilities of rich browsers. The idea is to have an extensible set of animation blocks that can be composed together and run either in sequence or in parallel. The animations to be played are declaratively specified using XML.

The *Animation* Extender

The *Animation* extender allows you to use the built-in animation framework in a mostly declarative and codeless fashion. The extender plays specified animations whenever a client event occurs on the target control. Supported events include *load*, *click*, *mouseover*, and *mouseout*. Here's an example:

```
<act:AnimationExtender ID="AnimationExtender1" runat="server"
    TargetControlID="Panel1">
  <Animations>
    <OnLoad>
      <OpacityAction Opacity=".2" />
    </OnLoad>
    <OnHoverOver>
      <FadeIn Duration=".25" Fps="20"
            MinimumOpacity=".2" MaximumOpacity=".8" />
    </OnHoverOver>
    <OnHoverOut>
      <FadeOut Duration=".25" Fps="20"
            MinimumOpacity=".2" MaximumOpacity=".8" />
    </OnHoverOut>
  </Animations>
</act:AnimationExtender>
```

The *Animations* tag fully describes the animation. It is made up of a list of actions bound to specific events. In the above preceding example, the events are *load*, *hover*, and *mouseout*. The tag *OnLoad* describes the animation performed when the extended control is loaded. Tags *OnHoverOver* and *OnHoverOut* describe what happens when the *hover* effect is to take place, which is typically delayed from the actual *mouseover* and *mouseout* events. To describe an animation, you use a combination of existing animation blocks: fade-in, fade-out, opacity, pulse, move, resize, color interpolation, and scaling. You can also specify actions using custom script. The sample code just shown applies a slight opacity filter to the extended control upon loading and then fades its area in when the mouse hovers over it and out of it. For more information on built-in animation blocks, take a look at *http://ajax.asp.net/ajaxtoolkit/Walkthrough/AnimationReference.aspx.*

The *UpdatePanelAnimation* Extender

The *UpdatePanelAnimation* extender applies animation to a very specific situation where custom events need to be handled—before and after an updatable region is refreshed. Using the extender is as simple as defining an updatable panel in the page and adding the following code for the extender:

```
<act:UpdatePanelAnimationExtender runat="server" ID="UpdatePanelAnimation1"
    TargetControlID="UpdatePanel1">
    <Animations>
        <OnUpdating>
            <Sequence>
                <EnableAction AnimationTarget="Button1" Enabled="false" />
                <FadeOut AnimationTarget="Panel1" minimumOpacity=".3" />
            </Sequence>
        </OnUpdating>
        <OnUpdated>
            <Sequence>
                <FadeIn AnimationTarget="Panel1" minimumOpacity=".3" />
                <EnableAction AnimationTarget="Button1" Enabled="true" />
            </Sequence>
        </OnUpdated>
    </Animations>
</act:UpdatePanelAnimationExtender>
```

As you can see, it is nothing more than an animation applied to panel-specific events such as *OnUpdating* and *OnUpdated*. Before the update begins, the area that contains the sensitive contents to update is faded out and a control, *Button1*, is disabled. You use the *FadeOut* animation block for this purpose. In the preceding example, *Panel1* is merely the HTML block that contains the *UpdatePanel* control.

```
<div ID="Panel1">
    <asp:UpdatePanel ID="UpdatePanel1" runat="server" ...>
        ...
    </asp:UpdatePanel>
</div>
```

The *EnableAction* animation block declaratively disables the specified control during the update. In Chapter 4, you learned how to accomplish the same thing programmatically—the extender now provides a declarative approach.

Once the region has been updated, you run a *FadeIn* animation to bring the panel content back to its full colors and re-enable previously disabled controls using the *EnableAction*. The *Resize* animation can also be used to implement a sort of collapse/expand effect during the update: the panel closes, gets updated, and then unfolds to show its new contents. Imagination is your only limit. (See Figure 5-30.)

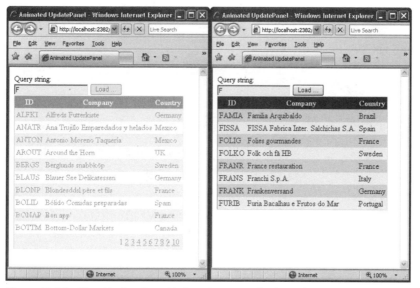

Figure 5-30   The *UpdatePanelAnimation* extender in action

Conclusion

No matter how many controls you have in your arsenal, you'll likely be always lacking just the one that is crucial for your current work. That's why the extensibility model of ASP.NET has been so successful over the years, and that's why so many component vendors crowd the market with excellent product offerings.

Anyway, always deriving new controls from existing ones might not necessarily be a wise strategy. A new control is required for a significant piece of server and client code that can be used to back up a good chunk of user interface. If you only need to filter the values in a text box, a custom text box control is hardly the best option. But until the arrival of ASP.NET AJAX and the AJAX Control Toolkit, there was no other way out.

With control extenders, you define the concept of a "behavior" and work with it as a distinct entity set apart from classic server controls. Extenders are server controls, but they work on top of bound controls and improve their overall capabilities by adding a new behavior.

An extender doesn't necessarily have to be an AJAX control. However, in the implementation of the AJAX Control Toolkit all extenders require a script manager, inject a good quantity of script code into the client pages, and take advantage of the client JavaScript library.

To take advantage of extenders and controls in the ACT, you don't have to import the binaries into your application. The ACT is an open-source project and, according to the license agreement you accept when you download the assembly, it can be incorporated piecemeal in your applications. This means, for example, that you can import only a few components through their source code and perhaps even adapt the code to your specific needs.

With this overview of controls and extenders, and armed with a strong knowledge of partial rendering, we're now ready to tackle an alternative programming model in ASP.NET AJAX—making remote procedure calls over the Web.

Part III
Client-Centric Development

Chapter 6
Built-in Application Services

The HTTP protocol is simple, effective, and ubiquitous, but it is not stateful. So two consecutive and logically related calls to the same URL (that is, a postback) are treated as independent calls, and for each of them a new and especially clean environment is created. To add some state and global data containment to Web applications, virtually all server-side runtime environments build an abstraction layer and provide additional services to applications. Common services for ASP.NET applications include session state, authentication, role management, caching, profiling and, in general, any operation that can manipulate an intrinsic ASP.NET object.

These application services are available only to server-side code and are not directly exposed to JavaScript; as such, they can't be invoked directly from the client page. Despite their rich and advanced user-interface capabilities, ASP.NET AJAX applications are primarily ASP.NET applications. So they still need a way to use traditional ASP.NET application services, such as Forms authentication, session state management, server-side caching, user profiling, and role and membership information verification. In the native server environment of ASP.NET, developers find a number of facilities such as the *HttpContext* object (including its child objects *Session*, *Cache*, *Profile*, and *User*) and static service-specific classes to accomplish common tasks such as managing a profile or authenticating a user. But on the client?

ASP.NET AJAX Extensions wraps some of these base application services into JavaScript classes defined in the Microsoft AJAX library. (See Chapter 2, "The Microsoft Client Library for AJAX.") Such wrapper classes expose server-side services through a number of built-in Web services, making services callable directly from the client.

In ASP.NET AJAX, you find client-side wrappers for two key and related server-side services: Forms authentication and user profiles.

 Note If you want to expose other system services to client script code, you have to use page methods or write ad hoc Web services, as we'll see in Chapter 7, "Remote Method Calls with ASP.NET AJAX." Note, though, that in the next version of ASP.NET a third built-in service will be added to the list—the *Role* service.

Forms Authentication Services

To protect Web pages from unauthorized users, you place some boilerplate code on top of each page and redirect the user to a login page. On the login page, the user is prompted for credentials. Next, if successfully authenticated, the user is redirected to the originally requested page. Forms authentication is the ASP.NET built-in infrastructure that implements the aforementioned pattern for login.

Server-side Forms authentication requires an additional login page and two HTTP redirect commands. Can you authenticate directly from the client without any page redirection? You bet.

The System Infrastructure for Authentication

The infrastructure of AJAX-accessible ASP.NET services is made of two key components: a client-side JavaScript class and a server-side Web service. Authentication and user profile services are both implemented according to this model.

A JavaScript class provides you with methods to send credentials to a built-in Web service. You receive a Boolean answer that indicates whether or not the user has been authenticated. The Web service uses the server-side ASP.NET authentication and membership API to validate the user information.

By using a client JavaScript class to command a remote Web service, you authenticate users more quickly because you incorporate login forms into the home page of the site (or any pages a user would visit regularly) rather than force a redirect to a specialized login page.

The Client-Side Authentication Service Class

To verify the credentials that a user typed in a client-side login box, you invoke the methods of a class defined in the Microsoft AJAX Library. The class is named *Sys.Services._AuthenticationService* and, as the leading underscore in the name suggests, it should be considered private to the library. More importantly, the class is a singleton, meaning that it has only one instance with a global point of access. You don't have to instantiate the *_AuthenticationService* class; you just use the global instance of it that is always available to your application and returned by the object named *Sys.Services.AuthenticationService*.

The global entry point is set in the Microsoft AJAX Library following the definition of the class. Here's an excerpt from the source code:

```
Sys.Services.AuthenticationService =
                new Sys.Services._AuthenticationService();
```

The authentication service class features the methods listed in Table 6-1.

Table 6-1 Methods of the *Sys.Services._AuthenticationService* Object

Method	Description
login	This method verifies credentials and issues an authentication ticket if the credentials are good.
logout	This method clears the authentication ticket.

Table 6-2 details the properties defined on the object.

Table 6-2 Properties of the *Sys.Services._AuthenticationService* Object

Property	Description
isLoggedIn	A Boolean read-only property, it indicates whether the current user is logged in.
path	This property gets and sets the URL to reach the authentication Web service.
timeout	This property gets and sets the timeout for the user authentication process.

The *Sys.Services._AuthenticationService* class acts as a client-side proxy for the remote Web service. It inherits from a class named *Sys.Net.WebServiceProxy* that is the base class for any JavaScript proxy of a remote Web service. As we'll see in Chapter 7, a class derived from *Sys.Net.WebServiceProxy* is generated on the fly for each ASP.NET Web service registered with the script manager. For the authentication Web service, this class is simply hard-coded in the Microsoft AJAX Library.

The Server-Side Authentication Web Service

The back end of the authentication service is implemented in the *AuthenticationWebService* class. The class is contained in the AJAX assembly within the *System.Web.Security.AuthenticationService* namespace. The *AuthenticationWebService* class is mapped to the following URL:

```
Authentication_JSON_AppService.axd
```

The URL points to an HTTP handler registered in the *web.config* file. The handler simply captures incoming requests, deserializes input parameters and method names, executes the call, and sends values back to the client in a JavaScript Object Notation (JSON) stream.

After the AJAX authentication service is enabled in the site configuration, any page served from the site includes the following script:

```
<script type="text/javascript">
<!--
Sys.Services._AuthenticationService.DefaultWebServicePath =
          '/Authentication_JSON_AppService.axd';
// -->
</script>
```

As you can see, a private member of the JavaScript _AuthenticationService_ class is set to the default path of the server Web service. However, by setting the path property via JavaScript, you can make the client invoke an authentication Web service elsewhere. The Web service, though, must support JSON and expose a contract identical to that of the _AuthenticationService_ class.

The Programming Interface of the Service

As you would expect, the _AuthenticationWebService_ class features the same two methods—_login_ and _logout_—that we have in the proxy client and with the same signatures. The login method, for example, has the following signature:

```
[WebMethod]
public bool login(
    string userName,
    string password,
    bool createPersistentCookie)
```

The first two arguments (_userName_ and _password_) set the credentials; the final Boolean argument indicates whether a persistent cookie is required. When you authenticate a user through Forms authentication, a cookie is created and attached to the response. This cookie is referred to as the _authentication ticket_, and its name defaults to _.ASPXAUTH_.

If you set the _createPersistentCookie_ argument to _false_, the issued authentication ticket expires after 30 minutes. If you opt for a persistent cookie, the authentication ticket lasts as long as 50 years. What if you need a ticket timeout that falls in between 30 minutes and 50 years? You can simply set the _timeout_ attribute in the _<authentication>_ section of the application's _web.config_ file to the desired number of minutes.

The _login_ method of the Web service uses the following code to do its work:

```
if (Membership.Provider.ValidateUser(userName, password))
{
    FormsAuthentication.SetAuthCookie(userName, createPersistentCookie);
    return true;
}
return false;
```

As you can see, it validates using the current membership provider and sets the cookie using the _SetAuthCookie_ method on the _FormsAuthentication_ class. This means that most settings defined in the _<authentication>_ section of the configuration file are taken into proper account while creating the authentication ticket.

Note The AJAX authentication service doesn't work with applications that use a cookieless authentication scheme. _SetAuthCookie_ works as it usually does for classic ASP.NET applications and modifies the return URL to include the authentication ticket. In classic ASP.NET, though, a system component intervenes, moving the ticket to a header and rewriting the URL to that

> originally requested. This component is an ISAPI filter (*aspnet_filter.dll*) that hooks up any ongoing request.
>
> If you authenticate through a Web service call, no new request is fired that the filter can intercept to extract the authentication ticket from the URL. As a result, when the user is successfully authenticated, the caller page receives a positive response, but no cookie (or equivalent information) is attached to the response. Any further requests for a secured resource are therefore destined to fail.

The *logout* method takes no arguments and simply removes the cookie from the response. Internally, the method ends up calling the *SignOut* method of the *FormsAuthentication* class.

> **Note**   ASP.NET AJAX authentication can happen only through a membership provider. If you need to implement custom logic to authenticate users, you must build a custom provider. For more information about ASP.NET Forms authentication and custom membership providers, refer to Chapter 15 of my book *Programming Microsoft ASP.NET 2.0 Applications: Core Reference* (Microsoft Press, 2005). More details on ASP.NET providers can be found in Chapter 4 of *Programming Microsoft ASP.NET 2.0 Applications: Advanced Topics* (Microsoft Press, 2006).

Configuration of the Authentication Service

The ASP.NET AJAX authentication service requires you to set a few attributes in the application's *web.config* file. In particular, you need to enable the service as follows:

```
<authenticationService enabled="true" />
```

Note that the service is disabled by default. A second attribute can be specified for the *<authenticationService>* node—the *requireSSL* Boolean attribute. Set to *false* by default, the attribute indicates whether a Secure Sockets Layer (SSL) connection is required to transmit the authentication cookie.

> **Warning**   A frequent security hole in too many Web applications is when a nonsecured HTTP page (for example, the site's home page) hosts the login box. If the submit button of the login form points to an HTTPS page, your credentials are sent out properly protected. However, can you be sure that you're sending out your credentials from a site that is really the site it claims to be? If you're a victim of a DNS-poisoning attack, you might have been redirected to an apparently identical Web site that is run by a hacker. In this scenario, it is easy for the hacker to steal your credentials and then redirect you to the right site. To be absolutely sure this cannot happen to users of your site, you should display a login box only within an HTTPS page.

When SSL is not required, credentials are sent out as clear text. This is a known limitation of Forms authentication. If this is a concern to you, use SSL or Transport Layer Security (TLS) to secure your login page.

The *<authenticationService>* section is located under a new AJAX-specific section:

```
<system.web.extensions>
  <scripting>
    <webServices>
      <authenticationService enabled="true" />
      ...
    </webServices>
  </scripting>
</system.web.extensions>
```

All sections must be properly registered, as discussed in Chapter 3, "The Pulsing Heart of ASP.NET AJAX." An ASP.NET AJAX application built using the Microsoft Visual Studio 2005 template already incorporates required settings in its default *web.config* file.

In addition to configuring AJAX-specific sections, to take advantage of ASP.NET AJAX out-of-band authentication you also need to have Forms authentication turned on in the *<system.web>* section of classic ASP.NET:

```
<system.web>
    <authentication mode="Forms" />
</system.web>
```

> **Note**   Why are two different settings needed to enable authentication in ASP.NET AJAX applications? ASP.NET AJAX applications are still ASP.NET applications, even though they add a lot of new functionalities. The runtime environment that processes requests is the same for classic and ASP.NET AJAX applications. You need two different settings because currently AJAX Extensions is implemented as a bolted-on framework that hooks up certain behaviors of ASP.NET. The next version of ASP.NET will fully incorporate AJAX functionalities and expose them as part of a unique framework. When this happens, you can expect to find settings for the AJAX authentication service directly in the *<authentication>* section of *<system.web>*.

Using the Authentication Service in an Application

In a classic ASP.NET application configured to use Forms authentication, you group secured pages in one or more subfolders with a local *web.config* file that contains the following:

```
<configuration>
    <system.web>
        <authorization>
            <deny users="?" />
            <allow users="*" />
        </authorization>
    </system.web>
</configuration>
```

The script blocks anonymous users—by using the question mark symbol (?)—and lets any other user pass. In this way, when the user navigates to any page in such a folder, the request is captured by the Forms authentication module. If the request has no valid ticket attached, or its URL hasn't been mangled to contain the ticket, the user is redirected to a login page. The key facts in this model are that the authentication occurs on demand and is automatically facilitated by the system. Sure, you can provide in the master page a link to a login page so that users can be authenticated before trying to access secured pages. However, this is a bonus feature you implement and is not strictly required from a functional point of view. Because the capability to execute Forms authentication is built into ASP.NET itself, this model works without needing to change anything in an ASP.NET AJAX application.

ASP.NET AJAX applications, though, make a point of reducing the number of page redirects and full postbacks. In an AJAX application, you typically incorporate the login form in the master page and call the authentication service when the user clicks the Log In button. In Figure 6-1, you see a sample ASP.NET AJAX page with a login panel.

Figure 6-1 Implementing authentication in an ASP.NET AJAX application

Anonymous and authenticated users both can access the page and use a number of features; only registered users can access other features.

The Login Process

The login form can be as easy to create as a table by using a couple of text boxes and a push button. Needless to say, you can decorate the input fields with as many extenders as you want. In an ASP.NET AJAX application, the Log In button is clearly a client button (so that it doesn't cause a postback) and points to some JavaScript code that invokes the authentication service:

```
<input type="button" id="LoginButton" value="Log In" onclick="OnLogin()" />
```

The *OnLogin* function looks like in the following code:

```
<script type="text/javascript">
    var currentUser = $get("LoggedUser"); // User friendly name...
    var username = $get("Login1_UserName");

    function OnLogin()
    {
        Sys.Services.AuthenticationService.login(
            username.value, password.value, false,
            null, null, onLoginCompleted);
        return false;
    }
    ...
</script>
```

As you can see, the *login* method of the JavaScript class includes a few arguments beyond the user name and password. Let's review the signature in detail. Table 6-3 lists the accepted parameters.

Table 6-3   Parameters of the *login* Method

Parameter	Optional	Description
userName	No	Indicates the user name to verify against the list of registered users.
password	No	Indicates the password of the specified user. The parameter can be null.
createPersistentCookie	Yes	Boolean value. It indicates whether a persistent cookie should be created.
customInfo	Yes	String value. It indicates any additional text you want to pass. *This property doesn't appear to be used in the current version of ASP.NET AJAX Extensions.*
redirectUrl	Yes	String value. It indicates the URL to redirect the user to after a successful authentication.
loginCompletedCallback	Yes	Indicates the JavaScript callback to invoke after a successful authentication.
failedCallback	Yes	Indicates the JavaScript callback to invoke if the authentication fails.
userContext	Yes	Any object you want the library to pass to the callbacks.

Only the user name and password are mandatory parameters and can't be omitted. Note that for the the password field a value of *null* is acceptable. You can indicate two callbacks: one for a successful completion of the login process and one to use in case of failure. Here's a possible implementation of a login-completed callback:

```
function onLoginCompleted(results)
{
    // On success, there will be a Forms authentication cookie in the browser
```

```
// Adjust the user interface to reflect the logged-in status of the user
HandleLoginLogoutState(results);

// Clean up the login form
if (results)
{
    username.value = "";
    password.value = "";
}
else
{
    alert("Sorry, your credentials appear to be invalid. Try again.");
}
}
```

In ASP.NET AJAX, any JavaScript callback used to process the results of a remote Web service call has the following prototype:

```
function methodCompleted(results, context, methodName)
```

The *results* argument contains the return value of the Web service method, whereas *context* mirrors the contents of the *userContext* parameter of the *login* method. Finally, *methodName* indicates the name of the client-side method that triggered the callback. Of course, *context* and *methodName* arguments can be null.

The return value of the authentication Web service method is passed to the callback. In this case, it is a Boolean value indicating the result of the authentication.

You can handle the possible failure of a login operation by using a made-to-measure callback, as shown here:

```
function onLoginFailed(results, context, methodName)
{
    alert("Login failed.\n<" + results.get_message() + ">");
}
```

In this case, the *results* parameter is the JavaScript transposition of the exception that was raised on the server. It is a JavaScript *Error* object with as many properties as the server-side exception object.

It should be noted, though, that the login-failed callback is triggered only if an exception occurs on the server while the credentials are being verified. If the credentials are simply invalid, no exception is thrown, a value of *false* is returned to the client, and the login-failed callback isn't invoked.

The Logout Process

Figure 6-2 shows the HTTP request and response for a login attempt. (The tool in the figure is Web Development Helper, which we briefly discussed in Chapter 4, "Partial Page Rendering.")

As you can see, the HTTP response contains an additional cookie, named *.ASPXAUTH*. That is exactly the authentication ticket issued on the server and delivered to the client. From now on, the user can access any secured pages in the application until the ticket expires.

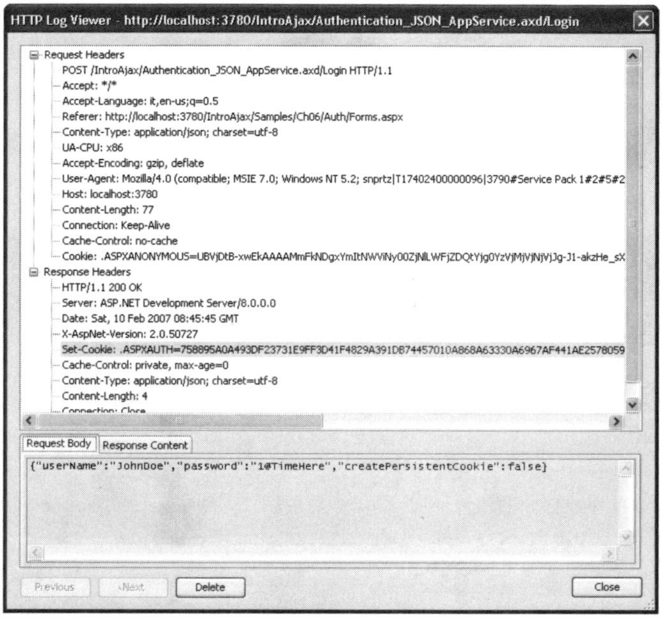

Figure 6-2   The HTTP response for a call to the *login* method on the authentication service

To give users a chance to log out directly from the client, you add another button to your client user interface and bind it to the following JavaScript code:

```
function Logout()
{
    Sys.Services.AuthenticationService.logout(onLogoutCompleted);
    return false;
}
```

When this function returns, the HTTP response looks like the one shown in Figure 6-3.

The .ASPXAUTH cookie now has an empty body and can no longer be used to enable access to the secured pages of the application.

Typical User Interface Enhancements

Any applications based on authentication services should provide optional user interface (UI) elements to welcome the logged-in user and give her a chance to log out. In addition, some pages might also include conditional controls that show up only if the current request is authenticated. How would you know whether the current request is authenticated?

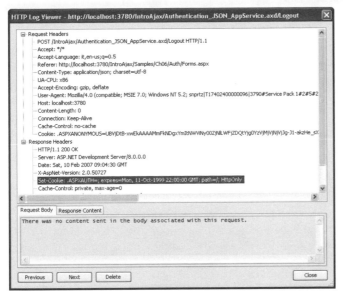

Figure 6-3   The HTTP response for a call to the *logout* method on the authentication service

In classic ASP.NET, you simply check the *Request.IsAuthenticated* property in *Page_Load* or wherever else you need to know it. In ASP.NET AJAX, things will be slightly different.

When the JavaScript *login* method returns, you know whether or not the current user is authenticated. Suppose that the user navigates to another page in the application and then clicks the Back button or any link that returns the user to the original page. Once back to the original page, the user's browser will have lost any information about the authentication status—in the end, the authentication status was simply the value of a JavaScript global variable. If not properly designed, the user interface might show that the user is not logged in, while the authentication module correctly handles her further requests for secured pages. Let's consider a block of user interface code that displays the name of the logged-in user:

```
<div runat="server" id="LoggedIn" style="display:none;">
    <h2>Hey, <asp:Label id="LoggedUser" runat="server" />  
    <input type="button" value="Log out" onclick="Logout()" /></h2>
</div>
<div runat="server" id="NotLoggedIn" style="display:none;color:red;">
    <h2>Not logged in</h2>
</div>
```

The first <*div*> will be used when any user is logged in; the second <*div*> block comes in handy when no user is connected. You toggle them based on the result of the *login* method and the authentication status of the request. To facilitate this, add the following code to the *Page_Load* event of the code file:

```csharp
protected void Page_Load(object sender, EventArgs e)
{
    if (Request.IsAuthenticated)
    {
        LoggedIn.Style["display"] = String.Empty;
        NotLoggedIn.Style["display"] = "none";
        LoggedUser.Text = User.Identity.Name;

        // Show any UI element specific to registered users
        ...
    }
    else
    {
        LoggedIn.Style["display"] = "none";
        NotLoggedIn.Style["display"] = "";
        LoggedUser.Text = "";

        // Hide any UI element specific to registered users
        ...
    }
}
```

The code ensures that UI elements are correctly initialized when the page first loads and every time the page is refreshed, loaded through a link, or loaded via the Back/Forward buttons. In addition, you will need to extend the client-side *onLoginCompleted* and *onLogoutCompleted* callback functions to update the user interface dynamically as the user connects or disconnects directly from the page. For example, you can use the following function:

```javascript
<script type="text/javascript">
    var currentUser = $get("LoggedUser");
    var loggedIn = $get("LoggedIn");
    var notLoggedIn = $get("NotLoggedIn");

    function HandleLoginLogoutState(userLogged)
    {
        if (userLogged)
        {
            notLoggedIn.style.display = "none";
            loggedIn.style.display = "";
            currentUser.innerHTML = username.value;

            // Show any UI element specific to registered users
        }
        else
        {
            loggedIn.style.display = "none";
            notLoggedIn.style.display = "";
            currentUser.innerHTML = "";

            // Hide any UI element specific to registered users
        }
    }
</script>
```

You can call the *HandleLoginLogoutState* function from both *onLoginCompleted* and *onLogoutCompleted* by passing *true* and *false*, respectively.

If the user has been successfully authenticated, you clear the user interface of the login form and enable the secured portions of the page. (See Figure 6-4.)

Figure 6-4   A typical user interface when the current user is logged in

Design Guidelines for Protected Resources

In ASP.NET, to guarantee that protected resources (for example, Web pages) are exclusively accessed by authorized users, you place them in a site folder controlled by a modified version of the *web.config* file. The configuration file requires that a valid authentication ticket is presented by requests aimed at any of the resources. From a UI perspective, you might or might not apply special measures to let users know about the requirements of a protected page. You can leave any links to such pages visible and active; if the user clicks, the system infrastructure blocks any unauthorized access.

More precisely, if the user follows the link to a protected page, ASP.NET first attempts to locate the authentication ticket. If no valid ticket is found, the user is automatically redirected to the configured login page. This behavior is good enough for classic ASP.NET pages; it's not a solution for AJAX-enabled sites. The redirect, in fact, will break the continuity between users and applications that is a characteristic of AJAX applications.

Although there's no way to prevent users from typing the URL of a protected page on the address bar—in that case, a full page reload is inevitable—there are two possible approaches to prevent users from blindly navigating to protected URLs from within the current page. You can hide links to protected pages, or you can add some script code to buttons to enable the operation only if the user is currently logged in. To hide protected resources to unauthenticated users, you set cascading style sheet (CSS) style attributes as shown in the preceding code snippet. To dynamically verify the status of the current user, you attach some script to the user interface element as shown here:

```
<a href="secured\listinvoices.aspx" onclick="return checkFirst()">
    <b>View invoices</b> (Must be logged in)
</a>
```

Next, you write a JavaScript function that checks the logged-in status and prevents the default action if the user is not authenticated:

```
function checkFirst()
{
    var loggedIn = Sys.Services.AuthenticationService.get_isLoggedIn();
    if (!loggedIn)
    {
        alert("You must be logged in to follow this link");
        return false;
    }
    return true;
}
```

To check the status of the user, you use the *isLoggedIn* property of the *Sys.Services.AuthenticationService* object.

User Profiling Services

To make your ASP.NET pages friendlier, more functional, and more appealing to use, you can build a personalization layer into your Web application that gives users a chance to set and retrieve their preferences. The personalization capabilities of ASP.NET 2.0 are built around the concept of the *user profile*.

The user profile is a collection of properties that the ASP.NET 2.0 runtime groups into a dynamically generated class. The application defines its own data model in the configuration file, and the ASP.NET runtime does the rest by parsing and compiling that model into a class. Each member of the class corresponds to a piece of information specific to the currently logged-in user. Any profile data is persisted on a per-user basis and is permanently stored on the server until someone with administrative privileges deletes it.

When the application runs and a page is displayed, ASP.NET dynamically creates a profile object that contains, properly typed, the properties you defined in the data model. The object is then added to the current *HttpContext* object and is available to pages through the *Profile* property. The ASP.NET profile service is implemented through an HTTP module. The module kicks in when the request has been authenticated and retrieves data for the specific user. (If the user is anonymous, a unique ID is generated for that user and stored in the *.ASPXANONYMOUS* cookie.) At the end of the request, the profile object is saved back to the data store ready for the next time.

From within a server page, you can read and write profile properties using the *HttpContext.Profile* object. Can you do the same from within an ASP.NET AJAX page in an out-of-band postback? In fact, you can.

The System Infrastructure for Profiling

Just as with the authentication service, the user profile service relies on a client-server infrastructure. A JavaScript class provides methods to load and save user-specific information to the server. You receive a collection of properties representing the profile of the current user and save it back to the server's data store with any changes made on the client. The underlying Web service uses the ASP.NET profile provider to persist information.

The user profile can be used to update properties used by server-side controls and page components. However, it also opens up a whole new world of possibilities. In fact, you can have client controls to persist a portion of their state to the server on a per-user basis.

The Client-Side Profiling Service Class

The Microsoft AJAX Library that wraps the user profiling service is named *Sys.Services._ProfileService* and is a private class that is available to programmers through a single point of access—the *Sys.Services._ProfileService* object. The global entry point is set in the Microsoft AJAX Library following the definition of the class, as the following code snippet shows:

```
Sys.Services.ProfileService = new Sys.Services._ProfileService();
```

The profile service class features the methods listed in Table 6-4.

Table 6-4   Methods of the *Sys.Services._ProfileService* Object

Method	Description
load	This method loads properties saved in the server's profile data store for the current user.
save	This method saves the current user profile to the data store.

Table 6-5 details the properties defined on the object.

Table 6-5   Properties of the *Sys.Services._ProfileService* Object

Property	Description
properties	This property returns the collection of properties that form the user profile.
path	This property gets and sets the URL to reach the profile Web service.
timeout	This property gets and sets the timeout for the user profile process.

Inherited from the *Sys.Net.WebServiceProxy* base class, the class *Sys.Services._ProfileService* acts as a client-side proxy for the remote Web service and is the bridge between the client page and the server-side *HttpContext.Profile* object.

> **Note** The data store for a given profile service can be configured in the *web.config* file through ad hoc components known as the *profile providers*. For more information on profile providers, take a look at Chapter 4 of my book *Programming Microsoft ASP.NET 2.0 Applications: Advanced Topics* (Microsoft Press, 2006).

The Server-Side Profiling Web Service

The ASP.NET AJAX profile service is a Web service coded through the class *ProfileWebService* located in the *System.Web.Profile* namespace. The class is mapped to the following URL:

```
Profile_JSON_AppService.axd
```

The URL points to an HTTP handler registered in the *web.config* file. The handler captures incoming requests and input parameters, executes the call, and then sends values back to the client in a JSON stream.

Once the AJAX authentication service is enabled in the site configuration, any page served from the site includes the following script:

```
<script type="text/javascript">
<!--
Sys.Services._ProfileService.DefaultWebServicePath =
            '/Profile_JSON_AppService.axd';
// -->
</script>
```

You can replace the default Web service with another of choice as long as the new Web service supports JSON and is an ASP.NET Web service in the same Internet Information Services (IIS) application as the caller.

The Programming Interface of the Service

Table 6-6 lists the methods of the server-side profile Web service.

Table 6-6 Web Methods of the Profile Web Service

Method	Description
GetAllPropertiesForCurrentUser	This method fills a dictionary of name/value pairs with values of all profile properties.
GetPropertiesForCurrentUser	This method takes a collection of property names and returns a dictionary filled with name/value pairs.
SetPropertiesForCurrentUser	This method takes a dictionary filled with name/value pairs and serializes such content to the profile data store. The method returns the number of properties updated.

The exact signatures of the *get* methods are shown in the following code segment:

```
[WebMethod]
public IDictionary<string, object> GetAllPropertiesForCurrentUser();

[WebMethod]
public IDictionary<string, object> GetPropertiesForCurrentUser(
    string[] properties)
```

The *properties* argument lists the profile properties that you want to load in the JavaScript *Sys.Profile* object.

The *SetPropertiesForCurrentUser* method has the following signature:

```
[WebMethod]
public int SetPropertiesForCurrentUser(IDictionary<string, object> values)
```

It takes a dictionary of name/value property pairs as the input argument and updates the data store.

Because the ASP.NET AJAX service works on top of the ASP.NET profile subsystem, you can choose to bring in only a portion of the application data model coded in the *web.config* file. This tactic is normally a good move because it lets you move only the profile data you need to access from the client.

Configuration of the Profiling Service

The profile service requires a bit of configuration work. In particular, you need to explicitly enable the service through the *<profileService>* section in the new *<webServices>* section under *<system.web.extensions>*:

```
<system.web.extensions>
    <scripting>
      <webServices>
        <profileService enabled="true" />
        ...
      </webServices>
    </scripting>
</system.web.extensions>
```

To allow profile properties to be retrieved and modified from within ASP.NET AJAX applications, you also need to list properties in the *readAccessProperties* and *writeAccessProperties* attributes. The value of the *readAccessProperties* attribute is a comma (,) separated list of property names that you want to read. The *writeAccessProperties* attribute is a comma (,) separated list of property names that you want to write. If you intend for all properties to be available, you can use an asterisk (*) or list all properties explicitly.

```
<profileService enabled="true"
      writeAccessProperties="propertyName1;propertyName2; ..."
      readAccessProperties="propertyName1;propertyName2; ..." />
```

The data model on which the profile service is based is defined through the *<profile>* section under *<system.web>*. Here's the data model we'll be using in the next example:

```
<profile>
  <properties>
    <group name="UI">
      <add name="BackColor" type="string" />
    </group>
    <add name="LastPane" type="integer" />
  </properties>
</profile>
```

Subsequently, the *<profileService>* section will take the form shown here:

```
<profileService enabled="true"
    writeAccessProperties="UI.BackColor,LastPane"
    readAccessProperties="UI.BackColor,LastPane" />
```

As mentioned, *writeAccessProperties* and *readAccessProperties* can list a subset of the properties defined in the data model. The two sets of properties don't have to match, meaning that you can enable a given profile property for reading from ASP.NET AJAX pages but not for writing (or vice versa). If your data model includes groups, you use the *Group.Property* convention to list the property in the *<profileService>* section. For example, in the preceding example the *BackColor* property belongs to the *UI* group; therefore, it is expressed as *UI.BackColor* in the configuration file.

Using the Profile Service in an Application

The profile service is tightly coupled with the authentication service in the sense that the profile object contains information specific to a given authenticated user. Anonymous users are allowed to have their own profile as long as you enable the anonymous user service in the configuration file. The anonymous user service will generate a Guid to identify the user; the profile of an anonymous user can then be migrated to the profile of a registered user when the anonymous user registers. In the next example, we consider only registered users.

> **Note** For more information on the ASP.NET profile subsystem, take a look at Chapter 5 of my book *Programming Microsoft ASP.NET 2.0 Applications: Core Reference* (Microsoft Press, 2005).

Profile-enabled applications should implement a number of features, including the following ones:

- Pages using profile information should have some server-side code in their *Page_Load* handler to ensure that child controls are correctly set up in case of full postbacks, redirects, or direct browser access.

- There should be one or more pages where registered users can edit their profile. These pages should then save changes to the profile data store.

- Login/Logout buttons should be provided to let users log in and log out at will.

If ASP.NET AJAX Extensions is employed, the user interface of profile-enabled pages should also be updated via script to immediately reflect a new logged-in user or changes to the profile object.

Initializing a Profile-Enabled Page

Figure 6-5 illustrates a sample page that uses the authentication service to let users log in and uses the profile service to read and update the profile.

Figure 6-5   A sample page requiring user authentication

After the user is connected, the user interface adapts to reflect the contents of the profile. The code-behind class can hide and display child controls based on the authentication state of the request. If a user is connected, the code in *Page_Load* typically applies profile information. In this case, it simply consists of setting the page background color:

```
protected void Page_Load(object sender, EventArgs e)
{
    if (Request.IsAuthenticated)
    {
        LoggedIn.Style["display"] = "";
        NotLoggedIn.Style["display"] = "none";
        LoggedUser.Text = User.Identity.Name;

        ApplyProfile();
    }
```

```
    else
    {
        LoggedIn.Style["display"] = "none";
        NotLoggedIn.Style["display"] = "";
        LoggedUser.Text = "";
    }
}
protected void ApplyProfile()
{
    // Set page background color
    string bgColor = Profile.UI.BackColor;
    if (!String.IsNullOrEmpty(bgColor))
        Body.Style["background-color"] = bgColor;
}
```

The preceding code is purely classic ASP.NET code. This ensures that the page works correctly if invoked from the address bar, if invoked from a hyperlink, or if the user navigates back or forward to it. The same logic must also be expressed through script code for when the user connects using the ASP.NET AJAX authentication service or edits the profile using the profile Web service from the client.

Loading the User Profile

The following script loads the profile data after the user logs in. It uses the *load* method on the *Sys.Services._ProfileService* object to connect to the server data store and download the user profile.

```
function OnLogin()
{
    Sys.Services.AuthenticationService.login(
        username.value, password.value, false, onLoginCompleted);
    return false;
}
function onLoginCompleted(result)
{
    if (result)
        loadProfile();
    else
        alert("Sorry, your credentials appear to be invalid. Try again.");
}
function loadProfile()
{
    Sys.Services.ProfileService.load(null,
        loadProfileCompleted, loadProfileFailed, null);
}
function loadProfileCompleted(result, context, methodName)
{
    var bgColor;
    bgColor = Sys.Services.ProfileService.properties["UI"]["BackColor"];
    $get("PageBody").style.backgroundColor = bgColor;
}
function loadProfileFailed(result, context, methodName)
```

```
{
    alert(result.get_message());
}
```

The first argument of the *load* method is an array that indicates the properties to load—a string array. If set to null, the method retrieves all properties in the profile. The *load* method works asynchronously. For this reason, you need a callback to execute any code that uses the profile information.

To access a particular profile property, you use the *properties* collection. You select an element in the collection using the property name as the indexer, as shown here:

```
var temp = Sys.Services.ProfileService.properties["MyProperty"];
```

If properties are grouped, you use a multidimensional array, as shown next:

```
var temp = Sys.Services.ProfileService.properties["Group"]["MyProperty"];
```

In the preceding code, the *loadProfileCompleted* function sets the page background color. The code assumes that the page's body is flagged *runat=server* and is given an ID named *PageBody*. The name of the ID is arbitrary. The *<body>* tag must be a server-side tag for you to change the background color programmatically from within an ASP.NET page. The tag isn't necessary if you only want to get and set the color via script. In this case, in fact, the sole ID would suffice. However, as mentioned, profile-enabled pages must also have a server-side version of any client code that manages profile data.

Updating the Profile

The sample application is completed by a page that allows each user to select a color to fill the page background. The page to edit colors is a pure ASP.NET server page that reads and saves profile data using the server *Profile* object. What would be necessary to save profile information directly from the client? Let's take a look at the markup at the bottom of the page in Figure 6-5:

```
<fieldset>
    <b><span>Background color </span></b>
    <input type="text" id="NewBgColor" value="" />
    <input type="button" value="Save profile" onclick="saveProfile()" />
</fieldset>
```

When the user clicks the Save Profile button (shown in Figure 6-5), the page saves the profile through the following code:

```
function saveProfile()
{
    // Proceed only if the user is authenticated
    var loggedIn = Sys.Services.AuthenticationService.get_isLoggedIn();
    if (!loggedIn)
    {
        alert("You must be logged in to try this");
        return;
    }
```

```
    // Save client data to the profile
    var clr = newBgColor.value;
    Sys.Services.ProfileService.properties["UI"]["BackColor"] = clr;
    Sys.Services.ProfileService.save(null,
        saveProfileCompleted, null, null);
}
```

The click event handler first checks whether the current user is authenticated. If so, it updates the profile properties and proceeds calling the *save* method on the *Sys.Services._ProfileService* client class. The first argument for the *save* method is an array with string/object pairs of properties to persist. If the argument is null, all properties in the data model will be saved. Figure 6-6 shows the page we saw in Figure 6-5 slightly updated (only background color) to reflect the profile of the logged-in user.

Figure 6-6 The user interface of the page changes to reflect the information in the user profile

> **Note** The *ProfileService* class in ASP.NET AJAX Extensions employs a built-in Web service to read and write profile properties on the server. It is just a client wrapper for the ASP.NET server *Profile* object which, in turn, uses a profile provider to store user-specific data. You can use server pages and AJAX pages in the same application that use the profile data. To be successful, though, do not rely on AJAX only; instead, make sure that your AJAX-enabled pages have a *Page_Load* event handler to apply profile data each time the page is loaded.

Conclusion

Web services are components hosted by Web applications whose functions are accessible using standard protocols. Web services represent black-box functionality that can be reused without worrying about how the service is implemented internally. In the context of ASP.NET AJAX applications, Web services also represent a neat way to access server-side functionality from the client. In the next chapter, we'll explore the techniques and machinery necessary to design and support new Web services that are callable from the client.

In this chapter, we reviewed a couple of built-in Web services that connect two pillars of ASP.NET development with JavaScript classes. User authentication and management of user profile information can be accomplished from the client thanks to a couple of built-in Java-Script proxies and hard-coded ASP.NET Web services. Although in ASP.NET AJAX Extensions the authentication and profile services are presented as two stand-alone pieces of functionality, they share the same pattern and machinery with user-defined Web services invoked from the client. In the next chapter, we'll focus on learning more about calling remote code from the client.

Remote Method Calls with ASP.NET AJAX

The chief factor for the success and rapid adoption of the AJAX model is that it enables most application tasks to be performed on the client with limited exchange of data with the server. Nonetheless, some data exchange with the server environment is necessary.

As discussed in Chapter 4, "Partial Page Rendering," ASP.NET AJAX applications can use asynchronous postbacks to refresh portions of the page and update the state of controls through lightweight server events. An AJAX postback is more lightweight than a full postback, but it's still a request that moves view state, event validation data, and any other input fields you might have around the page. Also, the AJAX postback is still a request that goes through the full server-side page life cycle. It differs from a regular ASP.NET postback only because it has a custom rendering phase and, of course, returns only a portion of the whole page markup. Put another way, an AJAX postback is definitely faster and much more beneficial than regular postbacks, but it's still subject to a number of constraints. And, more importantly, it doesn't fit just any scenario.

If the page has a huge view state, for example, the benefits of AJAX postbacks are quite watered down. With 50 KB of view state, can you really consider saving one or two KB of markup to be a success? On the other hand, the partial rendering model doesn't require the developer to learn new skills, has a surprisingly short learning curve, and has limited impact on existing code. It gives you an easy way of updating the state of controls during the roundtrip and, subsequently, on the user interface.

It turns out that there are situations in which the partial rendering model is not appropriate and other situations in which it is just perfect. When the client requires that a specific operation be executed on the server with no frills and in a purely stateless manner, you should consider other options. Enter remote server method calls.

Making a call to a remote server requires that a public, well-known application programming interface (API) be exposed and made accessible from JavaScript. ASP.NET AJAX Extensions supports two server APIs: Web services and page methods.

In this chapter, we'll explore the connections between the ASP.NET AJAX framework and the world of remote services. You'll learn how to configure an ASP.NET AJAX application to consume local services and bridge Web services hosted by other applications or deployed on external servers.

Designing the Server API for Remote Calls

As we saw in Chapter 6, "Built-in Application Services," ASP.NET AJAX Extensions sports a few built-in Web services for user authentication and profiling. These services are implemented as ASP.NET Web services local to the calling application. The Microsoft AJAX library also features two matching JavaScript classes acting as the proxies of such services. The same model is used to back client JavaScript calls to a custom ASP.NET remote API.

The first step entails that you design a public API to be invoked from the client. To define this API, an explicit contract is not required for version 1.0 of ASP.NET AJAX Extensions. However, I have a couple of good reasons to recommend that you start from this moment forward to design the public API as an interface. One reason is that it generates cleaner code. Another reason is that with the next version of ASP.NET (code-named "Orcas"), you'll be allowed to link primarily to Windows Communication Foundation (WCF) services, where an explicit contract for the interface is mandatory.

When you're done with the interface of the server API, you proceed with the creation of a class that implements the interface. Finally, you publish the remote API and let the ASP.NET AJAX runtime manage calls from the client. Let's expand on the various steps.

Important Too often, ASP.NET AJAX articles and documentation refer to the platform's ability to invoke Web services from the client. But this is a bit misleading. You can't just invoke any Web service you like. If this is so (and it is), one rightly wonders why the simple and clear Web service model is then subject to a number of seemingly arbitrary ASP.NET AJAX limitations.

For example, as you start working with Web services in AJAX, you quickly find that the Web services you can invoke are meant to be ASP.NET AJAX Web services, and what's more, they must be local to the host application. If your intention was to use a public Web service (say, Amazon), you realize that you need a separate download and a distinct (Amazon) programming model. And you probably will wonder why on earth is this the case? After all, the articles and documentation make it appear that any Web service will work.

In my opinion, all this confusion stems from a flawed approach to the question. ASP.NET AJAX doesn't just let you call into any Web service from JavaScript. Rather, the way to look at the situation is to imagine that ASP.NET AJAX lets you use JavaScript to place calls into some server code within your own application. The application server code, in turn, can be exposed as an ASP.NET AJAX Web service local to the application. External Web services, those being services outside your application's domain, cannot be invoked directly from the client for security reasons. This is by design.

Defining the Contract of the Remote API

A contract is used to specify what the server-side endpoint exposes to callers. An explicit contract is required for WCF services but is expressed in a less formal, implicit way for general Web services. In the context of an ASP.NET AJAX server API, a contract is mostly a way to write cleaner code. It's not required, but it can help and is definitely a practice worth pursuing. This is especially true in light of the next version of ASP.NET, where the integration with WCF services and the ability to invoke service endpoints from the client are the pillars.

The Contracted Interface

A contract is defined through an interface that groups methods and properties that form the server API. Here's an example of a simple service that returns the current time on the server:

```
using System;

public interface ITimeService
{
    DateTime GetTime();
    string GetTimeFormat(string format);
}
```

The contract exposes two methods: *GetTime* and *GetTimeFormat*. These methods form the server API that can be called from within the client.

Warning   Currently, you are on your own when implementing a given interface in an AJAX server API. There's no automatic runtime check to enforce the requirement that exactly those methods are exposed by the server API. If you think of the process in terms of contracts and operations within contracts however, having contracts helps a lot. You'll write cleaner code to begin with and find your code has laid the groundwork for migrating to future evolutions of the .NET and ASP.NET platforms.

What's Coming Out with "Orcas"?

From an AJAX perspective, the next innovation in the "Orcas" release of the .NET platform (presumably in late 2007) is the tight integration between the AJAX platform and WCF services. In the near future, WCF services will become the primary back-end environment for AJAX-driven client calls.

As we'll see in the remainder of the chapter, with the current version 1.0 of ASP.NET AJAX Extensions, remote calls target the contract that is either exposed by a local application-specific Web service or incorporated in the page's code-behind class. These two models will be joined, or even replaced, by a new model entirely based on WCF services and a new runtime infrastructure in ASP.NET "Orcas."

According to the upcoming model, you define your server API as a WCF service and give it a well-known contract. You expose the service to browser clients by registering the service's endpoint with the script manager. In the configuration file, then, you can make deployment-time decisions on bindings and behaviors for the service. The JavaScript proxy model in vogue today will work unchanged. For a page developer, all that apparently changes is merely the URL to register with the script manager. For a server developer, the change is all about a different set of attributes used to decorate the service class. The infrastructure in between the browser and the server environment, though, will be significantly enhanced.

In the end, you'll have a great server programming model with WCF that is also fully supported by DLINQ and Windows Workflow Foundation (WF). In addition, it can expose the same service, at the same time, as a service based on Simple Object Access Protocol (SOAP) to any client and as a JSON-based service to AJAX clients. Plus, and what an extraordinary feature this is, you get to reuse all the great features of the WCF platform: manageability, tracing, logging, throttling, timeouts, Denial-of-Service (DoS) protection quotas, and hosting options.

Why Not WSDL and SOAP?

You can use Web services to define the server API that an ASP.NET AJAX application can invoke via JavaScript, but this doesn't mean that you can call just *any* Web services from JavaScript. The JavaScript proxy class used by the page script is generated by the script manager class, and it requires the ASP.NET AJAX Extensions to be installed on the server. Why not use Web Services Description Language (WSDL) to expose the contract and use SOAP (instead of JSON) to compose messages?

Being XML-based, WSDL and SOAP are hard to manage from the client and when using the JavaScript language. JSON is a much simpler format that, more importantly, finds a natural serializer—the *eval* function— in any JavaScript engine. As we'll see later in the chapter, you need an extra layer of code to call any remote Web services, regardless of location and platform. This additional layer of code is managed code that runs on the server and that provides a proper JavaScript proxy for client-driven calls. We'll return to this point later in the "Bridging External Web Services" section and also, from an architectural perspective, in Chapter 8, "Building AJAX Applications with ASP.NET."

Implementing the Contract of the Remote API

Once you have defined the server API you want to invoke from the client, you implement and expose it. As mentioned, this can be done in either of two ways: using an application-local ASP.NET Web service, or using a set of static methods on the code-behind class of each page interested in making any calls.

Contract via Web Services

An ASP.NET Web service is usually implemented through a .NET class that derives from the *WebService* base class:

```
using System.Web.Services;

public class TimeService : WebService, ITimeService
{
    ...
}
```

To direct the Web service to support a given interface, you simply add the interface type to the declaration statement and implement corresponding methods in the body of the class.

Again, the implementation of a user-defined interface in an ASP.NET Web service is not strictly required. However, especially for Web services that represent the server API in the context of ASP.NET AJAX applications, the implementation of an interface is a good thing that keeps code neat and even elegant. And doing so prepares you and your code for future enhancements of the platform.

> **Note**   The *WebService* base class is optional and serves primarily to provide direct access to common ASP.NET objects, such as *Application* and *Session*. If you don't need direct access to the intrinsic ASP.NET objects, you can still create an ASP.NET Web service without deriving from the *WebService* class. In this case, you can still use ASP.NET intrinsics through the *HttpContext* object:

Contract via Code-Behind Classes

A Web service forms an extra layer of code in an ASP.NET application. If you don't want to define such a layer, you can still define your server API via static methods exposed directly by the code-behind class of a given page. Needless to say, if you opt for static methods you'll be able to call server methods only from within the page that defines them. No cross-page calls are supported. If you need a centralized location for the server API that is visible to all pages in the application, you have to go for the Web service interface.

By design and mostly because of performance considerations, client-callable page methods need to be static. In a .NET interface, though, static methods are not allowed. How can you then expose a contract out of a code-behind class? The following code shows the typical prototype of a code-behind class with a client-callable Web method:

```
public partial class SamplePage : System.Web.UI.Page
{
    [WebMethod]
    public static DateTime GetTime()
    {
        ...
    }
    ...
}
```

To ensure that all methods in a given interface are exposed by the page, you first define a base class with the desired set of static Web methods:

```
public class TimeServicePage : System.Web.UI.Page
{
    [WebMethod]
    public static DateTime GetTime()
    {
        return DateTime.Now.AddYears(1);
    }
}
```

Next, you change the parent of the code-behind class from *System.Web.UI.Page* to the contract-based class, as shown here:

```
public partial class SamplePage : TimeServicePage
{
    ...
}
```

All static methods are inherited, and the *WebMethod* attribute is automatically maintained on methods across class inheritance.

Publishing the Contract

Now that we have defined the formal contract and implementation of the server API of an ASP.NET AJAX application, one more step is left—publishing the contract. How do you do that?

Publishing the contract means making the server API visible to the JavaScript client page and subsequently enabling the JavaScript client page to place calls to the server API. From the client page, you can invoke any object that is visible to the JavaScript engine. In turn, the JavaScript engine sees any class that is linked to the page. In the end, publishing a given server contract means generating a JavaScript proxy class that the script embedded in the page can command.

When the server API is implemented through a Web service, you register the Web service with the script manager control of the ASP.NET AJAX page. In addition, you add a special HTTP handler for *.asmx* requests in the application's *web.config* file.

When the server API is exposed via page methods, you need to explicitly enable page methods on the script manager and also add an HTTP module to the configuration file.

Let's expand upon the topic of Web services and page methods by exploring a few examples.

Remote Calls via Web Services

Web services provide a natural environment for hosting server-side code that needs to be called in response to a client action such as clicking a button. The set of Web methods in the service refers to pieces of code specific to the application, including some parts of the application's middle tier. In this context, the Web service is part of the application and lives on the same machine and AppDomain. Keep in mind, however, that an ASP.NET AJAX application calls its server code via Web services; it does not call into just any Web service in a SOAP-based, platform-independent manner.

Creating an AJAX Web Service

A Web service made to measure for an ASP.NET AJAX application is nearly identical to any other ASP.NET Web service you might write for whatever purposes. Two peripheral aspects, though, delineate a clear difference between ASP.NET AJAX Web services and traditional ASP.NET Web services.

First and foremost, when working with ASP.NET AJAX Web services, you design the contract of an ASP.NET AJAX Web service to fit the needs of a particular application rather than to configure the behavior of a public service. The target application is also the host of the Web service. Second, you use a couple of new attributes to decorate the class and methods of the Web service that are not allowed on regular ASP.NET Web services.

The effect of this is, in the end, that an ASP.NET AJAX Web service has a double public interface: the JSON-based interface consumed by the hosting ASP.NET AJAX application, and the classic SOAP-based interface exposed to any clients, from any platforms, that can reach the service URL.

The *ScriptService* Attribute

To create an ASP.NET AJAX Web service, you first set up a standard ASP.NET Web service project and then add a reference to the *system.web.extensions* assembly. Next, you import the *System.Web.Script.Services* namespace:

```
using System.Web.Script.Services;
```

The attribute that establishes a key difference between ASP.NET Web services and ASP.NET AJAX Web services is the *ScriptService* attribute. You apply the attribute to the service class declaration, as shown here:

```
namespace IntroAjax.WebServices
{
    [WebService(Namespace = "http://introajax.book/")]
    [WebServiceBinding(ConformsTo = WsiProfiles.BasicProfile1_1)]
    [ScriptService]
    public class TimeService : System.Web.Services.WebService, ITimeService
    {
        ...
    }
}
```

The attribute indicates that the service is designed to accept calls from JavaScript-based client proxies. If the Web service lacks the attribute, no JavaScript proxy class will ever be generated for it, regardless of whether or not the Web service is registered with the page. Without a Java-Script proxy class, no client call is possible to the remote server API.

When flagged with the *ScriptService* attribute, an ASP.NET Web service supports two types of calls: classic calls via SOAP packets and client calls using JSON messages.

> **Important** If not properly handled, ASP.NET AJAX Web services, with their dual personalities, might result in you configuring a security issue. If you simply consider the Web service to be a constituent part of the ASP.NET AJAX application, you need no special security barrier to keep unauthorized users out. The application through its authentication layer is responsible for protecting pages.
>
> A Web service, though, is also exposed to SOAP clients and is a public endpoint. For this reason, you should be careful with the methods you expose. You should avoid exposing sensitive pieces of the middle tier to the public without a well-configured security barrier. It is recommended, then, that you add to the Web service only methods that form a sort of user interface–level business logic, where no critical task is accomplished. In addition, you should consider adding a validation layer in the body of Web methods and perhaps using network-level tools to monitor calling IP addresses and, if needed, block some of them.

The *ScriptMethod* Attribute

Public methods of the Web service class decorated with the *WebMethod* attribute are automatically added to the JavaScript proxy class and can subsequently be called from the client page. Any methods in the proxy class are invoked using the HTTP POST verb and return their values as JSON objects. You can change these default settings on a per-method basis by using an optional attribute—*ScriptMethod*.

The *ScriptMethod* attribute features three properties, as described in Table 7-1.

Table 7-1 Properties of the *ScriptMethod* Attribute

Property	Description
ResponseFormat	Specifies whether the response will be serialized as JSON or as XML. The default is JSON, but the XML format can come in handy when the return value of the method is *XmlDocument*. In this case, because *XMLHttpRequest* has the native ability to expose the response as an XML DOM, you save unnecessary serialization and deserialization via JSON.
UseHttpGet	Indicates whether an HTTP GET verb should be used to invoke the Web service method. The default is *false*, meaning that the POST verb is used. The GET verb poses some security issues, especially when sensitive data is being transmitted. All the data, in fact, is stored in the URL and is visible to everybody.
XmlSerializeString	Indicates whether all return types, including strings, are serialized as XML. The default is *false*. The value of the property is ignored when the response format is JSON.

Because of the repercussions it might have on security and performance, the *ScriptMethod* attribute should be used very carefully. The following code uses the attribute without specifying nondefault settings:

```
[WebMethod]
[ScriptMethod]
public DateTime GetTime()
{
    ...
}
```

The *WebMethod* attribute is required; the *ScriptMethod* attribute is optional. You should use it only when you need to change some of the default settings, as explained in Table 7-1.

Registering AJAX Web Services

To place calls to an ASP.NET Web service from the client, you need a JavaScript proxy class. More precisely, all that you really need is the *XMLHttpRequest* object, the URL of the target Web service, and the ability to serialize input data to JSON and deserialize any received JSON response. However, if any input or output parameters of a method require a complex type (for example, a *Customer* type), you should be able to handle it too, both to and from JSON. As you can see, a proxy class and, more than just this, a server-side framework that governs the generation of the proxy is required.

To trigger the built-in engine that generates any required JavaScript proxy and helper classes, you register the AJAX Web service with the script manager control of each page where the Web service is required. You can achieve this both declaratively and programmatically. Here's how to do it declaratively from page markup:

```
<asp:ScriptManager ID="ScriptManager1" runat="server">
    <Services>
        <asp:ServiceReference Path="~/WebServices/TimeService.asmx" />
    </Services>
</asp:ScriptManager>
```

You add a *ServiceReference* tag for each Web service bound to the page and set the *Path* attribute to a relative URL for the *.asmx* resource. Each service reference automatically produces an extra <*script*> block in the client page, as shown here:

```
<script src="~/WebServices/TimeService.asmx/js"
        type="text/javascript"></script>
```

The */js* suffix appended to the Web service URL instructs the ASP.NET AJAX runtime (specifically, an ad-hoc HTTP handler, as we'll see in a moment) to generate and inject the JavaScript proxy class for the specified Web service. If the page runs in debug mode (which is discussed in Chapter 3, "The Pulsing Heart of ASP.NET AJAX"), the suffix changes to */jsdebug* and a debug version of the proxy class is emitted.

By default, the JavaScript proxy is linked to the page via a *<script>* tag and thus requires a separate download. You can also merge any needed script to the current page by setting the *InlineScript* attribute to *true*. The default value of *false* is helpful if browser caching is enabled and multiple Web pages use the same service reference. In this case, therefore, only one additional request is executed, regardless of how many pages need the proxy class. A value of *true* for the *InlineScript* property reduces the number of network requests at the cost of consuming a bit more bandwidth. This option is preferable when there are many service references in the page and most pages do not link to the same services.

To register AJAX Web services programmatically, you add the following code, preferably in the *Page_Load* event of the page's code-behind class:

```
ServiceReference service = new ServiceReference();
service.Path = "~/WebServices/TimeService.asmx";
ScriptManager1.Services.Add(service);
```

Whatever route you take, to invoke the Web service you need to place a call to the proxy class using JavaScript. The proxy class has the same name as the Web service class and the same set of methods. We'll return to this topic in a moment.

Configuring ASP.NET Applications to Host AJAX Web Services

To enable Web service calls from within ASP.NET AJAX applications, you need to add the following script to the application's *web.config* file and register a special HTTP handler for *.asmx* requests:

```
<httpHandlers>
    <remove verb="*" path="*.asmx" />
    <add verb="*" path="*.asmx"
        type="System.Web.Script.Services.ScriptHandlerFactory" />
    ...
</httpHandlers>
```

This setting is included in the default *web.config* file that the Microsoft Visual Studio 2005 ASP.NET AJAX template creates for you.

In ASP.NET, a handler factory determines which HTTP handler is in charge of serving a given set of requests. The specialized ASP.NET AJAX Web service handler factory for *.asmx* requests distinguishes JSON calls made by script code from ordinary Web service calls coming from SOAP-based clients, including ASP.NET and Windows Forms applications. JSON-based requests are served by a different HTTP handler, whereas regular SOAP calls take the usual route in the ASP.NET pipeline.

Consuming AJAX Web Services

A referenced ASP.NET AJAX Web service is exposed to the JavaScript code as a class with the same name as the server class, including namespace information. As we'll see in a moment, the proxy class is a singleton and exposes static methods for you to call. No instantiation is required, which saves time and makes the call trigger more quickly. Let's take a look at the JavaScript proxy class generated from the public interface of an AJAX Web service.

The Proxy Class

To understand the structure of a JavaScript proxy class, we'll consider what the ASP.NET AJAX runtime generates for the aforementioned *timeservice.asmx* Web service. The full name of the Web service class is *IntroAjax.WebServices.TimeService*, and therefore it is the name of the Java-Script proxy as well. Here's the first excerpt from the script injected in the client page for the time Web service:

```
Type.registerNamespace('IntroAjax.WebServices');
IntroAjax.WebServices.TimeService = function()
{
   IntroAjax.WebServices.TimeService.initializeBase(this);
   this._timeout = 0;
   this._userContext = null;
   this._succeeded = null;
   this._failed = null;
}
IntroAjax.WebServices.TimeService.prototype =
{
    GetTime : function(succeededCallback, failedCallback, userContext)
    {
        return this._invoke(IntroAjax.WebServices.TimeService.get_path(),
                  'GetTime', false, {}, succeededCallback,
                  failedCallback, userContext);
    },
    GetTimeFormat : function(timeFormat, succeededCallback,
                             failedCallback, userContext)
    {
        return this._invoke(IntroAjax.WebServices.TimeService.get_path(),
                  'GetTimeAsFormat', false, {format:timeFormat},
                  succeededCallback, failedCallback, userContext);
    }
}
IntroAjax.WebServices.TimeService.registerClass(
      IntroAjax.WebServices.TimeService',
      Sys.Net.WebServiceProxy);
IntroAjax.WebServices.TimeService._staticInstance =
      new IntroAjax.WebServices.TimeService();
```

As you can see from the prototype, the *TimeService* class has two methods—*GetTime* and *GetTimeFormat*—the same two methods defined as Web methods in the server-side Web service class. Both methods have an extended signature that encompasses additional parameters other than the standard set of input arguments (as defined by the server-side methods). In particular, you see two callbacks to call—one for the success of the call, and one for failure—and an object that represents the context of the call. Internally, each method on the proxy class yields to a private member of the parent class—*Sys.Net.WebServiceProxy*—that uses *XMLHttpRequest* to physically send bytes to the server.

The last statement in the preceding code snippet creates a global instance of the proxy class. The methods you invoke from within your JavaScript to execute remote calls are defined around this global instance, as shown here:

```
IntroAjax.WebServices.TimeService.GetTime = function(
        onSuccess,onFailed,userContext)
{
   IntroAjax.WebServices.TimeService._staticInstance.GetTime(
        onSuccess, onFailed, userContext);
}

IntroAjax.WebServices.TimeService.GetTimeFormat = function(
        format, onSuccess, onFailed, userContext)
{
    IntroAjax.WebServices.TimeService._staticInstance.GetTimeFormat(
        format, onSuccess, onFailed, userContext);
}
```

The definition of the proxy class is completed with a few public properties, as described in Table 7-2.

Table 7-2 Static Properties on a JavaScript Proxy Class

Property	Description
path	Gets and sets the URL of the underlying Web service
timeout	Gets and sets the duration (in seconds) before the method call times out
defaultSucceededCallback	Gets and sets the default JavaScript callback function to invoke for a successful call
defaultFailedCallback	Gets and sets the default JavaScript callback function, if any, to invoke for a failed or timed-out call
defaultUserContext	Gets and sets the default JavaScript object, if any, to be passed to success and failure callbacks

If you set a default *succeeded* callback, you don't have to specify a succeeded callback in any successive call as long as the desired callback function is the same. The same holds true for the *failed* callback and the user context object. The user context object is any JavaScript object, filled with any information that makes sense to you, that gets automatically passed to any callback that handles success or failure of the call.

Note   The JavaScript code injected for the proxy class uses the *path* property to define the URL to the Web service. You can change the property programmatically to redirect the proxy to a different URL.

Executing Remote Calls

A Web service call is an operation that the page executes in response to a user action such as a button click. Here's the typical way of attaching some JavaScript to a client button click:

```
<input type="button" value="Get Time" onclick="getTime()" />
```

The button is preferably a client button, but it can also be a classic server-side *Button* object submit button as long as it sets the *OnClientClick* property to a piece of JavaScript code that returns *false* to prevent the default submit action:

```
<asp:Button ID="Button1" runat="server" Text="Button"
        OnClientClick="getTime();return false;" />
```

The *getTime* function collects any required input data and then calls the desired static method on the proxy class. If you plan to assign default values to callbacks or the user context object, the best place to do it is in the *pageLoad* function. As discussed in Chapter 2, "The Microsoft Client Library for AJAX," the *pageLoad* function is invoked when the client page ASP.NET AJAX tree has been fully initialized, and precisely because of this it is more reliable than the browser's *onload* event.

```
<script language="javascript" type="text/javascript">
    function pageLoad()
    {
        IntroAjax.WebServices.TimeService.set_defaultFailedCallback(
            methodFailed);
    }
    function getTime()
    {
        IntroAjax.WebServices.TimeService.GetTimeFormat(
            "ddd, dd MMMM yyyy [hh:mm:ss]", methodComplete);
    }
    function methodComplete(results, context, methodName)
    {
        $get("Label1").innerHTML = results;
    }
    function methodFailed(results, context, methodName)
    {
        $get("Label1").innerHTML = String.format(
            "Execution of method '{0}' failed because of the
             following:\r\n'{1}'",
            methodName, results.get_message());
    }
</script>
```

Because the Web service call proceeds asynchronously, you need callbacks to catch up in case of both success and failure. The signature of the callbacks is similar, but the internal format of the *results* parameter can change quite a bit:

```
function method(results, context, methodName)
```

Table 7-3 provides more details about the various arguments.

Table 7-3   Arguments for JavaScript Web Service Callback Functions

Argument	Description
results	Indicates the return value from the method in the case of success. In the case of failure, a JavaScript *Error* object mimics the exception that occurred on the server during the execution of the method.
context	The user context object passed to the callback.
methodName	The name of the Web service method that was invoked.

Based on the previous code, if the call is successful, the *methodCompleted* callback is invoked to update the page. The result is shown in Figure 7-1.

Figure 7-1   A remote call from the client

Error Handling

The "failed" callback kicks in when an exception occurs on the server during the execution of the remote method. In this case, the HTTP response contains an HTTP 500 error code (internal error) and the body of the response looks like the following:

```
{"Message":"Exception thrown for testing purposes",
 "StackTrace":"  at IntroAjax.WebServices.MyDataService.Throw() in
             d:\\IntroAjax\\App_Code\\Services\\MyDataService.cs:line
             62","ExceptionType":"System.InvalidOperationException"}
```

On the client, the server exception is exposed through a JavaScript *Error* object dynamically built based on the message and stack trace received from the server. This *Error* object is exposed to the "failed" callback via the *results* argument. You can read back the message and stack trace through *message* and *stackTrace* properties on the *Error* object.

You can use a different error handler callback for each remote call, or you can designate a default function to be invoked if one is not otherwise specified. However, ASP.NET AJAX still defines its own default callback, which is invoked when it gets no further information from the client developer. The system-provided error handler callback simply pops up a message box with the message associated with the server exception. (See Figure 7-2.)

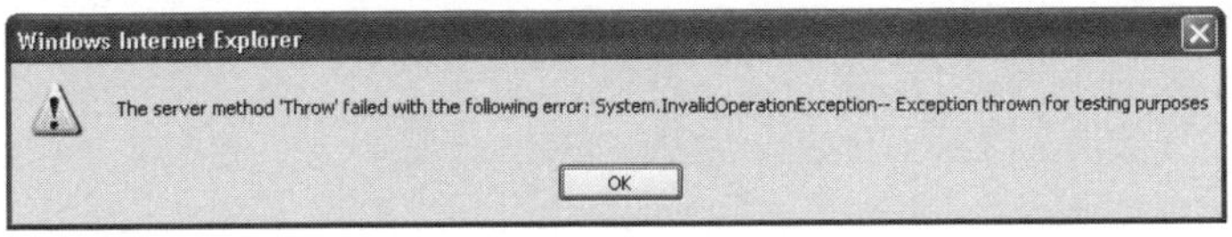

Figure 7-2   The system-provided JavaScript error handler

If you define your own "failed" callback, you can avoid message boxes and incorporate any error message directly in the body of the page.

Giving User Feedback

A remote call might take a while to complete because the operation to execute is fairly heavy or just because of the network latency. In any case, you might feel the need to show some feedback to the user to let her know that the system is still working. In Chapter 4, we saw that the Microsoft AJAX library has built-in support for an intermediate progress screen and also a client-side eventing model. Unfortunately, this functionality is limited to calls that originate within updatable panels. For classic remote method calls you have to personally take care of any user feedback.

You bring up the wait message, the animated GIF, or whatever else you need just before you call the remote method:

```
function takeaWhile()
{
    // In this example, the Feedback element is a <span> tag
    $get("Feedback").innerHTML = "Please, wait ...";
    IntroAjax.WebServices.MySampleService.VeryLengthyTask(
        methodCompletedWithFeedback, methodFailedWithFeedback);
}
```

In the "completed" callback, you reset the user interface first and then proceed:

```
function methodCompletedWithFeedback(results, context, methodName)
{
    $get("Feedback").innerHTML = "";
    ...
}
```

Note that you should also clear the user interface in the case of errors. In addition to showing some sort of wait message to the user, you should also consider that other elements in the page might need to be disabled during the call. If this is the case, you need to disable them before the call and restore them later.

Handling Timeouts

A remote call that takes a while to complete is not necessarily a good thing for the application. Keep in mind that calls that work asynchronously for the client are not necessarily asynchronous for the ASP.NET runtime. In particular, note that when you make a client call to an *.asmx* Web service, you are invoking the *.asmx* directly. For this request, only a synchronous handler is available in the ASP.NET runtime. This means that regardless of how the client perceives the ongoing call, an ASP.NET thread is entirely blocked (waiting for results) until the method is done. To mitigate the impact of lengthy AJAX methods on the application scalability, you can set a timeout:

```
IntroAjax.WebServices.MySampleService.set_timeout(3000);
```

The *timeout* attribute is global and applies to all methods of the proxy class. This means that if you want to time out only one method call, you have to reset the timeout for all calls you're making from the page. To reset the timeout, you just set the *timeout* property to zero:

```
IntroAjax.WebServices.MySampleService.set_timeout(0);
```

When the request times out, there's no response received from the server. It's simply a call that is aborted from the client. After all, you can't control what's going on with the server. The best you can do is abort the request on the client and take other appropriate measures, such as having the user try again later.

Considerations for AJAX Web Services

Now that we know how to tackle AJAX Web services, it would be nice to spend some time reflecting on some other aspects of them—for example, why use local services?

Why Local Web Services?

To make sure you handle AJAX Web services the right way, think of them as just one possible way of exposing a server API to a JavaScript client. You focus on the interface that must be exposed and then choose between ASP.NET Web services and page methods for its actual implementation. Looking at it from this angle, you might find it to be quite natural that the Web service has to be hosted in the same ASP.NET AJAX application that is calling it.

But why can't you just call into any Web services out there? There are two main reasons: security and required support for JSON serialization.

For security reasons, browsers tend to stop cross-site calls. Most browsers bind scripted requests to what is often referred to as the "same origin policy." Defined, it claims that no documents can be requested via script that have a different port, server, or protocol than the current page. In light of this, you can use the *XMLHttpRequest* object to place asynchronous calls as long as your request hits the same server that served the current page.

Because of the cross-site limitations of *XMLHttpRequest* in most browsers, ASP.NET AJAX Extensions doesn't allow you to directly invoke a Web service that lives on another IIS server or site. Without this limitation, nothing would prevent you from invoking a Web service that is resident on any platform and Web server environment, but then your users are subject to potential security threats from less scrupulous applications. With this limitation in place, though, an additional issue shows up: the inability of your host ASP.NET AJAX environment to build a JavaScript proxy class for the remote, non–ASP.NET AJAX Web service.

> **Note**   Because of the impact that blocked cross-site calls have on general AJAX develop-
> ment, a new standard might emerge in the near future to enable such calls from the browser.
> It might be desirable that the client sends the request and dictates the invoked server accept
> or deny cross-site calls made via *XMLHttpRequest*. As of this writing, though, the possibility of
> direct cross-site calls from AJAX clients (not just ASP.NET AJAX Extensions) remains limited to
> the use of IFRAMEs and finds no built-in support in ASP.NET AJAX Extensions 1.0.

Why JSON-Based Web Services?

A call to a Web service hosted by the local ASP.NET AJAX application is not conducted using SOAP as you might expect. SOAP is XML-based, and parsing XML on the client is very expensive in terms of memory and processing resources. It means that an XML parser must be available in JavaScript, and an XML parser is never an easy toy to build and manage, especially using a relatively lightweight tool such as JavaScript. So a different format is required to pack messages to be sent and unpack messages just received. Like SOAP and XML schemas together, though, this new format must be able to serialize an object's public properties and fields to a serial text-based format for transport. The format employed by ASP.NET AJAX Web services is JavaScript Object Notation, or JSON for short. (See *http://www.json.org* for more information on the origin and goals of the format.)

JSON is a text-based format specifically designed to move the state of an object across tiers. It is natively supported by JavaScript in the sense that a JSON-compatible string can be evaluated to a JavaScript object quite simply through the built-in JavaScript *eval* function. If the JSON string represents the state of a custom object, it's your responsibility to ensure that the definition of the corresponding class is available on the client.

The client-side ASP.NET AJAX network stack takes care of creating JSON strings for each parameter to pass remotely. The JavaScript class that does that is called *Sys.Serialization.Java-ScriptSerializer*. On the server, ad hoc formatter classes receive the data and use .NET reflection to populate matching managed classes. On the way back, .NET managed objects are serialized to JSON strings and sent over. The script manager is called to guarantee that proper classes referenced in the JSON strings—the Web service proxy class—exist on the client.

Runtime Support for JSON-Based Web Services

As a developer, you don't necessarily need to know much about the JSON format. You normally don't get close enough to the heart of the system to directly manage JSON strings. However, a JSON string represents an object according to the following example schema:

```
{
 "__type":"IntroAjax.Customer",
 "ID":"ANATR",
 "ContactName":"Ana Trujillo"
 ...
}
```

You'll find a number of comma-separated tokens wrapped in curly brackets. Each token is, in turn, a colon-separated string. The left part, in quotes, represents the name of the property; the right part, in quotes, represents the serialized version of the property value. If the property value is not a primitive type, it gets recursively serialized via JSON. If the object is an instance of a known type (that is, it is not an untyped JavaScript associative array), the class name is inserted as the first piece of information associated with the _type property. Any information being exchanged between an ASP.NET AJAX client and an ASP.NET AJAX Web service is serialized to the JSON format.

To the actual Web service, the transport format is totally transparent—be it SOAP, JSON, plain-old XML (POX), or whatever else. The runtime infrastructure takes care of deserializing the content of the message and transforms it into valid input for the service method. The ASP.NET AJAX runtime recognizes a call directed to an AJAX Web service because of the particular value of the *Content-Type* request header. Here's an excerpt from the Microsoft AJAX client library where the header is set:

```
request.get_headers()['Content-Type'] = 'application/json; charset=utf-8';
```

The value of this header is used to filter incoming requests and direct them to the standard ASP.NET Web service HTTP handler or to the made-to-measure ASP.NET AJAX Web service handler that will do all the work with the JSON string.

Why Not WCF Services?

Windows Communication Foundation (WCF) is the .NET 3.0 API for building service-oriented applications. WCF should be seen as the sum of a number of existing Microsoft connectivity technologies that are unified and extended into a single programming model. WCF is independent of underlying communications protocols, and it lets native applications interoperate with other applications using open standards and protocols.

From this concise but effective description, WCF seems to be the perfect partner for an ASP.NET AJAX client. However, in ASP.NET AJAX Extensions 1.0, there's no way to connect a JavaScript client to a WCF service. Well, not yet.

Starting with the next release of the .NET Framework (presumably in late 2007), the engine that allows ASP.NET AJAX clients to call remote methods will be redesigned to allow WCF services as yet another way to define the callable server API. An extended runtime engine will then capture local server calls and forward them to a remote WCF service hosted anywhere, even outside the ASP.NET AJAX application. The integration between ASP.NET AJAX and WCF services is on its way. It's just a matter of a few months now.

Remote Calls via Page Methods

As we've seen, ASP.NET Web services are a simple and effective way of implementing a server API. Once the ASP.NET AJAX runtime engine has generated the proxy class, you're pretty much done and can start calling methods as if they were local to the client. Web services, though, are not free of issues. They require an extra layer of code and additional files to be added to the project. Is this a big source of concern for you? If not, consider this instead: once deployed, the Web service is accessible via SOAP to any clients and from any platforms that can see the endpoint. This arrangement might or might not be a problem, as it mostly depends on what you expose through the Web service. In any case, you now have a less visible alternative—page methods—although it's still not immune from replay attacks.

Creating Page Methods

Page methods are simply public, static methods exposed by the code-behind class of a given page and decorated with the *WebMethod* attribute. The runtime engine for page methods and AJAX Web services is nearly the same. If you want an explicit container of endpoints, you choose Web services; if you want an implicit host, you go for the page class. Using page methods saves you from the burden of creating and publishing a Web service; at the same time, though, it binds you to having page-scoped methods that can't be called from within a page different from the one where they are defined. We'll return later to the pros and cons of page methods. For now, let's just learn more about them.

Defining Page Methods

Public and static methods defined on a page's code-behind class and flagged with the *WebMethod* attribute transform an ASP.NET AJAX page into a Web service. Here's a sample page method:

```
public class TimeServicePage : System.Web.UI.Page
{
    [WebMethod]
    public static DateTime GetTime()
    {
        return DateTime.Now;
    }
}
```

You can use any data type in the definition of page methods, including .NET Framework types as well as user-defined types. All types will be transparently JSON-serialized during each call.

> **Note**   The page class where you define methods might be the direct code-behind class or, better yet, a parent class. In this way, in the parent class you can implement the contract of the public server API and keep it somewhat separated from the rest of event handlers and methods that are specific to the page life cycle and behavior. Because page methods are required to be *static* (*shared* in Microsoft Visual Basic .NET), you can't use the syntax of interfaces to define the contract. You have to resort to abstract base classes.

Alternatively, you can define Web methods as inline code in the *.aspx* source file as follows. If you use Visual Basic, just change the *type* attribute to *text/VB*.

```
<script type="text/C#" runat="server">
    [WebMethod]
    public static DateTime GetTime()
    {
        return DateTime.Now;
    }
</script>
```

Note that page methods are specific to a given ASP.NET page. Only the host page can call its methods. Cross-page method calls are not supported. If they are critical for your scenario, I suggest that you move to using Web services.

Enabling Page Methods

When the code-behind class of an ASP.NET AJAX page contains *WebMethod*-decorated static methods, the runtime engine emits a JavaScript proxy class nearly identical to the class generated for a Web service. You use a global instance of this class to call server methods. The name of the class is hard-coded to *PageMethods*. We'll return to the characteristics of the proxy class in a moment.

Note, however, that page methods are not enabled by default. In other words, the *PageMethods* proxy class that you would use to place remote calls is not generated unless you set the *EnablePageMethods* property to *true* in the page's script manager:

```
<asp:ScriptManager runat="server" ID="ScriptManager1"
    EnablePageMethods="true" />
```

As a side note, consider that this property was added quite late in the development cycle of ASP.NET AJAX Extensions, just before the release-to-market (RTM) version. Code ported to the RTM version may require this property to be added and set to work correctly.

Runtime Support for Page Methods

For the successful execution of a page method, the ASP.NET AJAX application must have the *ScriptModule* HTTP module enabled in the *web.config* file:

```
<httpModules>
<add name="ScriptModule"
    type="System.Web.Handlers.ScriptModule, System.Web.Extensions" />
</httpModules>
```

Among other things, the module intercepts the application event that follows the loading of the session state, executes the method, and then serves the response to the caller. Acquiring session state is the step that precedes the start of the page life cycle. For page method calls, therefore, there's no page life cycle and child controls are not initialized and processed.

Why No Page Life Cycle?

In the early days of ASP.NET AJAX (when it was code-named Atlas), page methods were instance methods and required view state and form fields to be sent with every call. The sent view state was the last known good view state for the page—that is, the view state downloaded to the client. It was common for developers to expect that during the page method execution, say, a *TextBox* was set to the same text just typed before triggering the remote call. Because the sent view state was the last known good view state, that expectation was just impossible to meet. At the same time, a large share of developers was also complaining that the view state was being sent at all during page method calls. View state is rarely small, which served to increase the bandwidth and processing requirements for handling page methods.

As a result, starting with the beta stage, ASP.NET AJAX Extensions requires static methods and executes them just before starting the page life cycle. The page request is processed as usual until the session state is retrieved. After that, instead of going through the page life cycle, the HTTP module kicks in, executes the method via reflection, and returns.

Coded in this way, the execution of a remote page method is quite effective and nearly identical to having a local Web service up and running. The fact that static methods are used and no page life cycle is ever started means one thing to you—you can't programmatically access page controls and their properties.

Consuming Page Methods

The collection of page methods is exposed to the JavaScript code as a class with a fixed name—*PageMethods*. The schema of this class is similar to the schema of proxy classes for AJAX Web services. The class lists static methods and doesn't require any instantiation on your own. Let's take a look at the *PageMethods* class.

The Proxy Class

Unlike the proxy class for Web services, the *PageMethods* proxy class is always generated as inline script in the body of the page it refers to. That's a fairly obvious choice given the fixed naming convention in use; otherwise, the name of the class should be different for each page. Here's the source code of the *PageMethods* class for a page with just one Web method named *GetTime*:

```
<script type="text/javascript">
var PageMethods = function()
{
    PageMethods.initializeBase(this);
    this._timeout = 0;
    this._userContext = null;
    this._succeeded = null;
    this._failed = null;
}
PageMethods.prototype =
{
    GetTime:function(succeededCallback, failedCallback, userContext)
           {
               return this._invoke(PageMethods.get_path(),
                            'GetTime', false, {}, succeededCallback,
                            failedCallback, userContext);
           }
}
PageMethods.registerClass('PageMethods', Sys.Net.WebServiceProxy);
PageMethods._staticInstance = new PageMethods();

PageMethods.set_path = function(value) {
    var e = Function._validateParams(arguments,
                                     [{name: 'path', type: String}]);
    if (e) throw e;
    PageMethods._staticInstance._path = value;
}
PageMethods.get_path = function() {
    return PageMethods._staticInstance._path;
}
PageMethods.set_timeout = function(value) {
    var e = Function._validateParams(arguments,
                                     [{name: 'timeout', type: Number}]);
    if (e) throw e;
    if (value < 0)
       throw Error.argumentOutOfRange('value', value,
                                      Sys.Res.invalidTimeout);
    PageMethods._staticInstance._timeout = value;
}
PageMethods.get_timeout = function() {
    return PageMethods._staticInstance._timeout;
}
PageMethods.set_defaultUserContext = function(value) {
    PageMethods._staticInstance._userContext = value;
}
PageMethods.get_defaultUserContext = function() {
    return PageMethods._staticInstance._userContext;
}
PageMethods.set_defaultSucceededCallback = function(value) {
    var e = Function._validateParams(arguments,
                   [{name: 'defaultSucceededCallback', type: Function}]);
    if (e) throw e;
    PageMethods._staticInstance._succeeded = value;
}
```

```
PageMethods.get_defaultSucceededCallback = function() {
    return PageMethods._staticInstance._succeeded;
}
PageMethods.set_defaultFailedCallback = function(value) {
    var e = Function._validateParams(arguments,
        [{name: 'defaultFailedCallback', type: Function}]);
    if (e) throw e;
    PageMethods._staticInstance._failed = value;
}
PageMethods.get_defaultFailedCallback = function() {
    return PageMethods._staticInstance._failed;
}


PageMethods.set_path("/IntroAjax/Ch07/CallPageMethod.aspx");
PageMethods.GetTime= function(onSuccess,onFailed,userContext) {
    PageMethods._staticInstance.GetTime(onSuccess,onFailed,userContext);
}
</script>
```

As you can see, the structure of the class is nearly identical to the proxy class of an AJAX Web service. You can define default callbacks for success and failure, user context data, path, and timeout. A singleton instance of the *PageMethods* class is created and all callable methods are invoked through this static instance. No instantiation whatsoever is required.

Executing Page Methods

The *PageMethods* proxy class has as many methods as there are Web methods in the code-behind class of the page. In the proxy class, each mapping method takes the same additional parameters you would find with a Web service method: completed callback, failed callback, and user context data. The completed callback is necessary to update the page with the results of the call. The other parameters are optional. The following code snippet shows the *getTime* function bound to a client event handler. The function calls a page method and leaves the *methodCompleted* callback the burden of updating the user interface as appropriate.

```
function getTime()
{
    PageMethods.GetTime(methodCompleted);
}
function methodCompleted(results, context, methodName)
{
    // Format the date-time object to a more readable string
    var displayString = results.format("ddd, dd MMMM yyyy");
    $get("Label1").innerHTML = displayString;
}
```

The signature of a page method callback is exactly the same as the signature of an AJAX Web service proxy. The role of the *results*, *context*, and *methodName* parameters is the same as described in Table 7-3.

Timeout, error handling, and user feedback are all aspects of page methods that require the same programming techniques discussed earlier for Web service calls.

> **Note** From page methods, you can access session state, the ASP.NET Cache, and *User* objects, as well as any other intrinsic objects. You can do that using the *Current* property on *HttpContext*. The HTTP context is not specific to the page life cycle and is, instead, a piece of information that accompanies the request from the start.

Page Methods vs. AJAX Web Services

From a programming standpoint, no difference exists between Web service methods and page methods. Performance is nearly identical. A minor difference is the fact that page methods are always emitted as inline JavaScript whereas this aspect is configurable for AJAX Web services.

Web services are publicly exposed over the Web and, as such, they're publicly callable by SOAP-based clients. A method exposed through a Web service is visible from multiple pages; a page method, instead, is scoped to the page that defines it. On the other hand, a set of page methods saves you from the additional work of developing a Web service.

Whatever choice you make, it is extremely important that you don't call any critical business logic from page and Web service methods. Both calls can be easily replayed by attackers and have no additional barrier against one-click and replay attacks. Normally, the view state, when spiced up with user key values, limits the range of replay attacks. As mentioned, though, there's no view state involved with page and Web service method calls, so even this small amount of protection isn't available for these specific cases. However, if you limit your code to calling UI-level business logic from the client, you should be fine.

Bridging External Web Services

As mentioned, for security reasons the browser is often not allowed to make calls to an endpoint server that differs in port, protocol, or server name from the current one. This constraint might be relaxed to some extent in the future, but as of this writing any call to an external endpoint can't occur from the client unless an IFRAME block is used. ASP.NET AJAX Extensions 1.0 doesn't natively support an HTTP executor based on IFRAMEs. There was one in the early days of Atlas, but it was removed in the beta stage. You can manage to create your own, however, using the base classes in the Microsoft AJAX library infrastructure.

So what if you want to connect to a remote endpoint (for example, the Amazon or Yahoo Web service) and bring in some external data? What if you want to make your application a mash-up? There are two approaches. One is the classic server-to-server schema where the client calls its server and has the server get in touch with the remote URL. The other is based on an upcoming feature of ASP.NET AJAX known as *Futures*, which currently requires an additional download. Let's dig out more details.

Traditional Server-to-Server Approach

In classic ASP.NET applications, invoking a remote Web service has never been an issue. You import the Web reference to the endpoint in the project, save the WSDL of the service in the *App_WebReferences* special folder, and go. The ASP.NET runtime then generates the proxy class for you, including for each Web method both a synchronous and an asynchronous stub.

Invoking a Web service from a server ASP.NET page is not problematic from an implementation perspective, but it is a delicate point from a performance standpoint. The call might take a while to terminate, be it for the network latency or for the inherent complexity of the task. Making an asynchronous call to the Web service is not enough: you need it to occur from within an ASP.NET page bound to an asynchronous HTTP handler.

Digging out the details of asynchronous ASP.NET pages is beyond the purpose of this book. So I'll limit the discussion to calling Web services synchronously. However, for more information on how to create asynchronous ASP.NET pages, check out Chapter 4 of my book *Programming Microsoft ASP.NET 2.0 Applications: Advanced Topics* (Microsoft Press, 2006).

Using .NET Proxies

For a large share of .NET developers, using a proxy class is the most natural way to consume a Web service. The proxy class is created for you by Visual Studio 2005 when you add a Web reference. Created in C# or Visual Basic .NET, the proxy class mimics the interface of the remote service as prescribed in the WSDL file.

As a developer, all that you have to do is create an instance of the proxy, opt for a synchronous or asynchronous call, and invoke the appropriate proxy method. Here's a quick example of a synchronous call:

```
using IntroAjax.WebServices;
...
TimeServiceClient proxy = new TimeServiceProxy();
string formattedDate = proxy.GetTimeFormat("dd-mm-yyyy");
```

In ASP.NET, the call has to be synchronous if you need to incorporate any results in the response. For start-to-finish calls, asynchrony is not an advantage per se in ASP.NET. You get real benefits only if you can have an asynchronous handler to process the page request. In this case, in fact, the ASP.NET thread is returned to its pool until the Web service operation terminates.

Using an asynchronous method on the proxy class makes sense if the Web service operates in the fire-and-forget modality, meaning that the ASP.NET page starts the method but doesn't wait for it to terminate.

Using Plain Web Requests

As an alternative to proxy classes, if the Web service supports the plain-old XML model (POX), you can just send requests to a URL where input data is packed in the query string according to a service-specific syntax. Here's how to obtain a response in a synchronous manner:

```
WebRequest req = WebRequest.Create(url);
WebResponse response = req.GetResponse();
StreamReader reader;
string output = String.Empty;
using (reader = new StreamReader(response.GetResponseStream()))
{
   output = reader.ReadToEnd();
   reader.Close();
   response.Close();
}
```

The *output* variable contains the response as sent by the server. Parsing the response and extracting any useful information is now entirely up to you.

ASP.NET AJAX Futures Bridge Files

The ASP.NET AJAX *bridge* technology enables developers to create programmatic gateways to Web services on the Internet. Because bridge code runs inside the caller ASP.NET AJAX application, the browser communicates with just one server. The bridge code, in turn, can interact with any Web service available on the Internet and return data to the client page. Bridge code is the chief enabling technology for building *mash-ups*, which are applications that combine data from multiple remote services and serve it to clients in a usable form.

Functionally speaking, the bridge technology is equivalent to making direct calls to a Web service either through a proxy or a Web request. It provides a declarative programming interface and tends to hide as many details as possible from ASP.NET developers.

 Important The bridge technology is not included in ASP.NET AJAX Extensions 1.0. A pre-release version of it can be obtained under the terms of the Go-Live license by installing the ASP.NET AJAX Futures download from *http://ajax.asp.net*. The bridge technology will be part of the next version of ASP.NET slated for release in late 2007.

Configuration and Setup

The ASP.NET AJAX gateway to a third-party Web service is an *.asbx* file. The file contains XML data that describes how to make the call to the Web service. The primary reason for having an intermediary is that real-world Web services might not accept parameters as individual values but require an object instead. In turn, this object might include properties that are also complex types. Therefore, constructing requests and parsing return values might require some programming effort. This is where bridge files (*.asbx* files) fit in.

To connect to third-party Web services from ASP.NET AJAX, you need to register the *.asbx* extension in Internet Information Services (IIS) and make ASP.NET handle it. To see how this is done, open the configuration dialog box in the target IIS virtual folder, select the Mappings tab, and take a look at the contents of the Add/Edit Application Extension Mapping dialog box. (See Figure 7-3.)

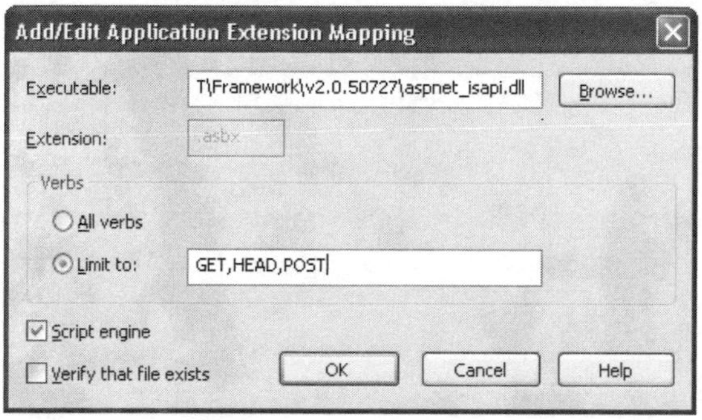

Figure 7-3 Registering the ASBX extension in IIS

Then you edit the mappings and bind *.asbx* resources to the *aspnet_isapi.dll* file—the ISAPI extension that handles ASP.NET calls within IIS.

To continue, you also need to register the HTTP handler for bridge files:

```
<httpHandlers>
   <add verb="*" path="*.asbx"
       type="System.Web.Script.Services.ScriptHandlerFactory" />
   ...
</httpHandlers>
```

You can also move this setting to a folder-level *web.config* file if all the bridge-based pages live in a subfolder.

Finally, you define a build provider for *.asbx* files so that a wrapper class can be silently generated around the source of the bridge file:

```
<compilation>
   <buildProviders>
      <add extension=".asbx"
          type="Microsoft.Web.Preview.Services.BridgeBuildProvider" />
   </buildProviders>
</compilation>
```

In addition to all these changes to the *web.config* file, you should make sure you add a copy of the *Microsoft.Web.Preview* assembly to the Bin folder of your application.

The Bridge File

As mentioned, a bridge file is simply an XML file with the *.asbx* extension. Through a bridge file, you declare how you connect to a remote Web service and how you intend to process any return value.

Currently, a number of popular Web services support two calling protocols: SOAP and POX. SOAP is the well-known Simple Object Access Protocol and defines the XML-based structure of the messages that appear in a distributed environment exchange. SOAP is the protocol that Web services use to interact with their callers. As we've seen, POX stands for plain-old XML and consists of a GET command that lists all parameters on the query string. Why is POX used by a number of popular Web services, including MSN Search and Amazon? The answer can be summed up in just one word: reach. More people can access these POX-based Web services if the complexity associated with SOAP is negated. (Make no mistake, SOAP is not necessarily simple—it's just easier to work with than predecessor protocols.)

Let's see how to create a bridge file that uses POX to access the Amazon Web service and query for books. (The Amazon Web service, however, also exposes a SOAP-based interface from which a proxy class can be created.)

Building a Bridge File for the Amazon Web Service

The Amazon Web service allows Web site developers to programmatically interact with the Amazon catalog, search engine, shopping cart, and merchandising tools. To download the necessary software developer's kit, go to the following URL:

```
http://associates.amazon.com/exec/panama/associates/join/developer/kit.html
```

You need a developer token to start using the Web service, and this page facilitates that. If you need to know about the books written by a given author, you place a call to the following URL and add a number of additional parameters:

```
http://xml.amazon.com/onca/xml2
```

Table 7-4 details some of the most frequently used parameters.

Table 7-4   Parameters to Search for Books with the Amazon Web Service

Parameter	Description
t	Indicates the tag of the query. Must be set to *webservices-20*.
f	Indicates the output format. Must be *xml*.
page	Indicates the page required. Set to 1 by default.
sort	Indicates the sorting required. Valid values are *+salesrank*, *+daterank*, and *+titlerank* (alphabetical).
dev-t	The developer's token.
mode	Indicates the catalog to search. Must be set to *books*.
type	Indicates how much information must be packaged in the response. Feasible values are *lite* or *heavy*.
keywordSearch	Indicates the query string.

In the bridge file, you create a programming interface around the capabilities of the Web service. For example, you can define a JavaScript wrapper with a *Find* method that accepts the keyword and returns some data. Here's the corresponding bridge file:

```
<bridge namespace="IntroAjax" className="AmazonPox" >
  <proxy type="Microsoft.Web.Preview.Services.BridgeRestProxy"
         serviceUrl="http://xml.amazon.com/onca/xml2" />
  <method name="Find">
    <input>
      <parameter name="t" value="webservices-20" />
      <parameter name="mode" value="books" />
      <parameter name="type" value="lite" />
      <parameter name="f" value="xml" />
      <parameter name="page" value="1" />
      <parameter name="sort" value="+salesrank" />
      <parameter name="dev-t" value="% appsettings : AmazonToken %" />
      <parameter name="KeywordSearch" />
    </input>
  </method>
</bridge>
```

In the *<bridge>* tag, the *namespace* and *classname* attributes define the full name of the resulting JavaScript class. In the *<proxy>* element, the *type* attribute indicates the component in charge of executing the remote call on behalf of your application. The *serviceUrl* attribute sets the URL to call.

The *<method>* elements define the programming interface of the bridge class. Any methods you define here are added to the *IntroAjax.AmazonPox* JavaScript wrapper you will use in your ASP.NET AJAX pages. Of course, you can have as many *<method>* elements as you like.

The preceding script defines a *Find* method that takes up to eight parameters. All the listed parameters (and only the listed parameters) will be added to the GET command that is sent to the service URL. The first six parameters are given fixed values. For the seventh argument—the *dev-t* parameter—the value is read from the *<appSettings>* section of the *web.config* file:

```
<appSettings>
    <add key="AmazonToken" value="..." />
</appSettings>
```

At this point, you're ready to write a piece of JavaScript code that calls into the Amazon Web service and gets some information about the books written by a given author. What information? That's the point!

Consuming Amazon Data through a Bridge

The following page adds a reference to the bridge file using the same syntax we used for local Web services. The sample page includes a text box and a button. The user will type an author name in the text box and click the button to search for that author's books.

```
<form id="form1" runat="server">
    <asp:ScriptManager ID="ScriptManager1" runat="server">
        <Services>
            <asp:ServiceReference Path="~/WebServices/Amazon.asbx" />
        </Services>
    </asp:ScriptManager>

    <h3>Find an author: <asp:TextBox ID="TextBox1" runat="server" /></h3>
    <input type="button" value="Go" onclick="findBooks()" />
    <hr />
    <asp:Panel runat="server" ScrollBars="Auto" Height="300px">
        <asp:label runat="server" ID="Output" />
    </asp:Panel>
</form>
```

Let's take a look at the *findBooks* function:

```
<script language="javascript" type="text/javascript">
    function findBooks()
    {
        var author = $get("TextBox1").value;
        IntroAjax.AmazonPox.Find( {KeywordSearch:author},
                                  findBooksCompleted);
    }
    function findBooksCompleted(results, response, context)
    {
        ...
    }
</script>
```

Try running this page. Then type **Dino Esposito** in the text box, and click the button. Figure 7-4 shows what you'll get.

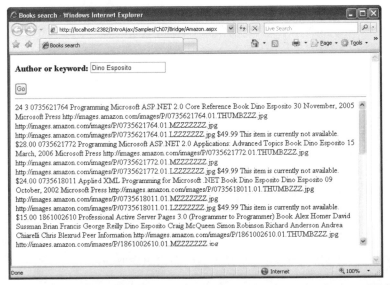

Figure 7-4 The bridge file retrieving information from the Amazon Web service

It works, but can you honestly say that you got just what you were hoping for? The returned value is a huge XML string in which all the requested information is packed according to a schema defined by Amazon developers. How would you transform this string into something usable by your users?

Transforming the Web Service Response

By default, the response of an AJAX Web service call is assumed to be a JSON data stream and is parsed to a JavaScript object. This is not necessarily true, though, when a non-AJAX Web service is invoked. Amazon, or any other third-party Web service, doesn't know about your JSON expectations and may just return XML or text data. In the end, the data is correctly downloaded, but it's not immediately usable by an AJAX client if it wasn't JSON encoded. By adding a *<transforms>* section to your bridge file, you instruct the ASP.NET AJAX infrastructure to post-process the return value and build a JavaScript object you can successfully interact with to present results to the user.

You can use a variety of *transformers* to post-process the return value of a Web service call. ASP.NET AJAX comes with a few built-in transformers, which are listed in Table 7-5.

Table 7-5   Built-in Bridge Transformers

Type	Description
ObjectMapperBridgeTransformer	When the return value is an object, this type maps properties in the returned object to a custom object.
XmlBridgeTransformer	This type runs the return data through the *XmlSerializer* and obtains an XML string that represents the output.
XpathBridgeTransformer	This type uses XPath queries to extract data from the response string and build a custom object.
XsltBridgeTransformer	This type applies an XSLT style sheet to the XML document that represents the return data.

The following code demonstrates how to parse the XML string returned by Amazon using XPath queries to extract significant information. To write a transformer, you need to know a lot about the format of the response text.

Amazon responses take the following format:

```
<ProductInfo>
   <TotalResults> ... </TotalResults>
   <TotalPages> ... </TotalPages>
   <Details>
      <Asin> ... </Asin>
      <!-- Other tags -->
   </Details>
   <Details>
      ...
   </Details>
```

```
    ...
</ProductInfo>
```

The *<TotalResults>* element indicates how many items your search selected, whereas *<TotalPages>* specifies the number of pages it takes, assuming a default size for the page. Finally, an array of *<Details>* blocks lists information about individual items—books, albums, and whatever. Each *<Details>* block contains at least the *<Asin>* tag, which indicates the Amazon identifier for the item. For books, that's just the ISBN code.

The following transformer processes the response into an array of simpler JavaScript objects:

```
<transforms>
    <transform type="Microsoft.Web.Preview.Services.XPathBridgeTransformer">
        <data>
            <attribute name="selector" value="Details" />
            <dictionary name="selectedNodes">
                <item name="ISBN" value="Asin" />
                <item name="Title" value="ProductName" />
                <item name="Publisher" value="Manufacturer" />
                <item name="CoverPicture" value="ImageUrlSmall" />
            </dictionary>
        </data>
    </transform>
</transforms>
```

The *selector* attribute instructs the XPath to select the specified node—in this case, *Details*. Next, the *selectedNodes* dictionary selects the node set that is rooted in the selected node. As a result, all nodes named *Details* are selected. The transformer creates a JavaScript dictionary that contains objects with four properties: *ISBN*, *Title*, *Publisher*, and *CoverPicture*. Each of these properties is mapped to a particular element under the nth *<Details>* element.

At this point, the value passed to the method-complete callback is an array of JavaScript objects with the preceding four properties. You can now build a nice user interface, as shown in Figure 7-5.

```
function findBooksCompleted(results, context, methodName)
{
    var builder = new Sys.StringBuilder("<table>");
    for(i=0; i<results.length; i++)
    {
        builder.append("<tr>");
        builder.append("<td><img src='");
        builder.append(results[i].CoverPicture);
        builder.append("' /></td>");
        builder.append("<td>");
        builder.append(results[i].ISBN);
        builder.append("<br/><b>");
        builder.append(results[i].Title);
        builder.append("</b><br/>");
        builder.append(results[i].Publisher);
        builder.append("</td></tr>");
    }
```

```
        builder.append("</table>");
        $("Output").innerHTML = builder.toString();
}
```

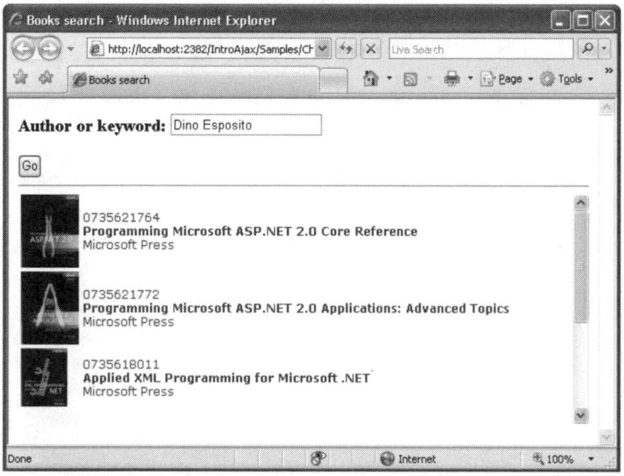

Figure 7-5   A quick but effective example of a mash-up application using listed books from Amazon

Conclusion

Of the two ASP.NET AJAX models of enhancing Web sites, partial rendering is the one with some hidden costs. Although it can still achieve a better performance than classic postbacks, partial rendering moves a lot of data around. In some worse cases, the savings in terms of markup are negligible compared to the quantity of bytes moved. On the other hand, AJAX was developed around the idea of making stateless server-side calls from the client and updating the page via the DOM.

Here's where the second model fits in—direct client-to-server calls. No hidden costs are buried in this model. As in a classic SOAP-powered Web service call, you send in only input data required by the method being invoked and receive only the return value. Traffic is minimal, and no view state or other hidden fields (for example, event validation) are roundtripped. On the down side, remote method calls require JavaScript skills. You command the execution of the method via JavaScript, and use a JavaScript callback to incorporate the results in the page.

You need a server API to plan and execute client-to-server direct calls. How would you expose this API? As per the current version of ASP.NET AJAX Extensions, you're not forced to define a contract (for example, an interface). However, it's a good software practice to define the server API as an interface. How would you implement such a server API? There are two options: as a local, application-specific Web service, or through page methods. In both cases, the ASP.NET AJAX client page is enriched with a system-generated proxy class to make calling the server easy and effective.

In the context of ASP.NET AJAX Extensions 1.0, Web services are instrumental to the implementation of a server API. Beyond this, is it possible for an ASP.NET AJAX client to call into any Web service out there? Security reasons dictate that most browsers stop cross-domain and cross-site calls via script. This reality is a huge hurdle for AJAX applications. For this reason, you need a bridgehead on the server to make a server-to-server call to a remote endpoint and return data to the client. In the future, the bridge technology will provide a declarative way of linking remote services to client pages; meanwhile, you have to code it yourself as you would do today in classic ASP.NET applications.

Chapter 8
Building AJAX Applications with ASP.NET

The primary purpose of ASP.NET AJAX is making the user's experience as rich as possible by providing a breakthrough programming environment to developers so that they can code what was impossible or impractical before. Partial page refresh and remote method calls are the key features of an AJAX-powered application. Together, these features enable developers to build mash-up applications, display real-time data, and update the user interface promptly and smoothly. All this is darned cool and effective, but it's also a little bit confusing when, having recovered from the initial hype, you think it over with a cold and fresh mind.

Where's the confusion? Partial rendering (covered in Chapter 4, "Partial Page Rendering") and remote method calls (covered in Chapter 7, "Remote Method Calls with ASP.NET AJAX") herald two neatly distinct approaches to AJAX. Which one is best, and when? Would one complement the other, and to what extent? What are the costs and benefits of bringing each into an existing application? What kind of work is required on the back end? What if several different user interfaces are expected to work, and what if the AJAX client is just one possible client? As you can see, a number of architectural issues arise as you move past the starting line of AJAX and make your way toward the finish.

What's the best way to move your application to AJAX? Should you just go with low-level ASP.NET AJAX controls such as the *UpdatePanel* control, or would you be better off adopting a third-party suite of controls? If you're building an AJAX application, or adding a new feature, from scratch, how should you design and code the client and server infrastructure?

From a pragmatic standpoint, you should clearly distinguish situations in which you're just migrating an existing application to AJAX from situations in which you need to design a brand-new system for AJAX. In the former case, ASP.NET AJAX has a number of shortcuts, some of which are really smart to use. In the latter case, you should spend some time developing a deep understanding of the client and server boundaries of your system and be sure to keep the client decoupled from the server. When writing new code using AJAX technology, you can expose server-side capabilities through contract-bound services, and you can consume services using JavaScript proxies. Clearly, creating and using contract-bound services and JavaScript proxies is not necessarily like building a classic ASP.NET application. AJAX is a new paradigm for Web development; it's not simply a new application programming interface (API) for writing applications.

In this final chapter, I'll first spend some time illustrating the pros and cons of the AJAX paradigm from an application perspective. Next, I'll move on to architectural considerations by separating partial rendering from true AJAX architectures. Finally, I'll take one of the most popular ASP.NET starter kits and update it to an ASP.NET AJAX starter kit.

AJAX in Perspective

AJAX propounds a pattern for applications that is fundamentally centered around the user. The two main approaches to AJAX development are often referred to as AJAX Lite and AJAX Deluxe. These two approaches define the extremes, and most applications fall somewhere in between.

In AJAX Deluxe, you use the set of AJAX features to the fullest. Your final goal is making the application feel nearly identical to a classic desktop Microsoft Windows application. The browser drives the interaction and goes to the server only when it needs to perform operations that require more processing than just JavaScript and collecting input data on the client can do. AJAX Lite, on the other hand, propounds a programming style in which applications look like conventional Web applications with some out-of-band calls sprinkled here and there. AJAX Lite is the ideal approach to migrate and upgrade existing applications; AJAX Deluxe is the philosophy you might want to embrace when you build a new application. However, not all applications fall so neatly into one approach or the other. It's mostly a matter of costs and time to develop. A "lite" approach doesn't require a full redesign, but still some subsystems may need a deep refactoring. In this case, you're just in the middle of the two approaches. Personally, I tend to use the "lite" approach and fall back to more complex AJAX when I have to.

Whatever approach, or combination of approaches, you take, though, it is essential that you understand which logical tasks around the application might take advantage of AJAX and which are the proper architectural choices and design patterns to adopt.

The Benefits of AJAX

In this book, I already mentioned that the term *AJAX* was coined in 2005, but I didn't mention *why* the term was invented. *Jesse James Garrett* was the first to refer to AJAX in the form we know it today, and he did so in a paper you can read at *http://www.adaptivepath.com/publications/essays/archives/000385.php*. Jesse argues that the typical responsiveness of desktop applications is out of reach for Web applications. The key factor to the rapid proliferation of Web pages is a sort of common denominator approach: you can reach zillions of people if you don't pose strict requirements on hardware and software. At the same time, the less you require, the smaller the set of features will be that you can build in pages.

The ultimate goal of AJAX is demonstrating that by using the proper set of (existing) tools, and without loss of simplicity and reach, you can fill (most of) the gap between Web and desktop applications as far as the user interface is concerned.

The last sentence contains three strategic qualifications, I believe, that were key in establishing the goals of the AJAX platform. First, *fill the gap* between Web and desktop applications. Second, fill *most of this gap* but not all. Third, fill most of the gap *as far as the user interface* is concerned. Let's see how the benefits AJAX provides allow us to target these strategic tenets.

AJAX Is a Real Breakthrough

AJAX is an important achievement for the Web software industry. It makes possible implementing features and functionalities that were impossible or impractical before. AJAX is neither a single technology, nor does it require an external plug-in. AJAX is not akin to Adobe Flash, Adobe Flex, or similar tools, including the Microsoft code-named WPF/E product based on the Windows Presentation Foundation (WPF) API. Rather, AJAX is a recipe of design patterns. You get to use AJAX if you need Web applications that do more things or do things better than technologies that are generally available today.

What are the fields in which AJAX can make a difference? AJAX is mostly concerned about the user interface and a user's perception of performance. What are examples of areas that can prove AJAX is a breakthrough? Here's a quick list: displaying live data, monitoring remote tasks, establishing zero page flickering, making smarter use of page real estate, making dynamic changes, and aggregating data from multiple feeds.

The Continuous Feel

In a traditional Web application, users click a button and submit a form. Then they hang out for a few seconds until the page redraws. When all is done, they can finally take a look at the new content. However, if they scrolled down a half page to find a button, they lose their position and have to rescroll. Although this behavior might be acceptable if you turn to a new page, or to a significantly modified version of the same page, it ends up being bothersome if you clicked just to page through grid data or flip through a photo album, only to lose your place when the page refreshes.

With the content-heavy pages of today's sites, going through a multistep operation such as a registration or an electronic purchase is like being stuck in traffic. In the end, it's a kind of Web stop-and-go. With AJAX, you have no full-page refreshes. The user experiences continuous interaction with the same page; she sends requests and receives responses, and it all happens smoothly. It's an easy ride all the way through—as long as nothing bad happens on the server. One thing AJAX can't do, in fact, is shield you from server failures and server-side scalability or performance issues. The responsibility to provide sound Web-based architectures is still a requirement.

The User's Experience and User Interface

AJAX is about the user interface and the user's experience. With AJAX, you can develop (or buy) powerful controls that incorporate out-of-band calls to expand or collapse views, page silently, detect ongoing changes, and refresh portions of the screen. If asked to justify their interest in AJAX, a large share of developers and managers would answer that they want or need to provide attractive and friendly user interfaces to customers. For example, expanding and collapsing views is much smoother with AJAX than without it. This is because ASP.NET AJAX and similar commercially available AJAX frameworks provide built-in objects and a client infrastructure to leverage for just this purpose.

More often than not, though, behind a cool and attractive user interface there's the need to build a rich user experience—which is somewhat different. A user's experience is the sum of many factors, including a gorgeous user interface. In addition to a rich set of user interface (UI) gadgets, you find data aggregation, prompt interaction with the server, personalizable graphics, information at the user's fingertips, and the possibility of building personalized views of pages using drag-and-drop functionality and other facilities. Giving the user a better experience is much easier with AJAX than without.

The Downsides of AJAX

AJAX has a number of positive aspects, but it also has some weaknesses. In the end, choosing AJAX should be the result of a careful and thoughtful process of evaluating the trade-offs. You weigh what's good and what's bad and decide the percentage of AJAX you need in your system and, more importantly, how to build it. In general, spicing up Web applications with AJAX is always a good thing. The recipe that works for you, though, might not be that obvious.

Comparing AJAX to Other Rich Clients

AJAX is the paradigm to use for building Web-rich clients. ASP.NET AJAX is a concrete framework you use to apply AJAX to your applications. How does AJAX compare to rich clients such as Windows applications deployed via ClickOnce or WPF browser applications in .NET 3.0? Let's see.

ClickOnce is a deployment technology that facilitates the deployment of a Windows Forms application. With ClickOnce, installing a Windows application is as easy as deploying a Web application; all that users have to do is click a link in a provided Web page. For administrators, installing or updating an application is only a matter of updating files on a server; there's no need to touch individual clients. (For further information, visit *http://msdn2.microsoft.com/en-us/netframework/aa497348.aspx.*)

WPF browser applications are essentially WPF applications that can be hosted inside a browser such as Internet Explorer. These applications are partially trusted and are not given full access to the local computer's resources. For example, they can't do any I/O. Although you get the perception of the application running in the browser, it is actually hosted outside the browser process. From a graphical point of view, though, it looks like a real WPF application with animation, media, and advanced graphics.

If ClickOnce and WPF browser applications are new to you, they probably sound very appealing at first glance, and they are compelling technologies. What about the differences between ClickOnce, WPF browser applications, and AJAX? We're basically talking about apples and oranges. AJAX clients are Web applications. ClickOnce clients are Windows Forms, .NET 2.0 applications with a number of nice features as far as deployment is concerned. Finally, WPF browser applications are .NET 3.0 WPF-powered applications that run in the sandbox within the graphical context of a browser.

All are valid options for adding a smart client to your enterprise systems. But each has its own role and application. AJAX (and ASP.NET AJAX as a concrete platform) is for pure, traditional Web applications.

Note   A browser plug-in currently codenamed WPF/E might be released by the time you read this. It is a product that, functionally speaking, is really close to Adobe Flash. It provides media capabilities without requiring Windows Media Player, vector graphics, and a rich user interface a là WPF in Web applications on Windows and Mac platforms. Based on XAML files, it comes with built-in controls for data binding and represents the natural way of extending AJAX with rich components fully scriptable through JavaScript.

Not Ready for Miracles as Yet

ASP.NET AJAX applications certainly let developers do things over the Web they never imagined possible in days past. However, there are still substantial restrictions to what one can achieve with AJAX and Windows applications. Want some examples? Multimedia capabilities, data storage, advanced graphics, hardware control. Plug-ins such as Adobe Flash and the upcoming Microsoft WPF/E can help developers to mitigate some of these limitations. However, a key fact shouldn't be forgotten or misconstrued: AJAX is not the desktop.

Note   Realistic AJAX applications do require good JavaScript skills. JavaScript is certainly not the most complex programming language you can learn, but it can be far less trivial than many suspect. More importantly, there's no alternative to JavaScript for the client portion of an AJAX application. ASP.NET AJAX does a good job of abstracting JavaScript intricacies as much as possible, but it's still script. And you shouldn't embark on a big AJAX project without a good working knowledge of JavaScript.

Continuous Connection

AJAX applications are virtually useless without an Internet connection. In other words, they still follow the classic Web application model and must remain connected to the network to function properly.

> **Note**   You can still run AJAX applications on the local host, as long as you have a local Web server that hosts the application. Which doesn't mean that AJAX applications, like regular Web applications, can sometimes work offline.

The major advantage of AJAX—the ability to connect to the server while bypassing the browser—can become its biggest drawback if abused. AJAX applications that ping servers almost constantly, multiplied by the order of magnitude of clients at peak time, certainly could create a boundary condition that can't be ignored. Such constant interaction between the browser and server can make an application appear slow or unresponsive.

Applying caching techniques and fine-tuning the frequency of updates might work in most cases, and it could even work in the case of high-demand applications such as stock-trading and live-score applications. This said, AJAX is obviously not a reliable fit for real-time processing and machine control applications.

One-Page Application

The life cycle of an AJAX application is amazingly more akin to that of a traditional desktop application than a classic Web site. In desktop applications, controls collect the user's input and developers establish a given behavior by handling their events; in AJAX applications, Document Object Model (DOM) elements play exactly the same role. Client event handlers command actions; and often they are actions that are then forwarded to the server. When this happens, though, the page remains up and running while waiting for the response.

When the server responds and the response is downloaded to the client, a request callback updates the DOM accordingly, much like a C# or Microsoft Visual Basic .NET handler updates a desktop-based form.

In light of this, can we consider AJAX applications as one-page applications where the presentation layer just does three-card tricks with user-interface panels? I remember that a similar "potential" problem arose when Microsoft shipped SQL Server 2005 with support for common language runtime (CLR) types. Quite a few developers, more or less seriously, wondered whether they were supposed to abandon database normalization and relational principles to work with one-table, one-column databases.

Of course, AJAX applications will be made of a number of pages linked together through a menu or a tree-view. Within the page, then, related microfunctions will be implemented to increase friendliness and time-to-last-byte, while limiting flickering, scrolling, redraws, and whatever else that can make a user unhappy.

Patterns, Practices, and Services

Building an AJAX application can be challenging. Don't be fooled by the apparent simplicity of the API involved with it—which includes the *UpdatePanel* control, Web service calls, Web methods, and so on. It is essential that you see the clear difference between AJAX and ASP.NET AJAX Extensions.

An AJAX application is a Web application architected and built according to AJAX concepts— such as the use of out-of-band calls, direct access to the DOM, regarding the GUI as a dynamically changing element, and the logical separation of the client and server APIs.

An ASP.NET AJAX application is an ASP.NET Web application that leverages the AJAX framework (whether that framework is ASP.NET AJAX or another third-party version). The framework has a client and server infrastructure and abstracts most of the AJAX principles by exposing it through concrete programming tools and techniques. If you opt for ASP.NET AJAX or any other framework, you opt for the AJAX architecture envisioned by the authors of the framework. You just get pragmatic and use whatever comes out of the box.

Despite the fact that building an ASP.NET AJAX application is not a complicated task, architecting one is definitely challenging. Why challenging? Mostly because you have to rethink functionalities and page structure and plan the allocation of functionalities to pages, the exposure of remote services, the format of data being exchanged, the level of coupling between client and server API, and testing.

Although this book is entirely dedicated to ASP.NET AJAX Extensions, it is good to stop and think a moment about common patterns and practices that lie behind AJAX programming. Then it should be easy to recognize many of them in the practical solutions offered by the ASP.NET AJAX Extensions framework.

Services and Web Services

For years, it has been natural for .NET developers to associate Web services with Simple Object Access Protocol (SOAP) and Web Services Description Language (WSDL). Now with ASP.NET AJAX support for ASP.NET Web services, one wonders why on earth the communication between the client and the Web service has to use JSON. And why there's no use of WSDL, neither explicit nor buried into the folds of the ASP.NET AJAX Extensions framework.

As mentioned in Chapter 7, you should think of the remote API exposed to JavaScript clients as plain services, possibly with a contract. Put in this way, the fact that ASP.NET AJAX lets you use ASP.NET Web services is a mere implementation detail. So you have a service with a contract.

A service with a contract is often referred to as an SOA service, where SOA stands for *Service-Oriented Architecture*. An SOA service can be like a classic Web service as long as we use SOAP and WSDL to implement it. On the other hand, a classic Web service can be an SOA service as long as it exposes its programming interface via a contract. Be pragmatic, think of functionality as a contract—that is, an interface—and expose it through a service. And try not to care too much about whether it is a Web service or an SOA service. What matters is that it works and can have its contract known and checked.

In the context of AJAX, you should use this principle to build the server-side, client-callable interfaces, as we demonstrated in Chapter 7.

> **Note** Services in an SOA environment are resources available as independent services that can be accessed without knowledge of the underlying platform implementation. SOA services are generally available and not targeted to the application in question and only that application. Clearly, services like those described in Chapter 7 and recalled here are specific to just one application. So, in this sense, they're not SOA at all. Again, be pragmatic: in AJAX all that you need is a service-oriented back end and services that are publicly exposed and have a well-defined contract.

REST vs. SOAP

Representational State Transfer (REST) is an architectural pattern used in the design of services. REST deals with the way in which you expose and make available to callers the contract of the service. REST is an alternative service implementation mechanism to SOAP.

A SOAP-based SOA or Web service uses a single URL to expose all functionalities and documents the service methods through WSDL or a contract name. Behind the URL, a single handler receives the request, examines the body, and forwards the call to the internal machinery for individual method processing.

A REST SOA or Web service uses distinct URLs to point to distinct functionalities. A REST service documents functionalities through links and HTTP headers. Each operation has a unique URL (plus, optionally, HTTP headers), and this URL is enough for the server-side handler to identify the requested resource and process it.

REST relies on HTTP verbs and URLs to express what operation is requested and on what data. SOAP, instead, relies on WSDL metadata to define the contract and data types. REST is more flexible and promotes decoupling of clients from the server. SOAP through WSDL defines a fixed contract. If this WSDL-based contract is extended or modified, all clients must be notified and adapted. A REST service can start supporting a new feature without the need of notifying all clients. Clients that become aware of this new feature (method) can then easily take advantage of it without changing existing code. And distinct clients can get data in different formats—JSON, XML, RSS, CSV, plain text, and so on—just by examining the HTTP header they use. This is not possible with SOAP, as SOAP is designed to convey all data types as XML, with consumer-specific type conversions taking place on the consumer's end.

Services consumed by AJAX applications should adhere to REST principles. The term *RESTful* is commonly used to indicate this.

Note   REST, SOAP, WSDL, remote procedure call (RPC), and flavors of services are all broad topics where personal opinions and attitudes blur and often generate either crude and sharp statements or long, tedious, semiphilosophical discussions. My advice is that you read as much as possible, but if you reach the point of being confused, stop. When every statement looks the same and you can no longer distinguish clearly where you are or who you are, it's about time to get pragmatic and start writing code! For your convenience, I'll recommend a few resources that I've found useful to clarify details and doubts. A good book is *Ajax and REST Recipes: A Problem-Solution Approach* by Christian Gross (Apress, 2006). Keep in mind that this is not an ASP.NET AJAX book; it's an AJAX book. A couple of good online articles can be found at *http://ajaxpatterns.org/RESTful_Service* and *http://webservices.xml.com/pub/a/ws/2002/02/06/rest.html*.

REST in ASP.NET AJAX

How much REST is in ASP.NET AJAX Extensions? There's some. All in all, I'd say that the services you can consume from ASP.NET AJAX clients are RPC-style services with some REST principles implemented. Because of the outermost RPC style, you—the programmer end-point—don't get many of the benefits of REST in terms of flexibility, loosely coupled client and server, and testing capabilities. These benefits are reserved for the framework for further extensions.

Hold on. This is not necessarily bad news. Once again, be pragmatic and look at what you get in return. ASP.NET AJAX Extensions gives you a familiar programming interface and, with Visual Studio "Orcas," ad hoc tools for testing. In addition, you can still use little-known classes in the JavaScript Microsoft Client Library for AJAX (discussed in Chapter 2, "The Microsoft Client Library for AJAX") to prepare and issue a Web request yourself, by modifying URLs and headers to make special requests to RESTful services you might have.

In the end, there's quite a few REST principles in ASP.NET AJAX even though they're not patently exposed to developers.

Quick Tour of AJAX Patterns

RESTful services is one of the key AJAX design patterns, but others are defined as well—many of which are silently implemented in the ASP.NET AJAX framework. Let's take a quick look at some of them in Table 8-1.

Table 8-1 lists only 10 patterns from a few areas. Each pattern brings with it a number of real-world applications, issues, and scenarios as well as multiple solutions and techniques. Building AJAX applications might not be easy, as I mentioned at the beginning of the chapter, if you want the application to be a deluxe one. Thankfully, a few patterns are taken care of by the ASP.NET AJAX framework and the components in the AJAX Control Toolkit. (See

Chapter 5, "The AJAX Control Toolkit.") But for the most part, deciding on a pattern is left up to you.

Table 8-1   A List of AJAX Patterns

Pattern	Category	Description
RESTful services	Services	Provides guidance on the most effective ways of exposing services to AJAX clients, and thereby minimizing the impact on testing, extensibility, client/server coupling, and data formats.
Cross-domain proxy	Services	Provides guidance on how to connect to Web services available remotely outside the boundaries of the current application.
Page rearrangement Display morphing	User interface	Related partterns that summarize the most common techniques to update the page structure and styles of DOM elements.
HTTP streaming	User interface	Provides guidance on how to push data from the server to the client.
Periodic refresh Progress indicator	Browser/Server communication	Related patterns that show common ways to implement periodic refresh of the page and monitor server-side operations.
Heartbeat Timeout	Browser/Server communication	Related patterns that show common ways to determine whether a user is still actively working with an application and give guidance on what to do once you know it.
On-demand JavaScript	Performance	Provides guidance on how to apply lazy-loading to JavaScript files and download them only when required.
Submission throttling	Performance	Provides guidance on how to retain posted data on the client and submit it at fixed intervals.
Predictive fetch	Performance	Provides guidance on how to make the browser more responsive by anticipating user actions and call the server in advance.

For more information, you can visit *http://www.ajaxpatterns.org*. If you prefer a book, my suggestion is *Ajax Patterns and Best Practices* by Christian Gross (Apress, 2006).

Revisiting ASP.NET Starter Kits

When a new programming paradigm is offered to the community, good and fully fledged examples are essential for a comprehensive understanding of the key facts and to get started on using it. ASP.NET Starter Kits play exactly this role in the context of classic ASP.NET 2.0 programming. You can find a number of them available for download at *http://www.asp.net/starterkits*.

To illustrate the application of AJAX techniques in a realistic scenario, I'll take one of them and upgrade some of the pages to ASP.NET AJAX Extensions. The result will be a partial rewriting of the starter kit, with some pages enhanced with partial rendering and remote calls.

The Jobs Site Starter Kit at a Glance

Adding AJAX capabilities to an existing application is seemingly a simple task. You just loop through the pages and add updatable panels where appropriate and where you want to limit page flickering and postbacks. The AJAX Lite approach seems to be lightweight and powerful overall.

As we'll see in a moment, though, not all that shines is necessarily gold. And not all that sounds easy on paper is as seamless in practice. The main point is the mechanics of the application. Their implementation is relatively cheap, adding AJAX to pages with a simple structure in which server controls generate the markup and event handlers dictate the behavior. In this case, you simply wrap blocks of server controls with updatable panels and go.

Fully templated pages and pages with a dynamically changing structure don't lend themselves well to AJAX. For example, porting to AJAX a page made of interchangeable templates or panels, which are shown and hidden via code, is challenging. These pages, therefore, already use the Page Rearrangement pattern, but they do it entirely on the server. In these cases, you have two options: either wrap the whole page in a single updatable panel or redesign the page from scratch.

For the purpose of this book, I picked up a relatively boilerplate sample site—the Jobs Site Starter Kit (JSSK). You can get it at *http://www.asp.net/downloads/starterkits/default.aspx?tabid=62#jobsite*.

Overview of JSSK

JSSK provides a Web platform for job seekers and employers to meet and share respective needs. After registering with the site, job seekers can post and edit their resume, search for job postings, and maintain a list of favorite searches. Registered employers, on the other hand, are allowed to enter a profile of their company, post and edit information about available positions, and search the resume database. Figure 8-1 shows the home page of the site.

Completely based on a three-tier architecture, the site employs forms authentication, role-based security, and user profiles. Users and roles are managed through membership and role providers. All pages are based on a master page. The master page defines a left sidebar with a navigation tree and a right sidebar with statistical information that reflects the current state of databases.

Log-in and navigation are managed using the ASP.NET *Login* and *TreeView* controls. Data binding is extensively used through the *ObjectDataSource* control and the site's middle tier.

Figure 8-1   The home page of a site built using the JSSK template

Setting up for AJAX

The first change to be made is editing the *web.config* file to make sure that ASP.NET AJAX Extensions assembly is successfully located and loaded. You can proceed in either of two ways. You can create a new ASP.NET AJAX-enabled Web site and merge the contents of the JSSK *web.config* file in the site's configuration. Alternatively, you can edit the JSSK *web.config* file to support AJAX if you are familiar with the configuration settings ASP.NET AJAX require. Either way, you must ensure that the configuration file contains the following information:

- A link to the *system.web.extensions* assembly in the *<compilation>* section

- Declaration of the new sections specific to ASP.NET AJAX

- In the *<pages>* section, an association that is defined between the *asp* tag and all controls in the *system.web.extensions* assembly

- Registration information for the ASMX handler and script module if you want to use remote calls and page methods

- Any scripting settings (compression, caching) that you might need

The latter two points are optional, and the information is required only if ASP.NET AJAX will use the features they refer to. Let's apply some changes to the JSSK site.

Reducing Page Flickering

The primary benefit of adding AJAX capabilities is reducing page flickering by limiting the number of full postbacks and subsequent page redraws. You conduct a page-by-page analysis and determine which portions of each page can be updated independently. Each partially updatable region will then be wrapped by an *UpdatePanel* control. To use the *UpdatePanel* control and any other ASP.NET AJAX controls, though, you need a script manager to be available to the page. For pages based on a master, though, you are better off adding the script manager directly to the master and using the script manager proxy in child pages.

Adding the Script Manager

For a site based on master pages, the first—and to some extent a step you are compelled to take—is adding a script manager to the master. All content pages will take advantage of the services the manager provides and, therefore, in all of them you can take for granted that a script manager exists.

In the master page, you typically give the script manager the configuration that fits the largest number of pages. For example, you commonly don't need to enable page methods in all pages. Will it really be a problem if you enable page methods globally for all pages? It's not a problem per se, but in this case all pages will get some script that only a few of them will actually use and need. So, in the end, you shouldn't set *EnablePageMethods* on a master page script manager.

Keep in mind that sometimes you might still want to register Web services and scripts through the master's script manager because Web service proxies and script files are downloaded once and then cached. However, a relatively large script that is only used by a very small percentage of pages is perhaps better managed if bound to the script manager of the specific page.

To override the settings of a master's script manager in a content page, you either use the *ScriptManagerProxy* control (discussed in Chapter 3, "The Pulsing Heart of ASP.NET AJAX") or programmatically invoke the static *GetCurrent* method on the *ScriptManager* class. The *GetCurrent* method returns the current instance of the script manager and provides full access to all of its properties and methods.

Adjusting the Log-in Process

In most ASP.NET 2.0 applications, the log-in process is implemented through a separate log-in page that collects credentials and posts back to the server to validate them. If the validation is successful, the user is redirected to the originally requested page with a valid authentication cookie attached to the request.

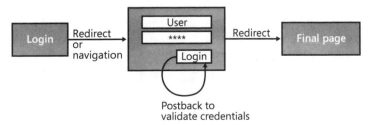

Figure 8-2   The typical log-in process of an ASP.NET 2.0 application

From an ASP.NET 2.0 perspective, the log-in process requires two page redirects and one post-back to validate credentials, as shown in Figure 8-2.

Usually, the user clicks to jump to a log-in page or to reach a protected page directly. In the latter case, the user is automatically redirected to the log-in page. After that, the user types in her credentials and clicks to validate. During the postback, if the user is recognized a page redirect is made to the return URL. In this process, there's not much that you can improve with AJAX. You can't control redirects and hyperlinking. As a result, two full-page redraws occur, and there's no way to prevent that. By wrapping the user interface of the log-in page in an *UpdatePanel*, you can save the page redraw in case an error occurs. Here's an example:

```
<asp:UpdatePanel runat="server" id="UpdatePanel1">
    <ContentTemplate>
        <asp:Login ID="Login1" runat="server" /><br />
        <asp:HyperLink ID="HyperLink1" runat="server"
            NavigateUrl="~/register.aspx">
            New user? Register here!</asp:HyperLink><br /><br />
        <asp:PasswordRecovery ID="PasswordRecovery1" runat="server" />
    </ContentTemplate>
</asp:UpdatePanel>
```

This code can be further improved by wrapping *only* the *Login* control in the updatable panel. The final effect is the same, but you move a bit less markup around.

Refactoring the Log-in Process

To take advantage of AJAX during the log-in process, you should design pages with a dual interface–for anonymous and registered users. In the *web.config* file, you don't associate the page with a *<location>* tag that rules out anonymous users. The page is always accessible, but it hides or disables portions of its user interface reserved to logged-in users.

The log-in form can be embedded in the home page or embedded directly in any such reserved pages. When the user logs in, the user interface of the page changes to reflect the user's preferences and enabled functions. You can wrap these user interface elements in an *UpdatePanel* control and use the *log-in* button as a trigger. No page redirection occurs, and the postback to validate and update the user interface can be easily managed by ASP.NET AJAX.

When dual pages are used, you can also consider a further level of integration with ASP.NET AJAX, as we demonstrated in Chapter 6, "Built-in Application Services." In this case, you replace the log-in server button of the log-in form with a client button. Next, you use Java-Script to command a remote authentication and refresh the page using script code. The Page Rearrangement and Display Morphing patterns provide guidance on the most effective ways to achieve this.

Warning   A log-in form directly hosted in the target page (or the home page) provides a smoother user experience, but it raises a security issue. In general, to be sure that nobody can intercept the user's credentials, the log-in form should be placed in an HTTPS page.

However, simply posting to an HTTPS-based URL doesn't fully protect you from possible DNS-poisoning attacks. To preserve security—and at least for certain categories of applications (for example, banking)—this is key: you should force users to navigate to an HTTPS page before they can enter credentials. Realistically, the log-in process is not the best scenario to consider for AJAX enhancements.

Users Registration

A common solution to letting users register with a site entails using a homemade wizard or an instance of the built-in *CreateUserWizard* control. The JSSK site employs the following code:

```
<asp:CreateUserWizard ID="CreateUserWizard1" Runat="server"
    CreateUserButtonText="Register Me"
    OnContinueButtonClick="CreateUserWizard1_ContinueButtonClick"
    OnNextButtonClick="CreateUserWizard1_NextButtonClick"
    OnCreatedUser="CreateUserWizard1_CreatedUser"
    OnActiveStepChanged="CreateUserWizard1_ActiveStepChanged">
  <WizardSteps>
    <asp:WizardStep runat="server" ID="Step1"
        Title="Please tell us about yourself">
        ...
    </asp:WizardStep>
    <asp:CreateUserWizardStep ID="CreateUserWizardStep1" runat="server"
        Title="Sign Up for Your New Account" />
    <asp:WizardStep runat="server" ID="Step2"
        Title="Choose your role">
        ...
    </asp:WizardStep>
    <asp:CompleteWizardStep ID="CompleteWizardStep1" runat="server"
        Title="Complete" />
  </WizardSteps>
</asp:CreateUserWizard>
```

By simply wrapping this code with an *UpdatePanel* control, you prevent full page refreshes without changing any other aspect of the code. The final effect is definitely worth the effort.

Searching for Jobs

The job search page allows logged-in users to search for positions. The page contains an input form to restrict the query—to city, skills, or country. Once you click the Search button, the page posts back, runs a database query, and returns the jobs it finds, listing them in a grid. This is the perfect scenario for setting up an updatable region with triggers and progress support. Here's an example:

```
<asp:UpdatePanel runat="server" ID="UpdatePanel1" UpdateMode="Conditional">
    <ContentTemplate>
        <asp:GridView ID="GridView1" runat="server"
            AutoGenerateColumns="False" AllowPaging="True" PageSize="3"
            DataKeyNames="PostingID" OnRowCommand="GridView1_RowCommand">
            <Columns>
```

```
                <asp:BoundField HeaderText="Date" DataField="PostingDate" />
                <asp:BoundField HeaderText="Title" DataField="Title" />
                <asp:BoundField HeaderText="Location" DataField="City" />
                <asp:BoundField HeaderText="Company" DataField="companyname" />
                <asp:ButtonField Text="View Details" CommandName="details" />
            </Columns>
        </asp:GridView>
    </ContentTemplate>
    <Triggers>
        <asp:AsyncPostBackTrigger ControlID="btnSearch" />
    </Triggers>
</asp:UpdatePanel>

<asp:UpdateProgress runat="server" ID="UpdateProgress1">
    <ProgressTemplate>
        <div>
        <div style="margin:20px; font-weight:bold;">
           <img alt="" src="/jobsite1/images/wizard.png" align="left" />
           <p align="right">Job Search Site in action looking for a good
                           job for you... It may take a while. <br />
           <img alt="" src="/jobsite1/images/indicator.gif" />
           <span id="Title1"> Please, wait ... </span>
           <img alt="" src="/jobsite1/images/indicator.gif" />
           </p>
        </div>
           <div>
    </ProgressTemplate>
</asp:UpdateProgress>
```

You wrap the grid in an updatable region and use triggers to bind it to the user's click on the Search button. Finally, the *UpdateProgress* control adds some animation during the search. (See Figure 8-3.)

Figure 8-3 The job-search function enhanced with AJAX capabilities

> **Tip**   The preceding code snippet for the *UpdateProgress* control has been edited for clarity and is missing the style information necessary to make the progress template appear at the center of the page as in the figure. To obtain the same results as in Figure 8-3, you should style the outermost *<div>* tag in the progress template as follows:
>
> ```
> width: 350px; height: 140px; top: 40%; left: 35%;
> position: absolute; border: solid 1px black;
> ```

The grid contains a button column that can be clicked to view details of a given job. In the JSSK implementation, when the user clicks, the page posts back and then redirects to a distinct page, as shown here:

```
void GridView1_RowCommand(object sender, GridViewCommandEventArgs e)
{
    if (e.CommandName == "details")
    {
        Response.Redirect("~/viewjobposting.aspx?id=" + e.CommandArgument);
    }
}
```

In this case, there's not much that ASP.NET AJAX can do to save you a full page loading. A more AJAX-friendly design of the page entails that you populate and display a user control with any job information. You embed the user control in the same page, manage its setup and visibility through server code, and let the *UpdatePanel* control silently download any related markup. Of course, doing so represents a major page design overhaul, so we'll stick with the current design and redirect to the job posting in formation page.

Posting a Resume

Posting a resume is a function that can be quickly adjusted to support the AJAX paradigm. The function is implemented as a set of input fields and a couple of buttons to save or cancel. By wrapping everything in an updatable panel, you prevent full page reloads in case of errors. In addition, you incur no postback overhead if you display a confirmation message to the user or bring up a little animation while the save operation occurs.

> **Note**   Only a few of the JSSK pages have been enhanced to support AJAX capabilities. In the new user interface, a double asterisk in the navigation tree indicates pages you can navigate to that have been enhanced with AJAX support.

Controlling Menus and Navigation

Many ASP.NET pages include a menu or a navigation panel. More often than not, these controls are declaratively bound to a site map; in this case, the navigation that occurs is out of your control. If you employ navigation controls to let users jump to other links, a full page loading is inevitable and by design.

Sometimes, though, a *Menu* control might have elements that just order a partial redesign of the current page. In this case, AJAX can help to minimize page flickering. You wrap the portion of the interface affected by a menu selection in an *UpdatePanel* and add a trigger:

```
<asp:UpdatePanel runat="server" ID="UpdatePanel1" UpdateMode="Conditional">
    <ContentTemplate>
        ...
    </ContentTemplate>
    <Triggers>
        <asp:AsyncPostBackTrigger ControlID="Menu1"
                                  EventName="MenuItemClick" />
    </Triggers>
</asp:UpdatePanel>
```

Whenever any menu items are clicked, the panel is refreshed. If the menu item is bound to an external URL, a full page transition is performed.

Unfortunately, the *MenuItemClick* event fires regardless of whatever selection is made. Is there a way to refresh only when a particular item is clicked? The only possibility I see entails creating a custom, application-specific menu control and firing ad hoc events—for example, *Item1Clicked*. Next, you use just this specialized event to trigger a panel update.

> **Note**   AJAX-oriented changes to the *Menu* and *TreeView* controls are expected to ship with the "Orcas" release of ASP.NET.

Periodic Screen Refresh

Nearly all Web sites have information on the home page that needs be updated frequently. Think, for example, of news Web sites that offer real-time updates on stock exchange markets. For years, many sites used the *meta refresh* tag to instruct the browser to reload the page periodically. Although it's easy to code and is effective, the solution doesn't get along with today's rich pages. Refreshing too often is boring for users; refreshing too little takes away most of the feature's value.

Today, a common solution consists of displaying a panel and updating it on each postback. In its home page, JSSK presents a panel with statistics about the current number of jobs, resumes, and companies featured in the site. As you can see, this number is subject to change as soon as concurrent users enter fresh data. In an AJAX-enabled application, that panel would refresh periodically without affecting the rest of the page. Easier said than done.

Periodic screen refresh is a delicate topic with a big potential drawback. Suppose you configure the panel to refresh every five seconds. Can you imagine the effect on the site of thousands clients that operate concurrently at peak times? On the other hand, if the goal of the panel is displaying real-time data, browser-side caching is simply not an option. In the end, you must refresh a piece of user interface periodically, while limiting the impact of frequent updates on the site's scalability.

Refreshing on Postback

The approach taken by JSSK is not particularly ambitious; instead, it is simple and effective. A user control is embedded in the page whose input fields are set during page loading. Here's the source code:

```
protected void Page_Load(object sender, EventArgs e)
{
    lblCompanies.Text = Company.GetCompanyCount().ToString();
    lblJobs.Text = JobPosting.GetJobPostingCount().ToString();
    lblResumes.Text = Resume.GetResumeCount().ToString();
    lblLastUpdate.Text = DateTime.Now.ToString();
}
```

Added to the master page, the user control is shared by a number of Web site pages. Each time one of these pages is refreshed or loaded, the panel is updated. In the end, in a typical browser session a user gets several updates. I modified the original JSSK source code to add a label with the time of the last update just to let you easily verify how often you get fresh data. (See Figure 8-4.)

Figure 8-4   The statistics panel with up-to-date information on jobs and resumes

Although it might not sound particularly exciting at first, this approach is still one of the most effective in terms of the cost/benefit ratio.

Using Updatable Panels

In its original form, the statistics panel won't get updated if the host page is partially updated through an AJAX postback. How can you detect partial updates, and what is necessary to programmatically update a panel?

As we saw in Chapter 4, an updatable panel always refreshes when another panel in the page is updated. In light of this built-in behavior, all that you have to do is wrap the statistics panel in an *UpdatePanel* control. However, an updatable panel defined in a user control has no way to detect partial updates that occur at the page level. Two *UpdatePanel* controls refresh sympathetically only if they are defined within the same container or if they are nested.

You don't have to wrap the markup of the statistics panel with an *UpdatePanel* control; instead, you wrap the user control in an updatable panel within the master page:

```
<asp:UpdatePanel runat="server" ID="UpdatePanel1">
   <ContentTemplate>
      <uc2:statistics id="Statistics1" runat="server" />
   </ContentTemplate>
</asp:UpdatePanel>
```

In this way, the contents of the *statistics* user control is updated each time a partial update occurs within any pages based on the master. Is there a way for you to base updates of a region on runtime conditions?

You can use triggers, either programmatically or declaratively, to specify under which conditions the update should occur. Alternatively, you can programmatically command the update of a given region by invoking the *Update* method on the *UpdatePanel* control that defines the region. (See Chapter 4.)

Finally, there's a third option that falls somewhere in between the other two. In the *Load* event of the page, or user control, that contains the partial-update region, you can check the ID of the postback element and decide whether or not, and even how, to update the user interface. Here's an example:

```
void Page_Load(object sender, EventArgs e)
{
    if (ScriptManager.GetCurrent(this.Page).IsInAsyncPostBack)
    {
        // Use the AsyncPostBackSourceElementID property on
        // ScriptManager to check the ID of the postback element
        ...
        return;
    }
    ...
}
```

To access properties such as *IsInAsyncPostBack* and *AsyncPostBackSourceElementID*, any script manager proxy you might have around the page won't work. You must use the *GetCurrent* static method on the *ScriptManager* class.

Using Server-Side Services

As we saw in Chapter 7, it's often desirable for the client of an AJAX site to call server-side services. Taken as a whole, the server-side services expose an API to the client that a JavaScript proxy will invoke. ASP.NET AJAX Extensions provides a framework that makes this easy. You expose the API either through a special ASP.NET Web service or a set of page methods. In general, you opt for a Web service if more than one page or client application is going to share the same server-side service; you go for page methods if that API serves the purpose of just one page.

Server-side services are generally invoked explicitly; however, you can also set up a client timer to trigger calls at regular intervals. To start out, let's design a contract for accessing the statistics you see in Figure 8-4:

```
public interface IStatistics
{
    JobStatistics GetStatistics();
}
public class JobStatistics
{
    public int CompanyCount;
    public int ResumeCount;
    public int JobCount;
    public string LastUpdate;
}
```

A Web service that implements the contract might look like the one shown next. Let's name the service *StatService.asmx*.

```
using System;
using System.Web.Services;
using System.Web.Services.Protocols;
using System.Web.Script.Services;
using JobSiteStarterKit.BOL;

namespace IntroAjax.WebServices
{
    [WebService(Namespace = "http://IntroAjax/")]
    [ScriptService]
    [WebServiceBinding(ConformsTo = WsiProfiles.BasicProfile1_1)]
    public class StatService : IStatistics
    {
        public StatService() {}

        [WebMethod]
        public JobStatistics GetStatistics()
        {
            JobStatistics stat = new JobStatistics();
            stat.CompanyCount = Company.GetCompanyCount();
            stat.JobCount = JobPosting.GetJobPostingCount();
            stat.ResumeCount = Resume.GetResumeCount();
            stat.LastUpdate = DateTime.Now.ToString();
            return stat;
        }
    }
}
```

To invoke the Web service, first you have to register it with the script manager. In the master page, make sure the script manager is configured as shown here:

```
<asp:ScriptManager id="ScriptManager1" runat="server">
    <Services>
        <asp:ServiceReference Path="StatService.asmx" />
    </Services>
</asp:ScriptManager>
```

At this point, you edit the user control to add a client button to explicitly request an update of the statistics:

```
<input type="button" value="Refresh" onclick="refreshStatistics()" />
```

The *refreshStatistics* JavaScript function will call a dynamically generated proxy class and download statistics data. The call is made asynchronously, and a user-defined callback gathers results and updates the user interface.

```
function refreshStatistics() {
    IntroAjax.WebServices.StatService.GetStatistics(methodCompleted);
}
function methodCompleted(results, context, methodName) {
    $get("ctl00_Statistics1_lblJobs").innerHTML = results.JobCount;
    $get("ctl00_Statistics1_lblResumes").innerHTML = results.ResumeCount;
    $get("ctl00_Statistics1_lblCompanies").innerHTML = results.CompanyCount;
    $get("ctl00_Statistics1_lblLastUpdate").innerHTML = results.LastUpdate;
}
```

It is worth noting that the ID of any user interface element you want to update has to exactly match the ID of the real DOM element. The user control contains a *Label* control named *lblJobs*. It would then be natural to assume that you can find its client-side DOM element using *$get("lblJobs")*. This worked in earlier examples because the *Label* was a direct child of the form. In this case, we have two further levels of containment—the master page and user control. In ASP.NET, containment is reflected in the client-side ID of the corresponding DOM elements. You can easily verify what the real client ID of the DOM element of an ASP.NET control is by looking at the page's source code.

> **Note** In server ASP.NET programming, you obtain the client ID of an ASP.NET control (or a portion of it) using the *ClientID* property of the *Control* object. On the client, though, there's no way to automatically match the server ID (for example, *lblJobs*) with the client ID. In case of control containment, you have to figure out what the real ID is.

Figure 8-5 shows the statistics panel updated by an explicit client request. The feature is used in addition to user control-managed updates triggered during postbacks and partial postbacks.

Figure 8-5 A Refresh button allows users to explicitly update the statistics making a Web service call

Using Server Timers

To schedule panel updates at a fixed time or periodically, you use timers. Timers are browser objects created and controlled using a couple of methods on the *window* object—*setTimeout* and *clearTimeout*. Once the interval has been set, the timer waits for the specified number of milliseconds and then fires a call to a user-defined function. To make the timer proceed indefinitely, you generally write a user-defined callback that performs its task and then restarts the timer.

In ASP.NET AJAX Extensions, you also have a server-side interface for the client timer object—the *Timer* control, which we discussed in Chapter 4. To periodically refresh the statistics box, you have two options: using the *Timer* server control in conjunction with an *UpdatePanel* or using a client-side timer. The former approach is really quick to implement. You add a *Timer* to the master page and bind the *Tick* event of the timer to the trigger list of the updatable panel we added earlier:

```
<asp:timer runat="server" id="Timer1" Interval="2000" Enabled="true" />
<asp:UpdatePanel runat="server" ID="UpdatePanel1">
   <ContentTemplate>
      <uc2:statistics id="Statistics1" runat="server" />
   </ContentTemplate>
   <Triggers>
      <asp:AsyncPostBackTrigger ControlID="Timer1" EventName="Tick" />
   </Triggers>
</asp:UpdatePanel>
```

This code will refresh the panel every two seconds. Can you embed the timer in the user control? The quick answer is yes, but there's a bit more to consider. You can certainly have a user control that encapsulates an updatable panel and a timer. Such a user control would hide all the details and just offer to the outside world an auto-refreshing statistics panel. However, this doesn't mean that the outermost *UpdatePanel* we have in the code snippet can be removed. In fact, the outermost *UpdatePanel* serves the purpose of updating statistics during partial postbacks. It can be argued that you probably don't need to worry about partial postbacks once you have an auto-refreshing user control. That's true.

So, in the end, you can certainly move *UpdatePanel* and *Timer* within the user control. If you also keep the *UpdatePanel* control that wraps the user control, you'll get an additional refresh whenever a partial update occurs within any page based on the master.

Using Client Timers

A server timer has just one drawback. It requires an *UpdatePanel* to refresh the user interface, and subsequently it moves a chunk of markup at every tick. A completely client-based timer, on the other hand, will use a Web service (or a page method) to get fresh data. In this case, only statistics will travel over the wire—just three numbers rather than an HTML table with data, markup, and perhaps auxiliary resources.

To manage a client timer, you can use direct calls to the browser's *window* object or, better yet, manage to create a Microsoft AJAX library JavaScript class. Here's the *SimpleTimer.js* class:

```
Type.registerNamespace('IntroAjax.Components');
IntroAjax.Components.Timer = function(userCallback) {
    this._interval = 10000;
    this._raiseTickDelegate = Function.createDelegate(this, this._tick);
    this._userCallback = userCallback;
    this._timer = null;
}
function IntroAjax$Components$Timer$get_interval() {
    return this._interval;
}
function IntroAjax$Components$Timer$set_interval(value) {
    this._interval = value;
}
function IntroAjax$Components$Timer$stop() {
    this._stopTimer();
}
function IntroAjax$Components$Timer$start() {
    this._startTimer();
}
function IntroAjax$Components$Timer$_tick() {
    if (this._userCallback !== null)
        this._userCallback();
    this._startTimer();
}
function IntroAjax$Components$Timer$_startTimer() {
    this._timer = window.setTimeout(
                    this._raiseTickDelegate, this.get_interval());
}
```

```
function IntroAjax$Components$Timer$_stopTimer() {
    if (this._timer !== null) {
        window.clearTimeout(this._timer);
        this._timer = null;
    }
}
IntroAjax.Components.Timer.prototype = {
    get_interval:    IntroAjax$Components$Timer$get_interval,
    set_interval:    IntroAjax$Components$Timer$set_interval,
    stop:            IntroAjax$Components$Timer$stop,
    start:           IntroAjax$Components$Timer$start,
    _raiseTick:      IntroAjax$Components$Timer$_tick,
    _startTimer:     IntroAjax$Components$Timer$_startTimer,
    _stopTimer:      IntroAjax$Components$Timer$_stopTimer
}
IntroAjax.Components.Timer.registerClass('IntroAjax.Components.Timer');
```

You register this file with the script manager using the *<Scripts>* tag:

```
<asp:ScriptManager id="ScriptManager1" runat="server">
    <Scripts>
        <asp:ScriptReference Path="simpletimer.js" />
    </Scripts>
</asp:ScriptManager>
```

The final step is arranging some code to start and stop the timer. In the user control, you can add a check box:

```
<input type="checkbox" id="chkEnableTimer" onclick="enableTimer()" />
```

The *onclick* event of the check box is bound to the following code:

```
var _timer = null;
function enableTimer()
{
    var chk = $get("chkEnableTimer");
    if (chk.checked) {
        if (_timer == null) {
            _timer = new IntroAjax.Components.Timer(refreshStatistics);
            _timer.set_interval(2000);
            _timer.start();
        }
    }
    else {
        _timer.stop();
        _timer = null;
    }
}
```

The function *refreshStatistics* is the same function we considered earlier that calls into the *StatService.asmx* Web service. As a result, the timer ticks every two seconds and invokes the Web service to get fresh data.

Note What if the Web service call takes more than two seconds to return? The timer and the Web service are two independent entities. The timer sends new requests every two seconds, and the associated callback processes Web service results when they are ready. As a result, the user interface might not be updated exactly every two seconds. Is there a way to synchronize the Web service and the timer so that a new request is placed only two seconds after receiving results? In this case, the problem is that the timer callback invokes a Web service method asynchronously. If you can make it run synchronously, then you're fine. A simple solution is to use a global variable and reset it only when the Web service callback is done. The timer callback fires the Web service call and loops until the variable is reset. If you do this, though, you might receive a warning from the browser stating that a script is probably slowing down your application. You have to change the browser's settings to avoid that message. Curiously, Internet Explorer measures timeouts based on the number of script statements executed, whereas Firefox reasons in terms of seconds. More information for Internet Explorer is at *http://support.microsoft.com/kb/175500*. For Firefox, visit *http://kb.mozillazine.org/ Unresponsive_Script_Error*.

Applying the Timeout Pattern

Combined use of timers and dynamic DOM changes make serving live data to users a breeze. However, live updates are potentially harmful for the application. This is not in any significant way the result of the inherent workload the feature will push to the server; the danger, rather, lies in the possible misuse of the feature. Assume that to get live data over the Web you can only poll the server, and then imagine a user that brings up a page that refreshes every two seconds. Then the user leaves for hours. What do you think will happen? The page keeps on sending requests for data that no user will ever consume.

The first aspect to emphasize is that when implementing real-time applications you should choose the timeout interval very carefully. You can still make it a customizable parameter, but make sure that the selected value falls in a reasonable range.

The second aspect is that you can't just leave end users with the final word. You should try to implement a sort of supervisor module that kicks in and stops scripts if no user activity is detected for a while. In other words, you should endow your applications with the same mechanism that allows Firefox and Internet Explorer browsers to detect long-running scripts. The Timeout pattern provides some guidance on how to do that.

You can use a global timer in the page that is stopped and restarted whenever clear signs of user activity are detected—for example, mouse clicks and keyboard typing. You set the timer to a few minutes and associate it with a timeout callback. If the user doesn't click the mouse or tap the keyboard for the entire time, the timeout callback is fired. What the callback does then is up to you. It could, for example, save the state of the application and blank the page. Another approach entails setting up a timer that every few minutes fires a call to the server and checks whether the server session is active. The two approaches can also be combined if need be. What really matters is that you find a way to stop applications that are loaded in the browser but not active from continuing to keep polling the server indefinitely and producing a massive waste of bandwidth.

Conclusion

Many AJAX commercial products advertise their ability of adding AJAX capabilities to sites with minimal impact on existing code. Zero-cost AJAX is a reality, and that's not just hype. So what's the problem?

AJAX applications are Web applications designed according to a new paradigm. Therefore, existing ASP.NET applications are not native AJAX applications, and they require a thorough and thoughtful refactoring to be fully considered true AJAX applications.

The *UpdatePanel* control, which we extensively covered in Chapter 4, is a powerful and interesting shortcut to using AJAX. To a large extent, it lets you maintain the same structure of the site and replace full postbacks with lightweight postbacks executed via *XMLHttpRequest*. The quickest way to implementing AJAX consists of wrapping regions of user interface in updatable panels, thereby maintaining the same pages and structure of the site. In doing so, you save a lot of postbacks, reduce flickering, and give users continuity. AJAX postbacks are not particularly lightweight, but they are certainly more lightweight than full postbacks. There's an obvious benefit in using *UpdatePanel* controls and a suprisingly low cost. Using updatable panels is hardly a bad solution.

However, as Jesse James Garrett—the man who coined the term AJAX—says, with AJAX the main challenge is not technical. The point is not so much making page operations smoother and seamless; the point is building richer and more powerful Web sites. From this perspective, *UpdatePanel* is easily the quickest ASP.NET way to using AJAX. A site that uses *UpdatePanel* is mostly an ASP.NET site with some cool features.

In this chapter, we took an existing typical ASP.NET 2.0 Web site and tried to add AJAX to it. We were able to improve quite a few page operations; however, we couldn't do much to improve the log-in process without a heavy redesign of the process because the ASP.NET log-in process is different from an AJAX log-in process. AJAX applications essentially are of two types—Lite and Deluxe. AJAX Lite refers to soliciting the help of *UpdatePanel* controls; AJAX Deluxe refers to building (or rebuilding) a new system. Both options are fine, but you need to be aware that they're different things.

Index

About the Author

Dino Esposito is a trainer and software consultant based in Rome, Italy. He is a member of the Solid Quality Mentors team (*www.solidq.com*). Dino specializes in Microsoft .NET technologies and spends most of his time teaching and consulting across Europe, Australia, and the United States.

Over the years, Dino developed hands-on experience and skills in architecting and building distributed systems for banking and insurance companies and, in general, in industry contexts where the demand for security, optimization, performance, scalability, and interoperability is dramatically high.

Every month, at least five magazines and Web sites throughout the world publish Dino's articles covering topics that range from Web development to data access, and from software best practices to Web services. A prolific author, Dino writes the monthly "Cutting Edge" column for MSDN Magazine (*msdn.microsoft.com/msdnmag*), the "CoreCoder" column for aspnetPRO Magazine (*www.aspnetpro.com*), and the *ASP.NET-2-The-Max newsletter* for the Dr. Dobb's Journal (*www.ddj.com/dept/windows*). Considered an authoritative and acknowledged expert in Web applications built with .NET technologies, Dino contributes to the Microsoft content platform for developers and IT consultants. Check out his articles on a variety of MSDN Developer Centers, such as *ASP.NET* (*msdn.microsoft.com/aspnet*), Microsoft Windows Vista, or data access.

Dino has written an array of books, most of which are considered state-of-the-art in their respective areas, including *Applied XML Programming with the .NET Framework* (Microsoft Press, 2002). Still requested, quoted, and, more importantly, used by developers worldwide is *Visual C++ Windows Shell Programming* (Apress, 1998). It remains the unique reference for anyone planning to extend the navigation capabilities of the Windows operating system.

His two most recent books are *Programming Microsoft ASP.NET 2.0: Core Reference"* and *Programming Microsoft ASP.NET 2.0 Applications: Advanced Topics* (Microsoft Press, 2006). An ASP.NET MVP, Dino regularly speaks at industry conferences all over the world (Microsoft TechEd, Microsoft DevDays, DevConnections, DevWeek, and Basta) and local technical conferences and meetings in Europe and the United States.

Dino lives with his family near Rome, Italy, and plays tennis or runs in the country when challenging technical issues knock at his door. The solution auto-magically appears a few minutes after his post-workout shower.

Additional Resources for Developers: Advanced Topics and Best Practices

Published and Forthcoming Titles from Microsoft Press

Code Complete, Second Edition
Steve McConnell • ISBN 0-7356-1967-0

For more than a decade, Steve McConnell, one of the premier authors and voices in the software community, has helped change the way developers write code—and produce better software. Now his classic book, *Code Complete*, has been fully updated and revised with best practices in the art and science of constructing software. Topics include design, applying good techniques to construction, eliminating errors, planning, managing construction activities, and relating personal character to superior software. This new edition features fully updated information on programming techniques, including the emergence of Web-style programming, and integrated coverage of object-oriented design. You'll also find new code examples—both good and bad—in C++, Microsoft® Visual Basic®, C#, and Java, although the focus is squarely on techniques and practices.

More About Software Requirements: Thorny Issues and Practical Advice
Karl E. Wiegers • ISBN 0-7356-2267-1

Have you ever delivered software that satisfied all of the project specifications, but failed to meet any of the customers' expectations? Without formal, verifiable requirements—and a system for managing them—the result is often a gap between what developers think they're supposed to build and what customers think they're going to get. Too often, lessons about software requirements engineering processes are formal or academic, and not of value to real-world, professional development teams. In this follow-up guide to *Software Requirements*, Second Edition, you will discover even more practical techniques for gathering and managing software requirements that help you deliver software that meets project and customer specifications. Succinct and immediately useful, this book is a must-have for developers and architects.

Software Estimation: Demystifying the Black Art
Steve McConnell • ISBN 0-7356-0535-1

Often referred to as the "black art" because of its complexity and uncertainty, software estimation is not as hard or mysterious as people think. However, the art of how to create effective cost and schedule estimates has not been very well publicized. *Software Estimation* provides a proven set of procedures and heuristics that software developers, technical leads, and project managers can apply to their projects. Instead of arcane treatises and rigid modeling techniques, award-winning author Steve McConnell gives practical guidance to help organizations achieve basic estimation proficiency and lay the groundwork to continue improving project cost estimates. This book does not avoid the more complex mathematical estimation approaches, but the non-mathematical reader will find plenty of useful guidelines without getting bogged down in complex formulas.

Debugging, Tuning, and Testing Microsoft .NET 2.0 Applications
John Robbins • ISBN 0-7356-2202-7

Making an application the best it can be has long been a time-consuming task best accomplished with specialized and costly tools. With Microsoft Visual Studio® 2005, developers have available a new range of built-in functionality that enables them to debug their code quickly and efficiently, tune it to optimum performance, and test applications to ensure compatibility and trouble-free operation. In this accessible and hands-on book, debugging expert John Robbins shows developers how to use the tools and functions in Visual Studio to their full advantage to ensure high-quality applications.

The Security Development Lifecycle
Michael Howard and Steve Lipner • ISBN 0-7356-2214-0

Adapted from Microsoft's standard development process, the Security Development Lifecycle (SDL) is a methodology that helps reduce the number of security defects in code at every stage of the development process, from design to release. This book details each stage of the SDL methodology and discusses its implementation across a range of Microsoft software, including Microsoft Windows Server™ 2003, Microsoft SQL Server™ 2000 Service Pack 3, and Microsoft Exchange Server 2003 Service Pack 1, to help measurably improve security features. You get direct access to insights from Microsoft's security team and lessons that are applicable to software development processes worldwide, whether on a small-scale or a large-scale. This book includes a CD featuring videos of developer training classes.

Software Requirements, Second Edition
Karl E. Wiegers • ISBN 0-7356-1879-8

Writing Secure Code, Second Edition
Michael Howard and David LeBlanc • ISBN 0-7356-1722-8

CLR via C#, Second Edition
Jeffrey Richter • ISBN 0-7356-2163-2

For more information about Microsoft Press® books and other learning products, visit: **www.microsoft.com/mspress** *and* **www.microsoft.com/learning**

Additional Resources for C# Developers

Published and Forthcoming Titles from Microsoft Press

Microsoft® Visual C#® 2005 Express Edition: Build a Program Now!
Patrice Pelland • ISBN 0-7356-2229-9

In this lively, eye-opening, and hands-on book, all you need is a computer and the desire to learn how to program with Visual C# 2005 Express Edition. Featuring a full working edition of the software, this fun and highly visual guide walks you through a complete programming project—a desktop weather-reporting application—from start to finish. You'll get an unintimidating introduction to the Microsoft Visual Studio® development environment and learn how to put the lightweight, easy-to-use tools in Visual C# Express to work right away—creating, compiling, testing, and delivering your first, ready-to-use program. You'll get expert tips, coaching, and visual examples at each step of the way, along with pointers to additional learning resources.

Microsoft Visual C# 2005 *Step by Step*
John Sharp • ISBN 0-7356-2129-2

Visual C#, a feature of Visual Studio 2005, is a modern programming language designed to deliver a productive environment for creating business frameworks and reusable object-oriented components. Now you can teach yourself essential techniques with Visual C#—and start building components and Microsoft Windows®–based applications—one step at a time. With *Step by Step*, you work at your own pace through hands-on, learn-by-doing exercises. Whether you're a beginning programmer or new to this particular language, you'll learn how, when, and why to use specific features of Visual C# 2005. Each chapter puts you to work, building your knowledge of core capabilities and guiding you as you create your first C#-based applications for Windows, data management, and the Web.

Programming Microsoft Visual C# 2005 Framework Reference
Francesco Balena • ISBN 0-7356-2182-9

Complementing *Programming Microsoft Visual C# 2005 Core Reference*, this book covers a wide range of additional topics and information critical to Visual C# developers, including Windows Forms, working with Microsoft ADO.NET 2.0 and Microsoft ASP.NET 2.0, Web services, security, remoting, and much more. Packed with sample code and real-world examples, this book will help developers move from understanding to mastery.

Programming Microsoft Visual C# 2005 *Core Reference*
Donis Marshall • ISBN 0-7356-2181-0

Get the in-depth reference and pragmatic, real-world insights you need to exploit the enhanced language features and core capabilities in Visual C# 2005. Programming expert Donis Marshall deftly builds your proficiency with classes, structs, and other fundamentals, and advances your expertise with more advanced topics such as debugging, threading, and memory management. Combining incisive reference with hands-on coding examples and best practices, this *Core Reference* focuses on mastering the C# skills you need to build innovative solutions for smart clients and the Web.

CLR via C#, Second Edition
Jeffrey Richter • ISBN 0-7356-2163-2

In this new edition of Jeffrey Richter's popular book, you get focused, pragmatic guidance on how to exploit the common language runtime (CLR) functionality in Microsoft .NET Framework 2.0 for applications of all types—from Web Forms, Windows Forms, and Web services to solutions for Microsoft SQL Server™, Microsoft code names "Avalon" and "Indigo," consoles, Microsoft Windows NT® Service, and more. Targeted to advanced developers and software designers, this book takes you under the covers of .NET for an in-depth understanding of its structure, functions, and operational components, demonstrating the most practical ways to apply this knowledge to your own development efforts. You'll master fundamental design tenets for .NET and get hands-on insights for creating high-performance applications more easily and efficiently. The book features extensive code examples in Visual C# 2005.

Programming Microsoft Windows Forms
Charles Petzold • ISBN 0-7356-2153-5

CLR via C++
Jeffrey Richter with Stanley B. Lippman
ISBN 0-7356-2248-5

Programming Microsoft Web Forms
Douglas J. Reilly • ISBN 0-7356-2179-9

Debugging, Tuning, and Testing Microsoft .NET 2.0 Applications
John Robbins • ISBN 0-7356-2202-7

For more information about Microsoft Press® books and other learning products, visit: **www.microsoft.com/books** *and* **www.microsoft.com/learning**

Additional SQL Server Resources for Developers

Published and Forthcoming Titles from Microsoft Press

Microsoft® SQL Server™ 2005 Express Edition
Step by Step
Jackie Goldstein • ISBN 0-7356-2184-5

Teach yourself how to get database projects up and running
quickly with SQL Server Express
Edition—a free, easy-to-use
database product that is based
on SQL Server 2005 technology.
It's designed for building simple,
dynamic applications, with all
the rich functionality of the SQL
Server database engine and
using the same data access APIs,
such as Microsoft ADO.NET, SQL
Native Client, and T-SQL.
Whether you're new to database
programming or new to SQL Server, you'll learn how, when, and
why to use specific features of this simple but powerful database development environment. Each chapter puts you to work,
building your knowledge of core capabilities and guiding you
as you create actual components and working applications.

Microsoft SQL Server 2005 Programming
Step by Step
Fernando Guerrero • ISBN 0-7356-2207-8

SQL Server 2005 is Microsoft's
next-generation data management and analysis solution that
delivers enhanced scalability,
availability, and security features
to enterprise data and analytical
applications while making them
easier to create, deploy, and
manage. Now you can teach
yourself how to design, build, test,
deploy, and maintain SQL Server
databases—one step at a time.
Instead of merely focusing on
describing new features, this book shows new database
programmers and administrators how to use specific features
within typical business scenarios. Each chapter provides a highly
practical learning experience that demonstrates how to build
database solutions to solve common business problems.

Microsoft SQL Server 2005 Analysis Services
Step by Step
Hitachi Consulting Services • ISBN 0-7356-2199-3

One of the key features of SQL Server 2005 is SQL Server Analysis
Services—Microsoft's customizable analysis solution for business
data modeling and interpretation. Just compare SQL Server
Analysis Services to its competition to understand the great
value of its enhanced features. One of the keys to harnessing
the full functionality of SQL Server will be leveraging Analysis
Services for the powerful tool that it is—including creating a cube,
and deploying, customizing, and extending the basic calcula-
tions. This step-by-step tutorial discusses how to get started, how
to build scalable analytical applications, and how to use and ad-
minister advanced features. Interactivity (enhanced in SQL Server
2005), data translation, and security are also covered in detail.

Microsoft SQL Server 2005 Reporting Services
Step by Step
Hitachi Consulting Services • ISBN 0-7356-2250-7

SQL Server Reporting Services (SRS) is Microsoft's customizable
reporting solution for business data analysis. It is one of the key
value features of SQL Server 2005: functionality more advanced
and much less expensive than its competition. SRS is powerful,
so an understanding of how to architect a report, as well as how
to install and program SRS, is key to harnessing the full functionality of SQL Server. This procedural tutorial shows how to use the
Report Project Wizard, how to think about and access data, and
how to build queries. It also walks through the creation of charts
and visual layouts for maximum visual understanding of data
analysis. Interactivity (enhanced in SQL Server 2005) and security
are also covered in detail.

Programming Microsoft SQL Server 2005
Andrew J. Brust, Stephen Forte, and William H. Zack
ISBN 0-7356-1923-9

This thorough, hands-on reference for developers and database
administrators teaches the basics of programming custom applications with SQL Server 2005. You will learn the fundamentals
of creating database applications—including coverage of
T-SQL, Microsoft .NET Framework, and Microsoft ADO.NET. In
addition to practical guidance on database architecture and
design, application development, and reporting and data
analysis, this essential reference guide covers performance,
tuning, and availability of SQL Server 2005.

Inside Microsoft SQL Server 2005:
The Storage Engine
Kalen Delaney • ISBN 0-7356-2105-5

Inside Microsoft SQL Server 2005:
T-SQL Programming
Itzik Ben-Gan • ISBN 0-7356-2197-7

Inside Microsoft SQL Server 2005:
Query Processing and Optimization
Kalen Delaney • ISBN 0-7356-2196-9

Programming Microsoft ADO.NET 2.0 Core Reference
David Sceppa • ISBN 0-7356-2206-X

For more information about Microsoft Press® books and other learning products,
visit: **www.microsoft.com/mspress** *and* **www.microsoft.com/learning**

Additional Resources for Web Developers

Published and Forthcoming Titles from Microsoft Press

Microsoft® Visual Web Developer™ 2005 Express Edition: Build a Web Site Now!
Jim Buyens • ISBN 0-7356-2212-4

With this lively, eye-opening, and hands-on book, all you need is a computer and the desire to learn how to create Web pages now using Visual Web Developer Express Edition! Featuring a full working edition of the software, this fun and highly visual guide walks you through a complete Web page project from set-up to launch. You'll get an introduction to the Microsoft Visual Studio® environment and learn how to put the lightweight, easy-to-use tools in Visual Web Developer Express to work right away—building your first, dynamic Web pages with Microsoft ASP.NET 2.0. You'll get expert tips, coaching, and visual examples at each step of the way, along with pointers to additional learning resources.

Microsoft ASP.NET 2.0 Programming
Step by Step
George Shepherd • ISBN 0-7356-2201-9

With dramatic improvements in performance, productivity, and security features, Visual Studio 2005 and ASP.NET 2.0 deliver a simplified, high-performance, and powerful Web development experience. ASP.NET 2.0 features a new set of controls and infrastructure that simplify Web-based data access and include functionality that facilitates code reuse, visual consistency, and aesthetic appeal. Now you can teach yourself the essentials of working with ASP.NET 2.0 in the Visual Studio environment—one step at a time. With *Step by Step*, you work at your own pace through hands-on, learn-by-doing exercises. Whether you're a beginning programmer or new to this version of the technology, you'll understand the core capabilities and fundamental techniques for ASP.NET 2.0. Each chapter puts you to work, showing you how, when, and why to use specific features of the ASP.NET 2.0 rapid application development environment and guiding you as you create actual components and working applications for the Web, including advanced features such as personalization.

Programming Microsoft ASP.NET 2.0
Core Reference
Dino Esposito • ISBN 0-7356-2176-4

Delve into the core topics for ASP.NET 2.0 programming, mastering the essential skills and capabilities needed to build high-performance Web applications successfully. Well-known ASP.NET author Dino Esposito deftly builds your expertise with Web forms, Visual Studio, core controls, master pages, data access, data binding, state management, security services, and other must-know topics—combining definitive reference with practical, hands-on programming instruction. Packed with expert guidance and pragmatic examples, this *Core Reference* delivers the key resources that you need to develop professional-level Web programming skills.

Programming Microsoft ASP.NET 2.0
Applications: *Advanced Topics*
Dino Esposito • ISBN 0-7356-2177-2

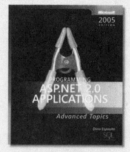

Master advanced topics in ASP.NET 2.0 programming—gaining the essential insights and in-depth understanding that you need to build sophisticated, highly functional Web applications successfully. Topics include Web forms, Visual Studio 2005, core controls, master pages, data access, data binding, state management, and security considerations. Developers often discover that the more they use ASP.NET, the more they need to know. With expert guidance from ASP.NET authority Dino Esposito, you get the in-depth, comprehensive information that leads to full mastery of the technology.

Programming Microsoft Windows® Forms
Charles Petzold • ISBN 0-7356-2153-5

Programming Microsoft Web Forms
Douglas J. Reilly • ISBN 0-7356-2179-9

CLR via C++
Jeffrey Richter with Stanley B. Lippman
ISBN 0-7356-2248-5

Debugging, Tuning, and Testing Microsoft .NET 2.0 Applications
John Robbins • ISBN 0-7356-2202-7

CLR via C#, Second Edition
Jeffrey Richter • ISBN 0-7356-2163-2

For more information about Microsoft Press® books and other learning products,
visit: **www.microsoft.com/books** *and* **www.microsoft.com/learning**

What do you think of this book?

We want to hear from you!

Do you have a few minutes to participate in a brief online survey?

Microsoft is interested in hearing your feedback so we can continually improve our books and learning resources for you.

To participate in our survey, please visit:

www.microsoft.com/learning/booksurvey/

...and enter this book's ISBN-10 number (appears above barcode on back cover*).
As a thank-you to survey participants in the United States and Canada, each month we'll randomly select five respondents to win one of five $100 gift certificates from a leading online merchant. At the conclusion of the survey, you can enter the drawing by providing your e-mail address, which will be used for prize notification only.

Thanks in advance for your input. Your opinion counts!

* Where to find the ISBN-10 on back cover

ISBN-13: 000-0-0000-0000-0
ISBN-10: 0-0000-0000-0

Example only. Each book has unique ISBN.

www.microsoft.com/learning/booksurvey/